WELL-BEHAVED WOMEN
SELDOM MAKE
HISTORY

The Age of Homespun: Objects and Stories in the Creation of an American Myth

A Midwife's Tale: The Life of Martha Ballard, Based on Her Diary, 1785–1812

Good Wives: Image and Reality in the Lives of Women in Northern New England, 1650–1750

Well-Behaved Women Seldom Make History

Laurel Thatcher Ulrich

Alfred A. Knopf   New York   2007

This Is a Borzoi Book Published by Alfred A. Knopf

Knopf, Borzoi Books, and the colophon are registered
trademarks of Random House, Inc.

Library of Congress Cataloging-in-Publication Data
Ulrich, Laurel.
Well-behaved women seldom make history / by Laurel
Thatcher Ulrich.—1st ed.
p. cm.
Includes bibliographical references.
ISBN 978-1-4000-4159-6
1. Women—History. 2. Women in literature. 3. Feminism.
4. Christine, de Pisan, ca. 1364–ca. 1431. Livre de la cité des dames.
5. Stanton, Elizabeth Cady, 1815–1902. Eighty years and more.
6. Woolf, Virginia, 1882–1941. Room of one's own. I. Title.
HQ1121.U517 2007
305.4209182'1—dc22   2006100581

Manufactured in the United States of America
Published September 7, 2007
Second Printing, October 2007

For my students

But the history of the world shows the vast majority, in every generation, passively accept the conditions into which they are born, while those who demand larger liberties are ever a small, ostracized minority, whose claims are ridiculed and ignored.

—ELIZABETH CADY STANTON, *Eighty Years and More,* 1898

For all the dinners are cooked; the plates and cups washed; the children set to school and gone out into the world. Nothing remains of it all. All has vanished. No biography or history has a word to say about it. And the novels, without meaning to, inevitably lie.

—VIRGINIA WOOLF, *A Room of One's Own,* 1929

If I wished to tell you all the great benefits which have come about through women, it would require much too long a book.

—CHRISTINE DE PIZAN, *The Book of the City of Ladies,* 1405

CONTENTS

ILLUSTRATIONS

15. Milking a cow. *Bestiary,* MS. Bodley 764, f. 41v., English, c. 1225–50. The Bodleian Library, University of Oxford

16. Boepetse Busang's *lelapa* wall. Tsetsebjwe, Botswana, 1990. Photo by Sandy Grant/Activepic

17. Mmashadi Sepotlo decorating a *lelapa* entrance. Odi, Botswana, 1992. Photo by Sandy Grant/Activepic

18. Annie Burke with her niece Marie Arnold. 1943. Mildred E. Van Every, photographer. McCurry Photo Collection, California History Section, California State Library

19. *Laura Somersal Twining a Basket.* National Women's History Week Poster, 1983. Photo by Scott M. Patterson courtesy Victoria Patterson

20. Annie Young and her great-granddaughter Shaquetta Young. Ronald Freeman, Alberta/Gee's Bend, Alabama, October, 1993

21. Jessie T. Pettway (b. 1929), *Bars and String-Pieced Columns.* Cotton, 95 × 76 inches, 1950s. From collection of Tinwood Alliance

22. *Jennie Pettway and Another Girl with the Quilter Jorena Pettway.* 1937. Arthur Rothstein, Farm Security Administration Photo Collection, Library of Congress

23. Women defending the Castle of Love. Walter de Milemete, *De Nobilitatibus, sapientiis, et prudentiis regum.* Ms. CH.CH.92, f. 4r. English, c. 1326. By kind permission of the Governing Body of Christ Church, Oxford

24. Radcliffe students demanding equal rights in front of the statue of John Harvard. Commencement, 1971. Photo by Peter Hunsberger. Courtesy Radcliffe Archives, Radcliffe Institute, Harvard University

25. Cover. First issue of *Exponent II,* 1974

26. Mary Yaeger, *Christine de Pisan at Her Computer.* Photo-transfer on satin with embroidered detail, 1999

THE SLOGAN

Some time ago a former student e-mailed me from California: "You'll be delighted to know that you are quoted frequently on bumpers in Berkeley." Through a strange stroke of fate I've gotten used to seeing my name on bumpers. And on T-shirts, tote bags, coffee mugs, magnets, buttons, greeting cards, and websites.

I owe this curious fame to a single line from a scholarly article I published in 1976. In the opening paragraph, I wrote: "Well-behaved women seldom make history." That sentence, slightly altered, escaped into popular culture in 1995, when journalist Kay Mills used it as an epigraph for her informal history of American women, *From Pocahontas to Power Suits*. Perhaps by accident, she changed the word *seldom* to *rarely*. Little matter. According to my dictionary, *seldom* and *rarely* mean the same thing: "Well-behaved women *infrequently*, or *on few occasions*, make history."[1] This may be one of those occasions. My original article was a study of the well-behaved women celebrated in Puritan funeral sermons.

In 1996, a young woman named Jill Portugal found the "rarely" version of the quote in her roommate's copy of *The New Beacon Book of Quotations by Women*. She wrote me from Oregon asking permission to print it on T-shirts. I was amused by her request and told her to go ahead; all I asked was that she send me a T-shirt. The success of her enterprise surprised both of us. A plain white shirt with the words "Well-behaved women rarely make history" printed in black roman type became a best-selling item. Portugal calls her company "one angry girl designs." Committed to "taking over the world, one shirt at a time," she fights sexual harassment, rape, pornography, and what she calls "fascist beauty standards."[2]

Her success inspired imitators, only a few of whom bothered to ask permission. My runaway sentence now keeps company with anarchists, hedonists, would-be witches, political activists of many descriptions, and quite a few well-behaved women. It has been featured in *CosmoGirl,* the *Christian Science Monitor,* and *Creative Keepsake Scrapbooking Magazine.* According to news reports, it was a favorite of the pioneering computer scientist Anita Borg. The Sweet Potato Queens of Jackson, Mississippi, have adopted it as an "official maxim," selling their own pink-and-green T-shirt alongside another that reads "Never Wear Panties to a Party."

My accidental fame has given me a new perspective on American popular culture. While some women contemplate the demise of feminism, others seem to have only just discovered it. A clerk in the Amtrak ticket office in D.C.'s Union Station told a fellow historian that all the women in her office wore the button. "I couldn't resist telling her that I was acquainted with you, and she just lit right up, and made me promise to tell you that the women at the Amtrak office thank you for all your 'words of wisdom.' "

I do, in fact, get quite a bit of fan mail. Recently a woman I had never met wrote to tell me she had seen someone wearing the T-shirt in a New York City subway. She wanted to know where to buy a shirt for herself, since she was one of the named plaintiffs in a gender discrimination suit against a major corporation. I have had notes thanking me for the slogan from a biology instructor at a community college on the White Mountain Apache Reservation in Arizona, from the program coordinator in a Massachusetts nursing home who started a "Wild Women's Group" for the residents there, and from the director of an Ohio homeless legal assistance program. A Massachusetts educator wrote to tell me she had painted my words and other inspiring quotations on the front hood of her 1991 Honda Civic, then covered the body of the car with the names of high-achieving women throughout history.

One of the most amusing e-mails was from an undergraduate who asked if I could give her the original source of the quotation. She wanted to use it in her honors thesis, and she didn't think her adviser would approve of a footnote to a T-shirt. The most surprising, given the origins of the quote, was from a woman named Lori Pearson who told me that my words had helped her write a funeral eulogy for her best friend, Kathy Thill, who was the first woman to become an electric designer for a public utility in Minnesota. She said Thill "was spunky, courageous, and just a helluva lot of fun."[3]

Other uses of the quote have been less inspiring. While standing at the check-out counter of an independent bookstore, I discovered my name and sentence on a dusky blue magnet embellished with one leopard-print stiletto-heeled shoe above a smoldering cigarette in a long black holder. Even more unsettling was finding a website selling T-shirts printed with both my name and a grainy photograph of me standing at a lectern. When I e-mailed to ask why the proprietors were selling my picture without permission, they responded, "I guess we are not very well-behaved girls."

The ambiguity of the slogan surely accounts for its appeal. To the public-spirited, it is a provocation to action, a less pedantic way of saying that if you want to make a difference in the world, you can't worry too much about what people think. To a few it may say, "Good girls get no credit." To a lot more, "Bad girls have more fun." Its popularity proves its point. Nobody has proposed printing T-shirts with any of the other one-liners in my article on funeral sermons. It is hard to imagine the women of Amtrak voluntarily wearing buttons that read, "The real drama is in the humdrum." Nor do I think the "Wild Women" of that Massachusetts nursing home would be cheered up by "They never asked to be remembered on earth. And they haven't been." Kay Mills certainly knew what she was doing when she picked one snappy sentence from that article about sermons.

But because I am a historian, I can't quite leave it at that. For some time now I've been collecting responses to the slogan, puzzling over the contradictory answers I have received, and wondering why misbehavior is such an appealing theme. It is hard to tell whether this is about feminism, post-feminism, or something much older. One thing it doesn't appear to have a lot to do with is history, at least not the kind that comes in books. For most people, the struggle is with the here and now, and with norms of good behavior that seem outdated yet will not go away.

Connie Schultz, a columnist for the *Cleveland Plain Dealer,* keeps a bumper sticker on her desk. She says that when men pass her desk, they "sometimes smile, sometimes snicker." One man read the words aloud, frowned, then pointed to a photo Schultz had on her desk of a friend with a newborn baby. " 'That's how women make history,' he huffed, then walked away." In contrast, women visiting her office usually have "an *a-ha* response." Schultz thinks they are remembering the lessons in good behavior they learned in girlhood, lessons she herself experienced: "Considerate meant deferential. Respectful was obedient. Polite was silent. 'No one likes a know-it-all,' we were told. And so we acted as if we knew nothing at all." As a journalist, Schultz had to overcome that conditioning to take on gritty topics usually reserved for male reporters. In 2005, her columns "in support of the weak, the oppressed, the underdog" won her a Pulitzer Prize.[4]

Jeanne Coverdale, the owner of an Iowa shop that sells quilting supplies both locally and online, was attending a conference in Puyallup, Washington, when she heard somebody use the "seldom" version of the quote. She immediately wrote it down, then went home and produced a snazzy blue-and-purple tie-dyed

T-shirt. The shirt was so popular she eventually created a whole line of products featuring the slogan, including a "leash" for keeping runaway scissors at home. When she wrote to thank me for the quotation, I was surprised: Hand-quilters hardly seem like candidates for rebellion. When I asked her about it, she responded that though most of her customers are indeed "salt-of-the-earth types, they like to see themselves as a little outrageous and naughty and out-of-control with their hobby."[5]

For the Sweet Potato Queens, being "outrageous and naughty and out-of-control" *is* a hobby. They adopt red wigs, false eyelashes, and sequined green dresses for the annual St. Patrick's Day parade in Jackson, Mississippi. Singer Kacey Jones recently performed their theme song on Garrison Keillor's radio show *Prairie Home Companion.* The first verse and the refrain go this way:

> *Now, I've been gettin' in trouble ever since I was a child*
> *Mama told me, "Girls like you turn into women that*
>   *run wild"*
> *But if I didn't do what I'd done, I wouldn't of had me so*
>   *much fun*
> *And Mama, life's too short to live it any other way*

> *Well-behaved women don't drink shots and beers*
> *That's why well-behaved women bore us all to tears*
> *They're politically correct but we invite them to defect*
> *'Cuz well-behaved women rarely make history.*[6]

The song continues with a rollicking roster of "historical chicks," mostly sirens of the stage and screen like Mae West, Sophia Loren, and Brigitte Bardot, though Golda Meir got into one verse because her name is a rough rhyme for Cher.[7]

At first glance, there is a chasm between the purposeful professionalism of Connie Schultz and the raucous "misbehavior" of the

SPQs. But some people see a connection. In May 2001, a reporter for a daily newspaper in South Carolina wrote to ask me if I was the author of the slogan. When I asked him why he wanted to know, he explained that a state Supreme Court justice, a woman "who has a historic career in public service here, hit a parked car, drove away, and later admitted she was drinking." When the reporter asked for a comment from one of the judge's supporters, a local leader famous for his wit, the man responded, "Well-behaved women seldom make history. Any further explanation is superfluous." To him it seemed obvious that any woman spunky enough to rise to the top of her profession was also likely to break other social norms.

Not long afterward, a friend sent me a clipping from the *Denver Post* that described the opposite case, a woman with a wild reputation who ended up in a responsible position. The newspaper reporter played the contrast for all it was worth, beginning with a description of Kathy "Cargo" Rodeman in a bar. The man sitting on the stool next to her did not know that she had once beaten her drunken father with a chair and a fireplace poker. So when he jabbed her one time too many, "she turned, hooked one long wiry arm around the guy's waist, and took him down." Weeks later, the town of Oak Creek, Colorado, elected her mayor. Some people wondered how a woman who had been arrested more than a dozen times and who was so poor her phone was about to be turned off could end up in such an office. "She's wild and crazy," said the local police chief, her major political rival. Rodeman doesn't deny it. "My momma started buyin' me cigarettes when I was 8 so I'd stop stealin' hers," she told the reporter. She said that when she was eighteen she tried hard drugs, but quit because she liked it too much. Rodeman may be wild, but according to the *Denver Post* she takes pride in two things: "I am a hard worker and a good mother." Her car, which is her second office, carries a familiar slogan. "That bumper sticker gets me in more trouble," she says.[8]

So what do people see when they read that well-behaved women rarely make history? Do they imagine good-time girls in stiletto heels or do-good girls carrying clipboards and passing petitions? Do they envision an out-of-control hobbyist or a single mother taking down a drunk in a bar? I suspect that it depends on where they stand themselves.

A manager in a Los Angeles development firm wrote to tell me that she and other members of the staff were outraged when the editor of their company magazine printed my sentence on T-shirts and coffee mugs distributed at a trade show. They thought the slogan was "disrespectful to women," that it was "sexist," "immoral and unethical," and a "horrible representation for our company." After a little research my correspondent discovered more positive implications of the slogan, but she still worried about its impact on the general public. "The ugly truth is, a regular joe would not know what your phrase means. People who are surrounded and involved in woman's issues and working to break the barriers women experience in the business world and in life in general, would be far more likely to look at your phrase in a different light," she wrote. In this case, history came to the rescue. Her company decided to keep the slogan but print it with a picture of a historical figure "such as Queen Elizabeth or Joan of Arc."

For some, history is a repository of edifying examples, for others a source of—if vague—vicarious rebellion. A custom-designed T-shirt for a women's camp-out in New England featured a cartoon of a long-lashed Lady Godiva perched on a bemused horse. When I asked the designer whether her drawing alluded to some forbidden activity, skinny-dipping perhaps, or an addiction to Belgian chocolate, she laughed and said she had no idea. It was just the first image that popped into her mind when she thought about the slogan.

A "Misbehaving Women Quilt" displayed at a national fiber arts festival in Nashua, New Hampshire, in the fall of 2002, featured nineteen meticulously embroidered and appliquéed mythical and historical figures ranging from Mother Eve to Gloria Steinem. Suzanne Bruno, who organized the project, admits that "the 'misbehaving' guidelines were pretty loose." One quilter featured her suffragist grandmother carrying a 1918 Armistice Day banner reading, WE MADE THEM SURRENDER. Another portrayed Katharine Lee Bates, the author of "America the Beautiful." The printed guide did not explain what qualified Bates as a misbehaving woman, but it must have been her lifelong partnership with fellow Wellesley College professor Katharine Coman. Bruno's own square featured Lizzie Borden with an ax and her favorite flower, a pansy.[9]

The historical content in *Cool Women: The Thinking Girl's Guide to the Hippest Women in History* is even more eclectic. The product of Girl Press, self-described publishers of "slightly dangerous books for girl mavericks," it splashes a green strip and the words "Well-behaved women rarely make history" across an orange cover filled with the names of famous—and infamous—women. There are lady pirates, suffragists, sports champions, Apache warriors, and samurai, as well as the "Fearless Flying WASPs" (female pilots) of World War II. The book is commendably multicultural, giving as much space to Queen Njinga of Angola as to Joan of Arc—though, unlike the edifying biographies parents and teachers might prefer, it does not discriminate between bandit queens and tennis greats, and it pays as much attention to fictional characters like Scarlett O'Hara as to historical figures like Harriet Tubman. An acknowledgment on the inside says the authors donate part of their royalties to Girls Inc. of Greater Santa Barbara, a "nonprofit organization dedicated to empowering girls to be strong, smart, and bold." The pervasive theme is rebellion. When deviance isn't apparent, the prose creates it. Georgia O'Keeffe was a "renegade artist." Martha Graham was the "ultimate wild girl of dance." Marie Curie "walked into the boys' club of the science world and basically tore the place apart."[10]

Cool Women suggests that "empowered" women are by definition "wild" women. That is a very old idea. Since antiquity, misogynists have insisted that females, being more emotional than males, are less stable, more likely to swing between extremes. Think of the old nursery rhyme that says, *when she was good, she was very, very good, but when she was bad she* . . . made history?

So how does a woman make history? Obviously, Marie Curie didn't win two Nobel Prizes by throwing tantrums in the lab. True, after her husband's death French tabloids pilloried her for having an affair with a married collaborator.[11] But she isn't remembered today because she was "bad" but because she was "very, very good" at what she did. So why doesn't high achievement in science qualify a woman as "well-behaved"? Could it be because some people still assume women aren't supposed to stand out in a crowd?

The "well-behaved women" quote works because it plays into longstanding stereotypes about the invisibility and the innate decorum of the female sex. Many people think women are less visible in history than men because their bodies impel them to nurture. Their job is to bind the wounds, stir the soup, and bear the children of those whose mission it is to fight wars, rule nations, and define the cosmos. Not all those who make this argument consider women unimportant—on the contrary, they often revere the contributions of women as wives, mothers, and caregivers—or at least they say so. But they also assume that domestic roles haven't changed much over the centuries, and that women who perform them have no history. A New Hampshire pastor captured this notion when he wrote in his commonplace book in 1650, "Woman's the center & lines are men." If women occupy the fixed center of life, and if history is seen as a linear progression of public events, a changing panorama of wars and kingdoms, then only those who through outrageous behavior, divine intervention, or sheer genius step into the stream of public consequence have a history.

The problem with this argument is not only that it limits women.

It also limits history. Good historians are concerned not only with famous people and public events but with broad transformations in human behavior, things like falling death rates or transatlantic migration. Here seemingly small actions by large numbers of people can bring about profound change. But this approach runs up against another imperative of history—its reliance on written sources. Until recent times most women (and a great many men) were illiterate. As a consequence their activities were recorded, if at all, in other people's writing. People who caused trouble might show up in court records, newspapers, or their masters' diaries. Those who quietly went about their lives were either forgotten, seen at a distance, or idealized into anonymity. Even today, publicity favors those who make—or break—laws.

But the difficulty is bigger than that. History is an account of the past based on surviving sources, but it is also a way of making sense out of the present. In the heat and confusion of events, people on all sides of an issue mine old stories for inspiration, enlightenment, or confirmation. Their efforts add to the layers of understanding attached to the original events, shaping what later generations know and care about. Scholars sometimes call these popular reconstructions of the past "memory" to distinguish them from formal history. But serious history is also forged in the tumult of change. History is not just what happened in the past. It is what later generations choose to remember.

The figure of Joan of Arc can rescue a controversial coffee mug today because office workers in Los Angeles in 2004 are no longer obsessed with the issues that fractured France and England when Joan put on her armor in 1429. Was she a saint, a witch, a virgin, a whore, a transvestite, or a simple peasant? Over time, she has been all these things. She was burned as a heretic in 1431, then posthumously reprieved in 1456. She was alternately venerated and vilified for the next four centuries. In *Henry VI*, Shakespeare portrayed her as a witch, a "dolphin or dogfish," a "Devil, or Devil's dam." In the introduction to his play *Saint Joan,* George Bernard Shaw called her "the most notable Warrior Saint in the Christian calendar, and the queerest fish among the eccentric worthies of the Middle Ages." Although the case for her beatification was first put forward in 1869, she wasn't canonized until 1920. Even then her meaning would not stay fixed. On one side of the English Channel, she inspired women suffragists; on the other, she became an icon of Catholic conservatism.[12] Clearly notions of good behavior vary from place to place, and they change over time.

The Angolan heroine Njinga Mbandi, known in some accounts as Queen Zhinga or Jinga, has gone through a similar transformation. In seventeenth-century sources, she spanned the spectrum from devout Christian to savage warrior. Portuguese missionaries were happy to claim her as an early convert, but changed their minds when she recanted and established a rebel kingdom. A book published in England in 1670 described her as dressed in animal skins with a feather stuck "through the holes of her bored Nose," hacking off a victim's head, then drinking "a great draught of his blood."[13] But all that had changed by the 1830s, when the American abolitionist Lydia Maria Child used her achievements to refute proslavery arguments about the incapacity of Africans for self-rule. "History furnishes very few instances of bravery, intelligence and perseverance equal to the famous Zhinga, the Negro queen of Angola," Child wrote. In the twentieth century, after Angolans once again won their independence from Portugal, Njinga became a national heroine. Today, some accounts refer to her as "an African Joan of Arc."[14] So she was, in more ways than one.

Sometimes fiction overwhelms history and people get remembered for things they didn't do. Consider that edifying, outrageous, and amusing character Lady Godiva. Historians still wonder how a pious eleventh-century Anglo-Saxon woman named Godgifu became known as an equestrian streaker. In her own lifetime, she was a well-behaved woman who endowed Christian monasteries and cathedrals. The story of her ride first appeared nearly two centuries after her death in the chronicle of an English monk, who portrayed her as a dutiful wife who undertook to ride unclothed only because her husband, as a cruel joke, said he would reduce taxes on his subjects on the day she rode naked through the streets of Coventry. Since Godgifu herself owned the lands around Coventry, she would have had no need for such a stratagem. But the monk's story prevailed. The story of an imagined woman devoted both to her people and obedient to her husband so entranced Queen Victoria that she gave Prince Albert a silver statue of the nude rider for his forty-eighth birthday. A re-enactment of Godiva's ride is the centerpiece of a popular festival in Coventry, England, to this day. Elsewhere the legend is losing its power, perhaps because nudity has become so commonplace. Perhaps in another generation Godgifu will be reincarnated as a wealthy philanthropist.[15]

Historians don't own history. But we do have a lot of experience sifting through competing evidence. Historical research is a bit like detective work. We re-create past events from fragments of information, trying hard to distinguish credible accounts from wishful thinking. One of our jobs is to explore the things that get left out when a person becomes an icon. Recent scholarship on the Sweet Potato Queens' heroine, Mae West, is a good example. There is no question about West's reputation for misbehavior. She said it herself: "When I'm bad, I'm better." Beginning her stage career at the age of six, she moved from playing the saintly Little Eva in *Uncle Tom's Cabin* to shimmying her way to fame. In uptight Boston, theater owners cut off the lights "with West's first ripple." But in New York she was the darling of urban sophisticates who wanted to explore the seamy side of life without leaving their theater seats. When she moved to Hollywood in the 1930s, censors tried to clean up her scripts, but she knew how to fill even the blandest lines with sexual innuendo. *Variety* complained that "Mae couldn't sing a lullaby without making it sexy."[16]

That is how Mae West made history. But what sort of history did she make? Some recent studies focus on her debts to the male homosexuals whose outrageous impersonations defined *camp* in the 1920s. Others claim that her largest debt was to African American entertainers. West's shimmy, for example, ultimately derived from West African traditions adapted in rural dance halls, or "jooks." Her ballad "Honey let yo' drawers hang down low" (which may have inspired the Sweet Potato Queens' "Never Wear Panties to a Party") was a favorite in southern jooks. In the early twentieth century, West, the sexually active, streetwise girl from Brooklyn, gave middle-class audiences a glimpse of worlds that both fascinated and repelled. Like the legendary Godiva, she allowed people to imagine the unimaginable. Because she was also a savvy businesswoman, she was able to live off other people's fantasies.[17]

A first-year student at a California university told me that to make history, people need to do the unexpected. She offered the example of civil rights activist Rosa Parks, "who would not leave her seat."[18] I like her emphasis on the unexpected. It not only captures the sense of history as the study of how things change, it offers a somewhat more complex way of understanding the contribution of a woman like Parks.

Was Parks a well-behaved woman? The Montgomery, Alabama, bus company did not think so. As the student from California recognized, Parks made history precisely because she dared to challenge both social norms and the law. Her refusal to obey the statute that required her to give up her seat to a white passenger sparked the 361-day-long boycott that thrust Martin Luther King into the public eye and led to a historic Supreme Court decision outlawing segregation on public transportation.[19] Yet Parks became an icon for the civil rights movement not only for her courage but because the media identified her as a hard-working seamstress who simply got tired of moving to the back of the bus. Few people outside Montgomery knew her as the politically conscious secretary of the local NAACP, nor understood how many years she and her husband had been working for social justice before that fateful day on the bus. In 1954 and 1955, Parks had attended workshops on desegregation sponsored by the radical Highlander Folk School in Tennessee, a public education project that Mississippi's Senator James Eastland excoriated as a "front for a conspiracy to overthrow this country."[20]

Nor has popular history recorded the names of other Montgomery women—teenagers—whose arrests that year for refusing to give up their seats failed to ignite a movement. Years later, E. D. Nixon, president of the Montgomery NAACP, explained why he hadn't chosen any of these other women to make a historic stand against segregation. "OK, the case of Louise Smith. I found her daddy in front of his shack, barefoot, drunk. Always drunk. Couldn't use her. In that year's second case, the girl, very brilliant but she'd had an illegitimate baby. Couldn't use her. The last case before Rosa was the daughter of a preacher who headed a reform school for years. My interview of her convinced me that she wouldn't stand up to pressure. She were even afraid of me. When Rosa Parks was arrested, I thought, 'This is it!' 'Cause she's morally clean, she's reliable, nobody had nothing on her, she had the courage of her convictions."[21] Parks's publicly acknowledged good behavior helped to justify her rebellion and win support for her cause. As one friend recalled, she "was too sweet to even say 'damn' in anger."[22]

After Parks's death in the fall of 2005, the airways were filled with tributes celebrating the life of the "humble seamstress," the "simple woman" who sparked a revolution because her feet were tired. Reviewing these eulogies, syndicated columnist Ellen Goodman asked, "Is it possible we prefer our heroes to be humble? Or is it just our heroines?" She wondered if it wasn't time Americans got over the notion that women are "accidental heroines," unassuming creatures thrust into the public eye by circumstances beyond their control. Goodman noted that Parks and her compatriots spent years preparing for just such an opportunity. She concluded: "Rosa Parks was 'unassuming'—except that she rejected all the assumptions about her place in the world. Rosa Parks was a 'simple woman'—except for a mind made up and fed up. She was 'quiet'—except, of course, for one thing. Her willingness to say 'no' changed the world."[23]

The California student said that in contrast to Parks a "well-behaved woman" is "a quiet, subservient, polite, indoors, cooking, cleaning type of girl who would never risk shame by voicing her own opinion." There is a delicious irony in this part of her definition. Notice that it associates a particular kind of work—cooking and cleaning—with subservience and passivity. Yet the boycott that made Parks famous was sustained by hundreds of African American domestic servants—cooks and maids—who walked to work rather than ride segregated buses. They too did the unexpected.[24]

Serious history talks back to slogans. But in the contest for public attention, slogans usually win. Consider my simple sentence. It sat quietly for years in the folds of a scholarly journal. Now it honks its ambiguous wisdom from coffee mugs and tailgates.

Not long ago, I received an e-mail from Austin, Texas. My correspondent told me that to her the slogan means that when women try to behave in a traditional "ladylike" way, they "miss the opportunity to really speak their minds" and become "passive and unimportant." Unfortunately, her husband disagrees. He thinks the saying "has more to do with being a 'bad girl' and getting attention from it, like Madonna and Britney Spears." Now she wonders "what my bumper sticker is really saying to my fellow Austinites." I wish I could tell her.

What I can do is explain what those words meant to me when I first wrote them.

In 1975, I was a thirty-six-year-old housewife enrolled in a graduate seminar in early American history. At the time, few historians of colonial America had much to say about women, and few historians of women had anything to say about the colonial period except to acknowledge the horror of the Salem witch hunts or lament the fate of Anne Hutchinson, the religious visionary who was banished from Boston in the 1630s. I wanted to know more about ordinary women, the ones who sustained the colonies day to day. In my search for sources for a seminar paper, I stumbled on a succession of funeral sermons celebrating the lives of pious women. These became the subject of my first scholarly publication. My objective was to dig beneath the pious platitudes that both celebrated and obscured their lives.

"Virtuous Women Found: New England Ministerial Literature, 1668–1735," appeared in *American Quarterly* in the spring of 1976.[25] It began this way:

> Cotton Mather called them "the hidden ones." They never preached or sat in a deacon's bench. Nor did they vote or attend Harvard. Neither, because they were virtuous women, did they question God or the magistrates. They prayed secretly, read the Bible through at least once a year, and went to hear the minister preach even when it snowed. Hoping for an eternal crown, they never asked to be remembered on earth. And they haven't been. Well-behaved women seldom make history.

My objective was not to lament their oppression, but to give them a history.

I may have had in the back of my mind a half-remembered line from an influential study of the rise of the novel—"Happy love has no history." (I had done graduate study in literature before I became a historian.) There are many versions of the same idea, including the famous opening sentence from Tolstoy's *Anna Karen-*

ina, "Happy families are all alike; every unhappy family is unhappy in its own way."[26] I could add my own mother's sardonic comment about housework: "Nobody notices it unless you don't do it." Or a friend's witty variant, "Nobody sees clean windows." However it happened, the words just slipped out, unbidden and without struggle.

Or so it seemed. But when I tell the story this way, I leave out several important facts. I was not only a thirty-six-year-old housewife enrolled in a graduate seminar in early American history. I was a thirty-six-year-old wife and mother who with a handful of friends in the Boston area had helped to found an independent periodical devoted to the "twin platforms of Mormonism and feminism." Both "isms" mattered: despite my flirtation with the women's movement, I too went to church even when it snowed. I didn't expect to have a career. For me, history was still a kind of hobby, though, like the quilters in Iowa, I was probably "a little outrageous and naughty and out-of-control" in its pursuit.

My friends and I called our feminist newspaper *Exponent II* to honor a nineteenth-century pro-suffrage periodical launched by Mormon women in Utah in 1872. Most of us had grown up knowing about the heroism of pioneer ancestors who had participated in the epic trek across the United States, but until we discovered old copies of the original *Woman's Exponent,* few of us knew anything about early Mormon feminism. We did not know that Utah women voted and held office fifty years before women in the eastern United States, nor that polygamists' wives had attended medical school, published newspapers, and organized cooperative enterprises. Reading their words, we were astonished at how confidently these pioneer women insisted on their right to participate in public life and work. In our enthusiasm, we no doubt missed many of the ironies in their stories (nobody wanted to think of polygamy as a liberating force). Still, we found in their lives models for religious commitment, social activism, and personal achievement that seemed far more powerful than the complacent domesticity portrayed in popular magazines or in our own congregations.

I originally thought of doing a dissertation on pioneer Utah, but since I was studying at the University of New Hampshire, where my husband taught engineering, I decided to focus instead on the colonial period, a particular strength of the history department there. Beyond that, I found it liberating to study a world seemingly disconnected from my own life and heritage. In researching that seminar paper on funeral sermons, I discovered the attractions of strangeness and the liberation in working with material that seemed opaque and alien. In the personal essays I wrote for *Exponent II*, I was all-present, accountable to the world and people I loved. Moving backward in time, I was able to establish a critical distance from my own life and culture. There was no point in advocacy. I had to sit back and try to understand.

Because my time and mobility were limited, I focused on women in northern Massachusetts, Maine, and New Hampshire near where I lived. Piecing together fragments of information gleaned from court records, gravestones, Indian captivity narratives, and men's account books, letters, and diaries, I attempted to see beyond the biblical archetypes employed in Puritan sermons. The dissertation led to my first book, *Good Wives: Image and Reality in the Lives of Women in Northern New England, 1650–1750*, which was published in 1982.

In my scholarly work, my form of misbehavior has been to care about things that other people find predictable or boring. My second book is a case in point. At a distance, the life of Martha Moore Ballard was the stuff from which funeral sermons were made. She was a "good wife" in every sense of the word, indistinguishable from all the self-sacrificing and pious women celebrated in Puritan eulogies. In conventional terms, she did not make history. She cherished social order, respected authority, and abhorred violence. As a midwife and healer, she relied on home-grown medicines little

different from those found in English herbals a century before her
birth. Her religious sentiments were conventional; her reading was
limited to the Bible, edifying pamphlets, and newspapers. Although
she lived through the American Revolution, she had little interest
in politics. She was a caregiver and a sustainer rather than a mover
and shaker.

Ballard made history by performing a methodical and seemingly
ordinary act—writing a few words in her diary every day.
Through the diary we know her as a pious herbalist whose curiosity about the human body led her to observe and record autopsies as
well as nurse the sick, whose integrity allowed her to testify in a
sensational rape trial against a local judge who was her husband's
employer, and whose sense of duty took her out of bed at night not
only to deliver babies but to care for the bodies of a wife and children murdered by their own husband and father. The power of the
diary is not only in its sensational stories, however, but in its
patient, daily recording of seemingly inconsequential events, strug-
gles with fatigue and discouragement, conflicts with her son,
and little things—like the smell of a room where a dead body lay.
In Ballard's case, the drama really was in the humdrum. The
steadiness of the diary provided the frame for everything else that
happened.

But it took at least two feminist movements to give significance
to her life. Nineteenth-century feminism sent her great-great-
granddaughter Mary Hobart to medical school in 1882. Hobart,
who believed she had inherited the mantle of her "gifted ancestor,"
lovingly cared for the diary, and shortly before her death, gave it to
the Maine State Library at Augusta. There it sat, of interest mainly
to local historians and genealogists, until a second women's movement launched a renaissance in history. I found it there in the summer of 1981 when I went to the Maine State Archives to research an
entirely different topic.[27]

To all appearances, Martha Ballard was a well-behaved woman.

Had she been better-behaved, however—more protective of her own and others' reputations—she would have inked out the family conflicts and neighborhood scandals that leaked into her record despite her best efforts to remain circumspect. Or she might never have kept a diary at all. Her occupation gave her a reason to keep records, but something else drove her to transform a list of births into a daily journal and a journal into a powerful assertion of her own presence and weight in the world. Most well-behaved women are too busy living their lives to think about recording what they do and too modest about their own achievements to think anybody else will care. Ballard was different. She was not a mover and shaker, but neither did she choose invisibility.

Although I have received mail addressed to Martha Ballard and have been identified on at least one college campus as a midwife, I am only a little bit like my eighteenth-century subject. Like her, I was raised to be an industrious housewife and a self-sacrificing and charitable neighbor, but sometime in my thirties I discovered that writing about women's work was a lot more fun than doing it. I remember thinking one winter day how ironic it was that I was wrapped in a bathrobe with the heat of a wood stove rising toward my loft as I wrote about a courageous woman who braved snow-storms and crossed a frozen river on a cake of ice to care for moth-ers in labor. I felt selfish, pampered, and decadent. But I did not stop what I was doing. I did not know why I needed to write Martha's story, and I could not imagine that anybody else would ever want to follow me through my meandering glosses on her diary. I was astonished at the reception of the book. Even more important than the prizes was the discovery of how important this long-dead midwife's story was to nurses, midwives, and anony-mous caregivers dealing with quite different circumstances today. These readers helped me to see that history is more than an engag-ing enterprise. It is a primary way of creating meaning. The mean-ing I found in Martha Ballard's life had something to do with my own life experience, but perhaps a lot more to do with the collective experiences of a generation of Americans coping with dramatic changes in their own lives.

When I wrote that "well-behaved women seldom make history," I was making a commitment to help recover the lives of otherwise obscure women. I had no idea that thirty years later, my own words would come back to me transformed. While I like some of the uses of the slogan more than others, I wouldn't call it back even if I could. I applaud the fact that so many people—students, teachers, quilters, nurses, newspaper columnists, old ladies in nursing homes, and mayors of western towns—think they have the right to make history.

Some history-making is intentional; much of it is accidental. People make history when they scale a mountain, ignite a bomb, or refuse to move to the back of the bus. But they also make history by keeping diaries, writing letters, or embroidering initials on linen sheets. History is a conversation and sometimes a shouting match between present and past, though often the voices we most want to hear are barely audible. People make history by passing on gossip, saving old records, and by naming rivers, mountains, and children. Some people leave only their bones, though bones too make history when someone notices.

Historian Gerda Lerner has written: "All human beings are practicing historians. . . . We live our lives; we tell our stories. It is as natural as breathing."[28] But if no one cares about those stories, they do not survive. People not only make history by living their lives, but by creating records and by turning other people's lives into books or slogans.

So here is another attempt to make history. Unlike my previous work, this book does not limit itself to early America. Ranging widely in time and space, and relying on the work of other scholars, I ask how and under what circumstances women have made history. I am interested in what women did in the past, how their actions were recorded, and how later generations remembered them. My objective is neither to prove nor to disprove the claims of my slogan, but to show the intersection of present and past in the making of history.

I begin with three classic works in Western feminism that were rediscovered about the time I began my own work: Christine de Pizan's *Book of the City of Ladies,* Elizabeth Cady Stanton's *Eighty Years and More,* and Virginia Woolf's *A Room of One's Own.* I begin with these three books, not only because they were important to my generation of scholars, but because all three authors turned to history as a way of making sense of their own lives.

I still have the dog-eared copy of *Eighty Years and More* that I used when I taught my first women's history course in 1975. Stanton's personal story of the struggle for women's rights helped to define what came to be called "first-wave feminism," the nineteenth-century movement that in the United States culminated with the passage of the women's suffrage amendment.

I discovered Christine's *Book of the City of Ladies* a few years later. Though known to specialists in medieval literature, it was virtually unknown to others until 1982, when it appeared in paperback in an accessible English translation. Readers were astonished. How was it possible that a woman living in fifteenth-century France could write so candidly about topics important to contemporary feminism?

Woolf's *A Room of One's Own* had been there all along. Never out of print since its publication in 1928, it nevertheless took on fresh meanings as a new generation of women began to "think back through their mothers."

This book is my gift to all of those who continue to make history—through action, through record-keeping, and through remembering.

WELL-BEHAVED WOMEN
SELDOM MAKE
HISTORY

Chapter One

۹

THREE WRITERS

$\mathcal{H}$ ere are the stories of three women making history. One was a poet and scholar attached to a French court, another was an American activist, the third an English novelist. None was a historian in the conventional sense, but all three were determined to give women a history. The settings in which they worked were radically different. The problems they faced were surprisingly—disturbingly—the same.

For each, a moment of illumination came through an encounter with an odious book.

Paris, France, c. 1400

Christine de Pizan sat in her study. Weary of serious reading, she opened a satire someone had given her for safekeeping. She knew better than to take its diatribes against women seriously, yet somehow its arguments disturbed her. Even the sight of the book made her wonder why so many learned men had "devilish and wicked thoughts about women." She took more volumes from their shelves. Men's opinions spilled out like a gushing fountain, filling her with doubt. "I could hardly find a book on morals where, even before I had read it in its entirety, I did not find several chapters or certain selections attacking women, no matter who the author was." She began to think God had made a vile creature when he created woman.[1]

In her despair she began to pray, asking why she could not have been born male. As she sat with her head bowed, tears streaming from her eyes, she discerned a beam of light falling on her lap just as a ray of sun might have done if it had been the right hour of the day. Looking up from her shadowed corner, Christine beheld a vision: standing before her were three radiant women. Terrified, she made the sign of the cross.

The first woman spoke. "Dear daughter, do not be afraid, for we have not come here to harm or trouble you, but to console you." Identifying herself as Lady Reason, the specter held up to Christine the mirror of self-knowledge. "Come back to yourself, recover your senses, and do not trouble yourself any more over such absurdities." She told Christine that she and her companions, Lady Rectitude and Lady Justice, had come to help her build a city in which the fame of good women would endure against all assailants. Together they would restore the reputations of those unjustly accused.[2]

Guided by her three visitors, Christine went back to books and discovered the lives of worthy women—queens, princesses, warriors, poets, inventors, weavers of tapestries, wives, mothers, sibyls, and saints. From their stories, she would build a city fit for the Queen of Heaven.

Johnstown, New York, c. 1825

Elizabeth Cady sat quietly in her father's law office listening to the complaints of his widowed clients. Absorbing their tales of woe, she wondered why her father couldn't do more to help them. When she asked him, Daniel Cady took a lawbook from its shelf and showed her the "inexorable statutes" that gave husbands the right to pass over their wives in favor of their sons. Married women, he explained, were civilly dead. Amused by Elizabeth's distress, the law students in Cady's office joined in the exercise, reading her "the worst laws they could find." One teased her by saying that if she should grow up to become his wife, her new coral necklace and bracelets should be his. "I could take them and lock them up, and you could never wear them except with my permission. I could even exchange them for a box of cigars, and you could watch them evaporate in smoke."[3]

Elizabeth puzzled over the power of her father's books. When he wasn't looking, she began to mark the offending statutes with pencil, planning "when alone in the office, to cut every one of them out of the books." Fortunately, she confided her secret to a housekeeper, who alerted her father. Without letting her know that he had discovered her secret, he explained how laws were made, telling her that even if his entire library were to burn, it would make no difference, because there were other books and other libraries. "When you are grown up, and able to prepare a speech," said he, "you must go down to Albany and talk to the legislators; tell them all you have seen in this office . . . and, if you can persuade them to pass new laws, the old ones will be a dead letter."[4]

Elizabeth vowed to do just that. When she grew up she would not only go down to Albany but journey across the Atlantic and throughout the United States in defense of women's rights.

London, England, 1928

Virginia Woolf, or one of her fictional personae ("call me Mary Beton, Mary Seton, Mary Carmichael or by any name you please"), sat in the domed reading room of the British Museum. She had returned from giving a lecture at Cambridge with her head full of questions. "Why was one sex so prosperous and the other so poor?" Surely the cached wisdom of a great library would provide answers. Surrounded by books, she lifted her pencil and prepared to begin, but no sooner had she written WOMEN AND POVERTY in block letters on a page of her notebook, than the enormity of her task confronted her.[5]

The more notes she took, the more confused she became. "Professors, schoolmasters, sociologists, clergymen, novelists, essayists, journalists, men who had no qualification save that they were not women, chased my simple and single question—Why are women poor?—until it became fifty questions; until the fifty questions leapt frantically into mid-stream and were carried away." Pausing in her labors, she began to doodle. Before she knew it, she had drawn a figure she called "Professor von X, engaged in writing his monumental work entitled *The Mental, Moral, and Physical Inferiority of the Female Sex*." The Professor was not a man attractive to women. "He was heavily built; he had a great jowl; to balance that he had very small eyes; he was very red in the face." Where had this phantom come from? Alas, from the morning's reading. Somewhere in that pile of books was a statement that had aroused a demon. That was hardly surprising. No woman likes to be told she is "naturally the inferior of a little man." Woolf looked at the unshaven student next to her and "began drawing cartwheels and circles over the angry professor's face till he looked like a burning bush or flaming comet—anyhow, an apparition without human semblance or significance. The professor was nothing now but a faggot burning on the top of Hampstead Heath."[6]

She returned the books to the center desk, and went to lunch. She had failed in her quest, but she had stumbled on anger—not just her own, but the anger of professors who liked to write about women. Why was it, she asked, that those who ruled the world felt the need to diminish women? Was anger, she wondered, "the familiar, the attendant sprite on power?"[7]

Little matter. For the moment at least, she had banished the Professor. With money and a room of her own, she would write her own books.[8]

Three Writers Making History

In each of these stories, a studious female discovers male disdain for women, and that discovery leads to a new mission. Christine de Pizan's story appears in the opening pages of her *Book of the City of Ladies,* a sophisticated allegory that remains, six centuries later, an accessible and provocative collection of female biographies. Elizabeth Cady Stanton told her story in Chapter II of *Eighty Years and More,* an autobiographical account of her fifty-year fight for women's suffrage. Virginia Woolf's vignette appears in *A Room of One's Own,* a semifictional essay that began as a pair of lectures given at the women's colleges at Cambridge University in 1928.

Christine lived in the age before printing. The books she read (and sometimes helped produce) were handwritten, and so precious that only those with great wealth or access to noble libraries might read them. Elizabeth Cady Stanton was born four hundred years later in a rural village in a new American republic. Her father's library, which contained classics of English literature as well as legal tomes, was a symbol of middle-class respectability in a nation proud of its revolutionary heritage. In contrast, the library where Woolf worked was an imperial behemoth. The British Museum prided itself on gathering under its roof the national literatures as well as the material artifacts of other nations. By 1912 it claimed to have not only the largest library in the world but the only one of any consequence possessing a complete printed catalog of its collections. Woolf was both impressed with and disdainful of its systems. "London," she wrote, "was like a workshop. . . . The British Museum was another department of the factory."[9]

Given such radical differences in setting, the similarity between the three stories is striking. There is no question of influence. Stanton and Woolf may have heard of Christine, but they could not have read her work. *The City of Ladies,* written in medieval French

British Museum Reading Room, *Illustrated London News*, 1857.
To Woolf, the massive room, with its spokes reaching out
from the central desk, felt like "part of the gallery."

in 1405, was not accessible in modern French or English until the 1980s. Only specialists consulted the manuscript compendium of Christine's work that had long been in the British Museum.[10] Nor is there any indication that Woolf read Stanton, or that if she had she would have been pleased. The narrator of *A Room of One's Own* dismisses old-fashioned suffragists and their cause, explaining that on the very day Parliament gave the vote to women, she received a legacy from an aunt who had died in India. "Of the two—the vote and the money—the money, I own, seemed infinitely more important."[11]

Yet there are intriguing parallels in the lives of the three writers. All had intellectual fathers, domestic mothers. All three were raised in settings that simultaneously encouraged and thwarted their love of learning. All three married men who supported their intellectual ambitions. All three lived through the wrenching deaths of loved ones and terrifying, fratricidal warfare—the Hundred Years War in Christine's case, the American Civil War in Stanton's, and World War I for Woolf. All three identified with women yet imagined becoming male. In their work and in their lives, all three writers addressed an enduring puzzle: Are differences between the sexes innate or learned? Using stories about the past to challenge history, they talked back to books.

Today, other writers talk back to them. Historians from regions Christine knew only through myth now return the European gaze. In the United States, descendants of the slaves Stanton wrote about with amused condescension now teach in leading law schools and preside in courts. In Woolf's London, books as well as legacies arrive from Bombay. Meanwhile, all three writers have become icons themselves. Images from Christine's illuminated manuscripts grace websites, datebooks, and calendars. Stanton's home in Seneca Falls, New York, is now part of a Women's Rights National Historical Park. Woolf's face appears on T-shirts and postcards.

Their canonical status ensures criticism as well as applause. Medievalists debate Christine's significance, and feminists tangle over the meaning of her books. Is her fame deserved, or an artifact of her sex? Were her ideas revolutionary or conventional? Did she, like many high-achieving women, secure her own reputation by validating traditions she herself surmounted? Students of the women's rights movement are no more settled about Stanton. Was she a path-breaker or a skilled publicist who exaggerated her own oppression and ignored the contributions of others? Woolf has provoked even more powerful reactions. Was she, like the writers she wrote about, a "madwoman in the attic" and a victim of patriarchy? If so, by what devious path did she become the repressed nightmare in Edward Albee's play *Who's Afraid of Virginia Woolf?* Or the inspiration for a supposedly liberated cigarette called "Virginia Slims"? In 1998, her life and death and her novel *Mrs. Dalloway* inspired Michael Cunningham's *The Hours,* which won a Pulitzer Prize for fiction and, in the film version, an Academy Award for Nicole Kidman. And yet, despite the affection they display for Woolf, the novel and the film have her drowning herself years before her actual death.

Christine de Pizan, Elizabeth Cady Stanton, and Virginia Woolf continue to make history. For those who would understand how and why their stories matter, their books are a place to begin.

The City of Ladies: Celebrating Exemplary Women

Born in Italy in 1365, Christine was three years old when her father, Tommaso di Benvenuto da Pizzano, became a "philosopher, servant, and counselor" to the French monarch, Charles V. As a consequence, she grew up in Paris in the shadow of a glittering but fragile court. The king and his three brothers—Louis, Jean, and Philippe—rivaled each other in their commitment to literature and the arts. They commissioned masterworks in stone, stained glass, textiles, and metal, and gathered around them writers, scholars, and poets. Charles's library at the Louvre eventually contained nine hundred volumes, an extraordinary achievement in a world where the richest man might own no more than fifty books. In an era when books were complex works of art encrusted with gold leaf and precious stones and bound in silk, royal patronage created work for preparers of parchment, paint-makers, goldsmiths, illuminators, scholars, translators, and scribes. Christine became part of this circle.[12]

Under her father's supervision, Christine had an unusually fine education, though she later wrote that she didn't really appreciate it until misfortune forced her to use it. When she was fifteen, she married Etienne du Castel, a twenty-four-year-old scholar of noble birth who became the king's clerk and notary. Of her marriage she later wrote, "We had so arranged our love and our two hearts that we had but one will, closer than brother and sister, whether in joy or in sorrow." But their happiness was precarious. At the king's death, Christine's father lost his position, then died. In 1389, her husband too passed away. At age twenty-five, she was left a widow with a mother, two brothers, and three children of her own to support.[13]

Christine began by using her skills in penmanship to work as a scribe and copyist, eventually becoming a writer herself. Scholars have identified at least fifty-five manuscripts written in whole or in part in her hand. She was proud of her work, and included in several of her own books an image of herself in her study. One now at the British Museum shows her dressed in a modest blue gown and white headdress, sitting at a cloth-covered table with a tiny dog at her side. Although she appears here as a solitary figure, she did not work alone. In *The City of Ladies* she praises a female artist named Anàstasia, noting that "she has executed several things for me which stand out among the ornamental borders of the great masters."[14]

Christine wrote in most of the major genres of her day. She

Christine de Pizan in her study, from
Collected Works of Christine de Pizan

penned the official biography of Charles V, produced love lyrics, history, and allegory, and even completed a manual on military strategy. She fully understood that in becoming a scholar and a writer, she had intruded into the world of men. In 1401, shortly before writing *The Book of the City of Ladies,* she was drawn into a literary debate over the merits of an allegorical poem called *The Romance of the Rose.* She deplored its portrayal of women as vain, inconstant, and lewd. In turn, the poem's defenders dismissed her as incompetent. One begged her, as a "woman of great ingenuity," not to exceed her talents; "if you have been praised because you have shot a bullet over the towers of Notre Dame, don't try to hit the moon."[15]

For a time, Christine did doubt her own abilities. In *The Book of Fortune's Transformation* (*Le Livre de la Mutacion de Fortune*), she described the period of her early widowhood as a kind of shipwreck. Under the command of her husband, her household, like a ship, had been safe. Then, without warning, "a sudden and powerful wind started up; the whirlwind was twisted like a corkscrew, and it struck against the ship." With her "good master" dead, she too wished to die. She lay on the deck sobbing until, exhausted, she fell into a fitful sleep or trance. Then Fortune came to her, stroking her body until she awoke. Miraculously, her voice was lower and her limbs more firm. Looking up at the broken mast, she had the courage to repair and take command of the ship. "Thus I became a true man (this is no fable)." Through her writing she supported her family and assured her own fame. As a scribe, translator, poet, historian, and essayist, she became, as one scholar has observed, "the son of her father," and, by extension, the daughter of herself.[16]

In *The City of Ladies,* written in 1405, Christine made peace with her sex by redefining the boundaries of womanhood. The key to the book is the puzzle she poses in the powerful opening scene in the library. Here we discover that learned authors slander women and that Christine is both a scholar and a woman. Is she, therefore, less a woman for being a scholar? Or less a scholar for being a woman? The problem, we learn later, is grounded in her own life experience. Because her father supported her intellectual interests and her mother did not, Christine was in the peculiar position of identifying with her father rather than her mother in her life's vocation. Hence, the need to become "male" in order to take up her father's work. But the three women who appear to her in the library break through this dilemma. They assure Christine that though her mother attempted to keep her busy "with spinning and silly girlishness," she was unable to destroy that "feeling for the sciences," which Christine, "through natural inclination, had nevertheless gathered together in little droplets."[17] With the help of her spiritual guides, Christine discovers that women are by "nature" capable of a great many more things than the scurrilous authors in her library—and her own mother—had claimed.

Led by Reason, Justice, and Rectitude, Christine discovers women's history. This exploration of the past not only solves her own problem, it refutes the slanders that had so upset her. *The City of Ladies* admits that "there are very different kinds of women, and some unreasonable."[18] But by the piling up of examples, it makes good women the rule.

Cleverly posing as an innocent inquirer, Christine speaks through her guides, allowing them to answer her queries: Why do men speak disparagingly of women? Have females ever been successful rulers? Are women capable of learning, and if so have they ever invented anything new? Lady Reason and her companions answer by telling stories. They claim that Ovid covered up his own sins by attacking women, that Blanche of France was one of many effective rulers, and that writers like Proba and Sappho proved women could be philosophers and poets. They remind Christine that Arachne taught the world how to process flax and linen, that Ceres was the first "to discover cultivation," and that Dido built and ruled the "marvelously beautiful, large, and strong city" of Carthage where she "lived a long time in glory."[19] If famous women sometimes suffered a sad end, that was no matter. Their achievements lived beyond them.

Christine chose her stories selectively and, when necessary, reframed their meaning. Her discussion of Xanthippe, the wife of Socrates, omitted a famous anecdote in which the philosopher's wife supposedly drenched him with water, provoking a witty response: "Did I not say that Xanthippe's thunder would end in rain?" (Later, Chaucer embellished the story by saying that Socrates' wife "cast piss upon his head.") Christine ignored this incident entirely, emphasizing instead the constancy of Xanthippe's devotion to her apparently absentminded and not-too-attentive husband. "Although Socrates was already quite old and cared more about searching for knowledge and researching in books than obtaining soft and new things for his wife, the valiant lady nevertheless did not stop loving him." Xanthippe appreciated her husband's virtues because she too "possessed great learning and goodness."[20]

The City of Ladies is a passionate defense of women's capacity for education. The opening scene in which Christine describes her dismay over misogynist ideas seems casual, almost chatty. Yet it is also artful. She lets the reader know that she is engaged in "the devoted study of literature" and that she is "surrounded by books on many different subjects." When she wants to bolster the reader's acceptance of her sometimes controversial interpretations, she invokes scholarly evidence, usually putting the words into the mouth of one of her guides. For example, in asserting the power of women warriors, Christine writes, "This would be fantastic to repeat and hard to believe if so many historical writings did not attest to it." Yet she is also critical of her sources, and she consistently reinterprets their meaning, nudged on by Reason, who in their first encounter gently scolds her for thinking that "all the words of the philosophers are articles of faith, that they could never be wrong." Responding to the claims of those who say women shouldn't be educated, Rectitude says bluntly, "Here you can clearly see that not all opinions of men are based on reason and that these men are wrong."[21]

Christine's independence ultimately derives from her piety. Her description of her vision deliberately echoes the New Testament account of the angel Gabriel's visit to the Virgin Mary. In Luke 1:30, the angel says to the Virgin, "Fear not, Mary." In *The City of Ladies*, the figure of Reason, emerging like Gabriel from a beam of light, tells Christine, "Dear daughter, do not be afraid." Mary exclaims, "For with God nothing shall be impossible." Christine similarly responds: "I know well that nothing is impossible for

God." Mary says to Gabriel, "Behold the handmaid of the Lord: be it done unto me according to thy word." Christine says to her three visitors, "Behold your handmaiden ready to serve. Command and I will obey, and may it be unto me according to your word."²²

In dedicating her city to the Virgin, Christine appropriated and redefined the highest ideal of womanhood in the Middle Ages. Yet she also made sophisticated use of secular texts. Three-quarters of her stories derive from Giovanni Boccaccio's *De mulieribus claris* (*Of Famous Women*), a work completed in Italy in the summer of 1362.²³ Christine seems to have known Boccaccio's book both in the original Latin and in one of the French translations produced in Paris by collectors and courtiers associated with the court of Charles VI. But though she borrowed many of Boccaccio's stories, she rejected his principles of selection and challenged many of his conclusions.²⁴

Unlike Boccaccio, who confined himself to classical sources, Christine mixed biblical stories and saints' lives with secular accounts. She paired the Old Testament paragons Sarah, Rebecca, and Ruth with Homer's Penelope, and followed her story of Queen Esther with an account of the Sabine women. She also took from the Bible the chilling stories of Susanna, who is accosted by three elders while bathing, and of Judith, the resolute widow who infiltrates the enemy camp and decapitates the Assyrian general Holofernes.²⁵ Christine infused pagan stories with Christian meaning, as in her account of Ceres, who through her invention of agriculture ultimately provides the Christian symbols of bread and wine. Jesus Christ himself "paid a great honor to the science which Ceres invented, that is, bread-making, when it pleased Him to give to man and woman such a worthy body in the form of bread."²⁶

She also recast the meaning of Boccaccio's stories by situating them in a larger argument about the nature of women. In her treatment of the Amazons, for example, she transformed what were choppy little stories in *De mulieribus claris* into the history of a powerful and forgotten kingdom. She did this by synchronizing the various accounts and calculating "the periods and epochs" in which they occurred. If Amazons were present at the destruction of Troy and the founding of Rome and were still around when Alexander the Great paid them a visit, then "this kingdom of women, founded and powerfully upheld, lasted more than eight hundred years." For Christine, the story of the Amazons affirmed the validity of female rule at a time when French law barred women from succeeding to the throne.[27]

Even when she followed Boccaccio's storyline, Christine revised his meaning. Her account of the assault on Lucretia, a Roman matron renowned for her chastity, differs little from his. Both authors explain how a man belonging to the Roman royal family, the Tarquins, comes to Lucretia's bedchamber in her husband's absence. When Lucretia says she would rather be killed than submit to him, her assailant threatens to kill both her and one of her manservants so he can cover up his rape by claiming to have found them committing adultery. Lucretia submits only to save her servant's life; then, the next day, after telling her husband, father, and other male relatives what has happened, she kills herself. In Boccaccio's telling, Lucretia "cleansed her shame harshly, and for this reason she should be exalted with worthy praise for her chastity, which can never be sufficiently lauded." He adds that Lucretia's action not only restored her reputation but helped to free Rome, because in retaliation the Roman people rose up against the Tarquins and established the Republic.[28]

Christine gives the story a different slant by situating it in a larger discussion with Lady Rectitude about the claim made by some male authors "that many women want to be raped and that it does not bother them at all . . . even when they verbally protest." Lucretia's despair over being violated becomes as central to the argument as her virtue. Like Boccaccio, Christine acknowledges the revolt against the Tarquins, but she gives this too a new twist, arguing that because "of this outrage perpetuated on Lucretia, so some claim, a law was enacted whereby a man would be executed for raping a woman, a law which is fitting, just, and holy."[29] In this way, Christine shifts the emphasis from the nobility of chastity to the horror of rape.

Scholars today debate the significance of Christine de Pizan in the history of feminism. Surely she raised issues, such as violence against women, that seem strikingly contemporary. Yet, as one critic argues, "it is not so much that Christine's consciousness is surprisingly modern, but rather that the problems facing women in our own time are surprisingly archaic."[30] Modern readers are sometimes puzzled by what they see as contradictions in Christine's writing. She asserts both the power and the piety of women. She praises warriors like the Amazons and Zenobia, but she also finds space in her city for long-suffering wives like Griselda, who even allows her own children to be killed rather than disobey a despotic husband. Despite Christine's willingness to stand up to misogynists, she upholds values alien to modern sensibilities. Other scholars argue that in the context of her own age, Christine's work is progressive. It claims political virtue not only for women who display male qualities, such as valor in war, but for those whose female virtues overcome evil.[31]

Christine reserves the highest spaces in her city for Christian saints and martyrs. Their fantastic and often grisly stories continue to engage and challenge modern readers. One of the most detailed concerns her own patron, Saint Christine, a virgin whose father shut her up in a tower and allowed her to be tortured because she would not worship his pagan gods. Her tormenters deprive her of food, tie her up with chains, and beat her. When she still refuses to submit, they invent increasingly horrendous punishments, covering her with boiling oil, attacking her with poisonous snakes, and cutting off her breasts and tongue. In every case, God and His angels intervene. When her torturers tie a rock around her neck and throw her into the sea, Saint Christine walks on water, sustained by angels. Her wounds bleed milk instead of blood. She speaks even without a tongue. In a final act of defiance, she spits a remaining fragment of her severed tongue in her torturer's face, blinding him. Christine's celebration of her patron's sacred tongue symbolizes the power of female speech, and by extension validates Christine's own role as a literary defender of women.[32]

The Book of the City of Ladies was part of an extraordinary scholarly output. In a little over a decade, Christine wrote fifteen major works. But in 1418, political events altered her life. After the English victory over French forces at Agincourt and in the midst of civil war, she fled Paris, taking refuge in the convent at Poissy, where her daughter was a nun. Abandoning literature, she now found strength in her hopes of an afterlife. At the time, there seemed no saving France. One faction, the Burgundians, had allied with England. Christine's party, the Armagnacs, seemed helpless to resist. Then, in 1429, a young peasant girl from Domremy donned armor, rallied French troops against the English, and had the young dauphin crowned as Charles VII. Two weeks after the coronation, Christine again took up her pen and composed her last work, *The Tale of Joan of Arc.*[33]

"The year of fourteen twenty-nine / The sun came out to shine again," she wrote. God had chosen a "little girl of sixteen years / (And doesn't that pass nature's ken?)." Like Moses, Joan had delivered a people. She was as strong as Joshua, even though she was but a woman, a "simple shepherdess." Like Esther, Judith, and Deborah, she cast honor on the entire female sex.

> *But as for us, we've never heard*
> *About a marvel quite so great,*
> *For all the heroes who have lived*
> *In history can't measure up*
> *In bravery against the Maid,*

> *Who strives to rout our enemies.*
> *It's God does that, who's guiding her*
> *Whose courage passes that of men.*

Joan had rescued a wasted kingdom—something a hundred thousand men could not do.[34]

As a still young and hopeful writer, Christine had imagined a city of ladies peopled with the women warriors of antiquity and the saints of Christian tradition. Now, living at Poissy in a convent that for her had become a "cage," she saw her dream come true. Joan was both an Amazon and a saint.

The Poem of Joan of Arc was Christine's last work. She probably did not live to see her heroine burned at the stake in 1431.[35]

Eighty Years and More: Remembering Rebellion

In comparison to Christine's elegant allegory, Elizabeth Cady Stanton's memoir, *Eighty Years and More,* is a grandmotherly chat. Part reminiscence, part sermon, and part travelogue, it was written to mollify her critics—there was little hope of that. When she published it in book form in 1898, she was an eighty-three-year-old widow with failing vision and limited mobility who was still one of the most outrageous women in America. The publication of *The Woman's Bible* in 1895 had not only enlivened her opponents in the clergy (they jumped around, she said, "like parched peas on a hot shovel"), it had embarrassed and dismayed her allies. In 1896, the National American Women's Suffrage Association officially disclaimed any connection with a book that alienated potential supporters by denying the divinity of Jesus, dismissing much of the Old Testament as mere Hebrew mythology, and condemning Christianity for persecuting women as witches. Although Stanton praised Jesus as the "great leading Radical of his time," she claimed that no book other than the Bible so fully taught "the subjection and the degradation of women."[36]

Eighty Years and More, like many memoirs written in the late nineteenth century, was filled with amusing stories about a childhood spent in a picturesque rural village. It alluded to ancestors who had fought in the American Revolution, honored the influence of an aged pastor, and described family gatherings in ancestral mansions. Stanton's vision of history was surely shaped by the nineteenth-century ideas she absorbed as a child running in fear from the fireworks in Fourth of July celebrations, or reading about the Revolution in standard textbooks. This was not a history that included women, but it did honor rebellion, the dominant theme in her life story. The vignettes she wove into *Eighty Years and More* were intimate and domestic, but they described the making of a revolutionary.

Elizabeth was the third of five daughters born to Daniel Cady, a country lawyer, and Margaret Livingston, a descendant of New York's old Dutch aristocracy. All but one of the male children born into the family died in infancy or early childhood. In 1826, when Elizabeth was eleven years old, her only living brother, a young man in his twenties, also died. In the first chapter of *Eighty Years and More,* she described walking into the darkened parlor where her father sat, totally silent, beside his son's coffin. The room seemed a foreign place with "the casket, mirrors, and pictures all draped in white." Her father, too, was "pale and immovable." She slipped onto his lap and rested her head "against his beating heart." He responded with a mechanical embrace, at length sighing, "Oh, my daughter, I wish you were a boy!" Elizabeth threw her arms around his neck and promised to be all that her brother had been. That night, she lay pondering her new commitment. How did a girl become the equal of a boy? Thinking about the boys she knew, she decided that the trick was to become both "learned and courageous." She needed "to study Greek and learn to manage a horse."[37]

And so she did. Elizabeth was assisted in her study of Greek by a kindly pastor who offered to give her lessons. Later she studied Latin, Greek, and mathematics with the boys at the local academy. When after earnest study, she finally displaced a boy at the head of the class, she ran down the hill to her father's office with her prize, a Greek New Testament, in her hands. "There, I got it!" she cried. Her father kissed her on the forehead "and exclaimed, with a sigh, 'Ah, you should have been a boy!' " Elizabeth's sense of injustice was augmented when the boys who had been her competitors in class and her partners in sports and games rode off to Union College, while she was left at home to endure the banter of the students in her father's office. They read to her from those odious lawbooks and from Shakespeare's *Taming of the Shrew*. "The Bible, too, was brought into requisition. In fact it seemed to me that every book taught the '*divinely ordained*' headship of man, but my mind never yielded to this popular heresy."[38]

Stanton claimed that her will to rebel came from her mother's side of the family. Her maternal grandfather, James Livingston, a veteran of the American Revolution, had narrowly escaped court-martial when, in the absence of senior officers, he had ordered his soldiers to fire into "a suspicious looking British vessel that lay at anchor" opposite the American fort at West Point. Washington sternly reprimanded him for acting without orders, then admitted that his action had saved the day. Stanton and her siblings, who, "like their grandfather, were disposed to assume the responsibility of their own actions," resisted their mother's "military idea of government." In retrospect, Stanton believed that what her parents called tantrums "were really justifiable acts of rebellion against the tyranny of those in authority." She even blamed her dislike of red flannel on her grandfather's hatred of red coats.[39]

One of the few benevolent figures in Stanton's account of her childhood is a black servant named Peter. "Like Mary's lamb, where'er he went we were sure to go. His love for us was unbounded and fully returned." When Peter took the Cady girls to church, they sat with him, much to the dismay of conservative parishioners who thought that it was beneath the dignity of Judge Cady's children to sit in the "Negro pew." In Elizabeth's memory, she and her sisters stood up for Peter and refused to leave him.[40] The girls got a second lesson in racial matters in the home of their cousin, Gerrit Smith, whose house, Elizabeth recalled, was "one of the stations on the 'underground railroad' for slaves escaping from bondage." One day, Cousin Gerrit hushed the Cady sisters into a closed room on the third story of his house where they found "a beautiful quadroon girl, about eighteen years of age," who told her story while they "all wept together as she talked." When their cousin returned, the girls "needed no further education to make us earnest abolitionists."[41]

At her parents' insistence, Elizabeth continued her education at Miss Emma Willard's Female Seminary in Troy, New York. Here she faced the terrors of Calvinism. During her girlhood, upstate New York was a center of evangelical fervor stimulated in part by the preaching of Charles Grandison Finney, who sometimes preached at Troy. During revivals, Elizabeth was the first to step forward to declare herself a sinner, but try as she might she could not feel assurance of salvation. Her parents and her liberal brother-in-law rescued her from despair by taking her on a pleasure trip to Niagara Falls. In old age, the meaning of this experience was clear. It had been a crime "to shadow the minds of the young with these gloomy superstitions; and with fears of the unknown and the unknowable to poison all their joy in life."[42]

Despite its casual structure, *Eighty Years and More* makes a clear argument: The revolutionary generation won political liberty for white men, but they left untouched structures of male authority that oppressed women and persons of color. In Stanton's view, the only possible hope for change lay in principled opposition to those she sometimes sardonically referred to as the "Lords of Creation." Since quite a number of these self-important men hung around her father's law office, studying for the bar or looking for wives among the judge's daughters, Elizabeth and her sisters learned how to charm and manipulate their seeming betters. When one pompous law student annoyed Madge, Elizabeth's older sister, she invited him to go horseback-riding, making sure he got the orneriest nag in the family stable. "Now do not waste your arguments on these prigs from Union College," she told Elizabeth. "Take each, in turn, the ten-miles' circuit on 'Old Boney' and they'll have no breath left to prate of woman's inferiority."[43]

For Elizabeth, a horseback ride with Henry Stanton, "a fine-looking, affable young man, with remarkable conversational talent," led instead to a proposal of marriage. Elizabeth's father was outraged. Stanton was not only ten years his daughter's senior, he was an abolitionist. Even if his politics had been acceptable, he had only limited prospects for supporting a family. But, as in most things, Elizabeth prevailed. In May 1840, she and Henry were married by a befuddled clergyman who not only had to overcome his superstitions by marrying them on a Friday but at Elizabeth's insistence left the word *obey* out of the ceremony.[44]

The Stantons spent their honeymoon in London, where Henry was a delegate to the World's Anti-Slavery Convention. Although the radical wing of the American abolitionist movement allowed women to participate as speakers and delegates, the London convention after earnest debate refused to seat them. "Deborah, Huldah, Vashti, and Esther might have questioned the propriety of calling it a World's Convention, when only half of humanity was represented there," Elizabeth recalled. As a consequence, all of the women sat in the observation gallery together. Elizabeth was especially impressed with the Quaker abolitionist Lucretia Mott. "These were the first women I had ever met who believed in the equality of the sexes and who did not believe in the popular orthodox religion," she recalled.[45]

After their European journey, Elizabeth and Henry returned to Johnstown, where Henry studied law with Daniel Cady. Here their first child was born. Motherhood offered Elizabeth new lessons in self-reliance. When the lying-in nurse tried to dose her baby with traditional nostrums, she resisted. When two physicians suggested treatments that she deemed harmful, she invented her own. When the doctors patronized her by saying, "Well, after all, a mother's instinct is better than a man's reason," she responded, "Thank you, gentlemen, there was no instinct about it. I did some hard thinking."[46]

When Henry secured a position in Boston, Elizabeth threw herself into housekeeping with the same energy. "Even washing day— that day so many people dread—had its charms for me," she remembered, though part of that charm must be attributed to an income that allowed her to hire help. "I inspired my laundress with an ambition to have her clothes look white and to set them out earlier than our neighbors, and to have them ironed and put away sooner." During these same years, Elizabeth also found time to attend all the "lectures, churches, theaters, concerts, and temperance, peace, and prison-reform conventions within my reach," though she admitted that one Sunday, after walking two miles from her home in Chelsea to Marlborough Street in Boston to hear the renowned Unitarian minister Theodore Parker speak, she fell asleep during the opening prayer and didn't wake until the sexton came to tell her it was time to close the doors.[47]

Stanton's stories are chatty and often humorous, and some of the time the joke is on her. Taken together, however, they form a narrative of triumphant advancement from ignorance to self-knowledge and from dependence to self-reliance. In her hands, the familiar

American story about political and economic progress became a narrative about women's rights. For her the Revolution began in Seneca Falls, New York, where she and Henry moved in 1847.

After the stimulation of living in Boston, Elizabeth found it difficult to settle into this sleepy market town. Henry was frequently away, and the novelty of housekeeping had begun to wear off. She now understood "the practical difficulties most women had to contend with in the isolated household." Her duties were "numerous and varied," but neither "exhilarating or intellectual" enough to call on her higher faculties. "I suffered with mental hunger, which, like an empty stomach, is very depressing." Rescue came when Lucretia Mott arrived in nearby Waterloo for a visit and invited her to spend the afternoon with other "earnest, thoughtful women." The next day they published in the *Seneca County Courier* a call for a Woman's Rights Convention.[48]

The most enduring product of that convention was the "Declaration of Sentiments and Resolutions," in the drafting of which Elizabeth played a major role. The Declaration proclaimed, "We hold these truths to be self-evident: that all men *and women* are created equal." It went on to recount a long list of grievances, some of them innocuous, but one—denial of the franchise—so radical that Henry Stanton, who had helped draft part of the document, refused to attend the convention, perhaps for fear it would ruin his political career. In *Eighty Years and More*, Elizabeth has less to say about the work of the convention than about the hostility it aroused. "All the journals from Maine to Texas seemed to strive with each other to see which could make our movement appear the most ridiculous." But the antislavery press stood by them. Frederick Douglass, who had escaped from slavery to become a powerful advocate for human rights, was one of the signers of the Declaration, and he continued to support it in his paper, *The North Star.*[49]

The Revolutionary generation had blamed George III for their troubles. The Seneca Falls delegates, a few of whom were male, signed on to a more radical claim. "The history of mankind is a history of repeated injuries and usurpations on the part of man toward woman, having in direct object the establishment of an absolute tyranny over her." The rhetoric was Elizabeth's adaptation of Jefferson in the Declaration of Independence, and it was bold language; but when she stood up to speak, so a friend recalled, she spoke so softly that no one could hear her. Many years later, she would remark that if she had known all that was to follow the launching of the women's crusade, she might not have risked it.[50]

The Seneca Falls Convention began Elizabeth Cady Stanton's public career. She still had three little boys and a house to care for, and in the next eleven years would give birth to four more children, but she would never again devote all her energies to what she later described as "a narrow family selfishness." She used what leisure time she had to write "articles for the press, letters to conventions held in other States, and private letters to friends." Eventually she began to give speeches. On one occasion when she spoke, a group of women asked her "in a deprecating tone" what she had done with her children. "Ladies," she said, "it takes me no longer to speak, than you to listen; what have you done with your children the two hours you have been sitting here?"[51]

Her public work became easier after Susan B. Anthony, a temperance reformer from nearby Rochester, New York, joined the cause. She and Elizabeth first met in 1851. They became friends and co-agitators for life. Theodore Tilton called them "two sticks of a drum, keeping up what Daniel Webster called 'The rub-a-dub of agitation.' "[52] After Anthony had thoroughly canvassed their home state of New York in behalf of women's property rights, Stanton delivered a speech before the state legislature. When her father saw a notice in the evening paper that his daughter was about to speak in Albany, he asked her to stop by and read him the speech. She knew that he disapproved of her campaign, but she could not deny him. Finding him alone in his office, she sat down and began to read. As she described widows in their first hour of grief "subject to the intrusions of the coarse minions of the law," she noticed tears begin to form in his eyes. He asked how she could know so much about widows' suffering when she herself had never experienced such injustice. She told him she had learned it all as a child sitting in his office listening to the entreaties of his clients. He then agreed to help her revise her draft. It was one in the morning before they finished and kissed each other good night.[53]

In *Eighty Years and More,* this is the triumphal finale to a story that had begun many years before. It may well have happened just as she described it, but in a letter to Anthony written in 1855, she reported a quite different visit to Johnstown in which she received a "terrible scourging." Stanton may have become her father's son, but that did not please him. "I cannot tell you how deeply the iron entered my soul. I never felt more keenly the degradation of my sex. To think that all in me of which my father would have felt a proper pride had I been a man is deeply mortifying to him because I am a woman. That thought has stung me to a fierce decision—to speak as soon as I can do myself credit. . . . I will both write and speak."[54]

As if their ideas weren't threatening enough, Stanton and her fellow reformers created additional controversy by adopting the so-called Bloomer costume. The name came from Amelia Bloomer, another resident of Seneca Falls, who popularized the new form of dress in her temperance periodical *The Lily.* Stanton explained that the idea for the new costume actually came from Gerrit Smith's daughter, Elizabeth Miller, who in the winter of 1852 arrived in Seneca Falls "dressed somewhat in the Turkish style—short skirt, full trousers of fine black broadcloth; a Spanish cloak, of the same material, reaching to the knee; beaver hat and feathers and dark furs." Stanton was entranced. Miller's garb was not only attractive but amazingly practical. "To see my cousin, with a lamp in one

"Woman's Emancipation," *Harper's New Monthly Magazine,* August 1851. Periodicals
satirized the "Bloomer costume" that Stanton and others championed.

hand and a baby in the other, walk upstairs with ease and grace,
while, with flowing robes, I pulled myself up with difficulty, lamp
and baby out of the question, readily convinced me that there was
sore need of reform in woman's dress."

Stanton and her friends experimented with the costume until
they created an ensemble that usually included a skirt falling just
below the knees under which they wore full trousers tapered
toward the ankle. Although their innovative clothing was comfortable, it attracted unwanted attention. People on the street pointed
and laughed. Cartoonists lampooned "strong-minded women" in
Bloomers, sometimes with men's hats and cigars. Although Miller
held out for seven years, Stanton and most of her friends gave up
after a couple of years, in part because the men in their lives were
unwilling to be seen with them in public.[55]

Some of the most amusing stories in *Eighty Years and More* come in the latter half of the book, where Elizabeth describes her experiences as an itinerant lecturer. With her children grown and Henry's income falling, she had signed on as a Lyceum speaker. On one occasion, she was invited to speak in a small town on the same evening when the Christy Minstrels, a popular blackface singing troupe, were due to perform. She was assigned the hour from seven to eight o'clock; the Minstrels were to have the rest of the evening. It was a warm night. The hilarity of the crowd came in through the open windows as Stanton began her speech, while backstage the singers were running around, getting into their costumes and laughing at one another's jokes. "I felt like laughing at my own comical predicament," Stanton recalled, "and I decided to make my address a medley of anecdotes and stories, like a string of beads, held together by a fine thread of argument and illustration."[56]

This description of her speech describes her memoir. It is a seemingly random string of anecdotes and stories, but it is held together by an argument. Stanton situated her life in a larger American story, framing her crusade for women's rights as part of a continuing struggle for the liberation of the individual from the tyranny of family government, religious superstition, and ignorance. *Eighty Years and More* modeled a kind of feminist history that remains popular today, and is certainly reflected on those mugs and bumper stickers of today which proclaim that well-behaved woman seldom make history. Stanton might have written that motto herself. She lamented that when most people seem happy with their circumstances, the discontent of a minority can easily be dismissed: "the history of the world shows the vast majority, in every generation, passively accept the conditions into which they are born, while those who demand larger liberties are ever a small, ostracized minority, whose claims are ridiculed and ignored."[57] These ridiculed minorities, she believed, made history. In her case, at least, she was right.

A Room of One's Own: Looking for Anon.

In 1882, the year his daughter Virginia was born, Sir Leslie Stephen became the founding editor of England's massive *Dictionary of National Biography*. Before he was finished, there were sixty-three volumes encompassing 19,120 biographical sketches. Although several hundred of these sketches were of women, Sir Leslie was no champion of women's rights.[58] He sent his sons to Cambridge, but refused to spend money on his daughters' education. Even worse, he required unquestioning affection from his children. Virginia resented his insensitivity, his imperious commands, and his pomposity. Yet, like Elizabeth Cady Stanton, she was bound to her father by admiration and love as well as obligation. Late in life she admitted that she had probably gotten a good education reading the books in his study. But had he lived into his nineties, she wrote, "His life would have entirely ended mine."[59]

Virginia's mother, Julia Prinsep Duckworth Stephen, who died when her daughter was eleven, exemplified the highest ideals of refined and domestic womanhood. She was an "angel in the house," to use the language of an influential Victorian poem. Because she and Sir Leslie had both been married before, their family eventually included children from three marriages. Virginia's half brothers, George and Gerald Duckworth, were the serpents in this Victorian Eden. Gerald began abusing Virginia sexually when she was still a child. She remembered him lifting her onto a slab beneath the mirror outside the dining room door and exploring her body. Although she "stiffened and wiggled," he would not stop. She thought this experience accounted for a recurring dream in which she saw behind her shoulder in a looking glass "a horrible face—the face of an animal." The other brother's abuse began when Virginia and her sister Vanessa were in their teens. George insisted on taking them to parties, then when they returned would force his attentions on Virginia.[60]

Much has been written about the effects of these experiences on Woolf's sexual identity and on her recurring mental illness. She had five major mental breakdowns in her life, four of them between the ages of thirteen and thirty-three. Had she been born a half-century earlier or later, she might have joined a crusade against male sexual license. Instead, in 1904, at the age of twenty-two, she took her inheritance from her father, joined her sister Vanessa and brother Adrian in a bohemian flat in the Bloomsbury district of London, and became a writer of fiction.[61] In 1912, she married Leonard Woolf, who had recently returned from a stint in the Civil Service in Ceylon. Together they founded the avant-garde Hogarth Press, which published *A Room of One's Own* in 1929. Virginia was then in her late forties and at the height of her literary powers. Her novels *Mrs. Dalloway* (1926) and *To the Lighthouse* (1927) had established her literary reputation. *Orlando* (1928) gave her financial security as well.[62]

Orlando, loosely based on the life of her flamboyant, aristocratic, cross-dressing friend and sometime lover, Vita Sackville-West, was a rollicking spoof of conventional biography. The title character, who lives for four hundred years, begins life sometime in the sixteenth century as a male, then mysteriously, after an adventure in Turkey, awakens as a woman. She has curiously, unmistakably switched sexes, yet she is without question the same person, with the same face, the same consciousness and memories. Only when she feels "the coil of skirts about her legs," and discovers the solicitude of men as she boards a ship, does she realize "the penalties and the privileges of her position." Among the penalties is a lawsuit claiming "(1) that she was dead, and therefore could not hold any property whatsoever; (2) that she was a woman, which amounts to much the same thing."[63]

Through *Orlando,* Woolf satirized legal, literary, and social conventions. She also lightly, and somewhat covertly, explored the nature of sexual desire. As a male, Orlando loves women. As a female, "it was still a woman she loved; and if the consciousness of being of the same sex had any effect at all, it was to quicken and deepen those feelings which she had had as a man." In the nineteenth century, as romance permeates the very walls of Orlando's house, she discovers her one true love. He appears to be male, but she cannot be sure. "You're a woman," she cries. "You're a man," he responds. To both, it is "a revelation that a woman could be as tolerant and free-spoken as a man, and a man as strange and subtle as a woman."[64]

Like Christine and Stanton before her, Woolf challenged seemingly impermeable boundaries between male and female identity. In the closing chapter of *A Room of One's Own,* she developed some of the same ideas more cerebrally. Pondering the poet Samuel Taylor Coleridge's notion that a great mind is androgynous, she suggested that in each soul "two powers preside, one male, one female." In a man's brain, the male predominates; in a woman's, the female. Yet both are there, and in the "normal and comfortable state of being . . . the two live in harmony together." The writing of her contemporaries, she feared, had lost this balance. There was too much virility in men's writing, too much special pleading in women's. "The Suffrage campaign was no doubt to blame," she concluded. "It must have roused in men an extraordinary desire for self-assertion." Men were now writing only with the male side of their brains. Women too had been warped, for it is "fatal to lay the least stress on any grievance; to plead even with justice any cause; in any way to speak consciously as a woman."[65]

Taken out of context, these passages might seem to invalidate the book in which they appear. *A Room of One's Own* is both highly conscious of sex and powerful in pleading a cause. Woolf's invocation of androgyny conveyed her ambivalence about the British women's suffrage movement. In *Jacob's Room,* published in 1922, she parodied "Miss Julie Hedge, the feminist," who, sitting in the reading room of the British Museum, dips her pen in bitterness and leaves her shoelaces untied. Dismayed that the gilded ring of names painted around the ceiling contains not even one name of a woman, Miss Hedge grimly applies herself to her work. "Death and gall and bitter dust were on her pen-tip."[66] Seven years later, in *A Room of One's Own*, Woolf rewrote this scene more sympathetically. Through her caricature of Professor von X, she admitted her own anger, then scratched it out with humor and a self-confidence born of success.

A Room of One's Own originated as a pair of lectures titled "Women and Fiction" given in October 1928 at Cambridge's two women's colleges, Girton and Newnham. When Woolf revised the lectures for publication, she added a description of an imagined visit to a fictional women's college called "Fernham," which she located in an equally fictional university called "Oxbridge."[67] Employing "all the liberties and licences of a novelist," she produced a work that, as her nephew and biographer Quentin Bell has observed, "is that rare thing—a lively but good-tempered polemic."[68]

Readers do not forget her narrator's encounter with the beadle when she absentmindedly steps on the grass at Oxbridge ("Only the Fellows and Scholars are allowed here"), or her description a few pages later of being turned away from a famous library ("for instantly there issued, like a guardian angel barring the way with a flutter of black gown instead of white wings, a deprecating, silvery, kindly gentleman, who regretted in a low voice as he waved me back that ladies are only admitted to the library if accompanied by a Fellow of the College or furnished with a letter of introduction"). These rejections, each of which interrupts her thinking about women and fiction, define her as an outsider to the male worlds of scholarship and privilege. They prepare us for the contrast between the sparkling wine served at luncheon in the men's college and the gravy soup at Fernham, and they set up the opening question of the next chapter, "Why was one sex so prosperous and the other so poor?"[69]

Although its central concern is literature, *A Room of One's Own* is also a provocative statement on the relationship of women to history. On a superficial level, Woolf offers a linear argument, much like Stanton's, that emphasizes the disabilities of women in the past. Women are poor, she argues, because in past centuries land and estates went to men and to men's colleges and libraries. Tied down by childbearing and -rearing, and without education, leisure, or freedom to explore, women had little hope of producing great literature even if they had the inclination. Any woman born "with a gift of poetry in the sixteenth century, was an unhappy woman, a woman at strife against herself." Although toward the end of the eighteenth century, middle-class women began to write, they still faced obstacles, she argued. Great literature required experience of life and freedom from the personal censure that dogged novelists like George Eliot, who had to pretend to be a man in order to sell her books. Had Tolstoy lived in a priory, could he have written *War and Peace?*[70]

But laced through this progressive narrative is a more complex encounter with history. It begins with Woolf's fantasy about "Judith Shakespeare." Wondering what Shakespeare's work would have been like if he had been a girl, she gives him a sister. Judith "was as adventurous, as imaginative, as agog to see the world as he was. But she was not sent to school." She may have picked up a book, even attempted to write, but more likely was given stockings to mend; "before she was out of her teens, she was to be betrothed to the son of a neighbouring wool-stapler." Rebelling, she ran away to London and found her way to a stage door, where she was laughed at and sent away, until the actor-manager took pity on her and got her with child. Because her poet's heart beat in a woman's body, she "killed herself one winter's night and lies buried at some cross-roads where the omnibuses now stop outside the Elephant and Castle." Woolf returns to this grim story at the very end of the book, telling the young women at Fernham that Judith Shakespeare, who died young and never wrote a word, still lived. "She lives in you and in me, and in many other women who are not here tonight, for they are washing up the dishes and putting the children to bed." If women could achieve five hundred pounds a year and rooms of their own and free themselves from the opinions of others, in a century or so Shakespeare's sister might "put on the body she has so often laid down."[71]

Adding Judith Shakespeare to the narrative changed its meaning. The challenge for women writers was not to extend a tradition established by male writers but to create one of their own. Their task was not to mimic Shakespeare but to pick up the body of his dead sister. "It would be a thousand pities if women wrote like men, or lived like men, or looked like men, for if two sexes are quite inadequate, considering the vastness and variety of the world, how should we manage with one only?"[72] An androgynous mind was not a male mind. It was a mind attuned to the full range of human experience, including the invisible lives of women.

Woolf's invocation of Judith Shakespeare is both a lament and an invitation, an acknowledgment of absence and a call for a new kind of history, one that begins with an imaginative recognition of all that has been lost. She didn't know what form that history might take, but she thought it worth seeking. Surely genius of a sort must have existed among women of the past. "Indeed, I would venture to guess that Anon., who wrote so many poems without signing them, was often a woman." True, it wouldn't be easy to find Anon., but it was worth trying.[73]

Her proposal to the women at Fernham was both witty and coy: "It would be ambitious beyond my daring, I thought, looking about the shelves for books that were not there, to suggest to the students of those famous colleges that they should re-write history, though I own that it often seems a little queer as it is, unreal, lop-sided; but why should they not add a supplement to history? calling it, of course, by some inconspicuous name so that women might figure there without impropriety?" Woolf believed that with proper attention, historians might find women. "For one often catches a glimpse of them in the lives of the great, whisking away into the background, concealing, I sometimes think, a wink, a laugh, perhaps a tear."[74] She thought of an old woman seen crossing a street in London on the arm of her middle-aged daughter. If one asked the old lady what her life had meant to her, she might be able to remember the guns firing in Hyde Park for the king's birthday, but she probably wouldn't be able to say what she herself was doing on a given day. "For all the dinners are cooked; the plates and cups washed; the children set to school and gone out into the world. Nothing remains of it all. All has vanished. No biography or history has a word to say about it. And the novels, without meaning to, inevitably lie."[75]

In her novels, Woolf turned plates and cups and the crossing of London streets into a new kind of fiction. In *A Room of One's Own*, she suggested that a similar realignment of vision might do the same for history.

Three Writers, Three Visions

Christine de Pizan, Elizabeth Cady Stanton, and Virginia Woolf each used history to argue against narrow definitions of womanhood. They did so by reading against the grain of existing narratives and by writing new ones of their own. All three breached the equality/difference divide: Pizan invited women warriors into a city dedicated to the Virgin Mary. Stanton turned grandmothers' tales into a political argument. Woolf allowed an androgynous mind to comprehend a women's culture. All three demonstrated that women were both like and unlike men, and they argued that stories told from a female perspective changed presumably universal notions of human behavior.

They talked back to books, but they did so in different ways. Christine's method was to gather biographies of remarkable women from every source she could find. She wasn't interested in chronology, nor did it concern her that stories about courage in battle might contradict stories of pious passivity. The chaos of her collection made its own argument—that women were as varied as the virtues they exemplified. Elizabeth Cady Stanton did care about time and place. Like other nineteenth-century writers, she believed in progress. Her story unfolded, event by event, in a linear progression from the crises of girlhood to the triumphs of old age. Her history had a plot, and she herself was its heroine. Virginia Woolf imagined a history that challenged the very foundations of history by exposing all that was missing from great libraries and archives. Her argument that women needed rooms of their own was both literal and metaphorical. Women needed psychic as well as physical space. Weighted down by traditions that excluded them, they needed to think back through their mothers.

Pizan's biographies of exceptional women, Stanton's narrative of women's rights, and Woolf's search for anonymous women challenged the subjects and methods of history as they knew them. Their stories have in turn been challenged by a new generation of activists, scholars, and writers. In the chapters to follow, I will explore this new work by revisiting selected episodes from *The City of Ladies, Eighty Years and More,* and *A Room of One's Own.* I begin with Christine's Amazons, move on to Woolf's myth of Judith Shakespeare, explore the brief appearance of a runaway slave in Stanton's memoir, then join in the search for the forgotten woman whom Woolf called "Anon." The book ends where all this new work began, with the revival of feminism in the 1970s.

In the past three decades, there has been a true renaissance in history, one driven by amateurs and activists as well as by professional historians. This book is a celebration of that work, a tribute to all those who have been making history.

Chapter Two

کر

AMAZONS

*I*n classical mythology, Amazons were female warriors who fought against the Greeks in the Trojan War. They ruled their own kingdom, mated with men only when they chose, and gave boy babies away. By Greek standards, they were not well-behaved women. Perhaps they weren't women at all. Some accounts said they cut off one breast to facilitate handling a bow. In a world where boundaries between the sexes seemed fixed, Amazons refused to stay put.[1]

None of this bothered Christine de Pizan. Amazons were among the first heroines she introduced into her imagined city of ladies. She praised them extravagantly, claiming that nowhere in the world could one find "as many people who accomplished such noteworthy deeds than among the queens and ladies of this kingdom." Following classical sources, she located them in a "country called Scythia" that lay beyond Europe, "near the great ocean which surrounds the entire world." She explained that when enemies killed Scythian men and raped their wives, the surviving women "courageously assembled and took counsel among themselves." Overthrowing their conquerors, they vowed never again to be subject to men. By Christine's calculation, their kingdom lasted more than eight hundred years and became one of the most admirable in history.[2]

Christine's Amazons slip easily into feminist plots. But in other accounts they look different. In literature and history, there have been good Amazons and bad Amazons, virginal heroines who served God and the state and lustful viragoes who fought against men and social order. When the Spanish Armada threatened England in 1588, Elizabeth I rallied her troops, so it was said, "habited like an Amazonian Queene, Buskined and plumed, having a golden Truncheon, Gantlet and Gorget."[3] But when a character in Shakespeare's *Henry VI* referred to Joan of Arc as an Amazon, he wasn't offering a compliment. During the American Revolution, Abigail Adams promised her husband that if men were unable to fight, he "would find a Race of Amazons in America."[4] In contrast, during the socialist uprising in Paris in 1870, opponents dismissed female combatants as "Amazons of the rabble," their very existence provoking one writer to ask "from what slime the human species is made and what animalistic instincts, hidden and ineradicable, still crouch in the dark soul of mankind."[5]

Stories about Amazons have never been about gender alone. Over the centuries, they have signified whatever is marvelous or alien. Ancient Greeks sought them beyond the boundaries of the known world. Europeans found them in Africa, Asia, and the Americas. In the thirteenth century, the Venetian explorer and chronicler Marco Polo located the Amazon kingdom on an island off the northwestern coast of what is now India. In 1493, Columbus discovered what he thought was the same island off the continent he mistook for India. In the sixteenth century, Spanish explorers named the *rio grande de las Amazonas* (the great river of the Amazons) for the women warriors they believed they had seen on its banks. In the eighteenth and nineteenth centuries, Europeans gawked at and sometimes fought the supposed "Black Amazons" of the African kingdom of Dahomey.[6]

Today, writers use the word *Amazon* narrowly to refer to the heroines of Greek mythology, broadly to designate any female warrior, and metaphorically to describe a wide range of female attributes, from physical prowess to disdain for the other sex. In contemporary usage, an "Amazon" might be an Olympic athlete, a female soldier, a lesbian separatist, a comic-book heroine, or the proprietor of a women's bookstore in Minneapolis suing the online giant Amazon.com for rights to a name.[7]

Amazon stories survive because they are capable of so many interpretations. Some see the old legends as flickering evidence of a now lost encounter between Greek soldiers and horseback-riding women from the steppes. Others read them as parables of patriarchy, cautionary tales in which women warriors always lose. Although there is no agreement on their meaning, the power of the old stories is unmistakable. They will not go away.

In the past thirty years, Amazons have inspired archaeologists, historians, poets, scriptwriters, feminist activists, and pencil-toting travelers. A subject that Christine de Pizan dealt with in a few pages has become its own library.

Women Warriors All Over the World

Jeannine Davis-Kimball didn't go to the Soviet Union in 1991 looking for Amazons. She just wanted to know more about the ancient nomads whose art had long intrigued her. Her journey to the Kazakh steppes had been a long one. Born in eastern Idaho, she had raised six children and worked for years in southern California as a nurse and hospital administrator when she decided to go back to school. She completed a B.A. in art history at the age of forty-nine, and a Ph.D. at Berkeley the year she turned sixty. Now she was realizing a dream—excavating in the Eurasian steppes alongside the Russian archaeologist Leonid Yablonsky. She had little idea that when she returned to California and began turning her meticulous notes into talks and papers, she would become something of a celebrity. A presentation at a local archaeological forum led to an article in the journal *Archaeology*, then to a story in the *New York Times*, an interview on National Public Radio, and eventually television documentaries for PBS, the History Channel, the Canadian Discovery Channel, the National Geographic Society, and British and German television. Ancient Amazons were the hook. The teaser for the NPR story claimed she had found "evidence that Amazonian women did exist, contrary to belief that ancient female warrior societies are mythological."[8]

The sentence was carefully constructed. It said she had found *Amazonian women*, not Amazons themselves. The nuance was lost on most audiences. Davis-Kimball became known as the woman who had confirmed the old Greek stories. What she had actually done was discover women buried with weapons in ancient mounds called *kurgans* near the present-day Russian town of Pokrovka. Her article in *Archaeology* explained that since the Pokrovka nomads lived 2,500 miles east of any group the Greeks could have known, they themselves could not have inspired the Greek tales; but she suggested that groups much like them may have been "the far-flung contemporaries of the Amazons."[9] That was enough to engage the press.

Davis-Kimball's excavations are an important example of a new approach in archaeology. At one time, archaeologists unthinkingly identified any skeleton found with weapons as male. DNA analysis and the presence of women in the field have changed that assumption.[10] After identifying 182 adult skeletons by sex, Davis-Kimball categorized them according to the objects buried with them. The results for men were predictable. Over 90 percent were buried with arrowheads, swords, and daggers. The surprise was in the female burials. Although 75 percent contained domestic tools, such as spindles, 15 percent had weapons and armor. The weapons buried with women were more than symbolic. One female skeleton was pierced through by an arrow. Another had bowed legs that indicated years spent on horseback. Even more surprising, the most prestigious burials, those highest in the *kurgans*, were of women.

These contained both weapons and ritual artifacts.[11] Davis-Kimball hadn't discovered a kingdom of women, but she had found female warriors. She was not alone.

In the past thirty years, scholars have discovered female soldiers in every region of the world and in virtually every historical period. Some impersonated men. A Muslim account of the battle of Acre during the Third Crusade reported among the prisoners "three Frankish women who had fought from horseback and were recognized as women only when captured and stripped of their armor." During the American Civil War, a female sergeant disguised her sex until, to the horror of her commander, she *"was delivered of a baby* . . . in violation of all military law and of the army regulations." With or without disguise, women fought in the French Revolution, the Haitian Revolution, and the Spanish Civil War. They carried guns in the successful Mexican Revolution of 1910 and the failed Hungarian Revolution of 1956. In Vietnam in the 1960s, they slung machine guns over their shoulders as they worked in the fields.[12]

For Christine de Pizan, stories like these were enough to sustain a larger argument: "in many women God has made manifest enormous courage, strength, and boldness to undertake and execute all kinds of hard tasks."[13] Contemporary scholars want to know more. If armies have been dominated by men, what induces women to join the fight?

One sociologist approached that question by identifying fourteen variables that she grouped under three broad categories— military factors, social structure, and culture. If her study demonstrated anything, it was the impossibility of extracting simple rules from history. She discovered that women's participation in war increased in times of high threat, but also in periods of low threat when cultural values encouraged it. She found that equality in the civilian economy encouraged women to enlist. But so did inequality—in periods when jobs were strictly segregated by sex, the military recruited women to act as nurses, telephone operators, and the like. Technology also played a contradictory role. The use of advanced weapons encouraged the recruitment of women (brains presumably negating brawn), but guerrilla warfare had a similar effect. When wars were fought close to home, women joined in.[14]

In short, women showed up in all kinds of political and cultural weather. The reason is not hard to find. Even if nature induces men to fight (and some challenge that assumption), circumstances do not always allow them to do so. Death, illness, catastrophic events like earthquakes or famine, new opportunities for economic gain, and a whole range of social and psychological differences lead women to war. A closer look at some of the circumstances in which that has happened helps us to see similarities in stories that come from different parts of the world and different centuries.

In societies where leadership is hereditary, one of the roles of women has been to stand in for men when needed. That was surely the case in 59 C.E., when Britain's Boudicca, queen of the Iceni, mounted a chariot and roused her people after Roman soldiers killed her husband and raped her daughters.[15] Something similar happened in eighteenth-century Peru during the "revolt of the Incas," when Micaela Bastida Pnynchua commanded men in her husband's absence. "I will die where my husband dies," she said.[16] In thirteenth-century India, a Delhi ruler dressed his daughter, Raziya, in male clothes and trained her in military affairs. She became a "female Sultan," but she was also a substitute son, standing in for a brother who died.[17] The same thing can be said of the Vietnamese sisters Tru'ng Trac and Tru'ng Nhi, who in the third century C.E. led a revolt against the Chinese governor of the region near modern-day Hanoi.[18] Elizabeth I, and other women who ascended European thrones in the sixteenth century, were also surrogates for missing or underaged sons and brothers. Stories like these show how an occasional deviation in the gender order can preserve hierarchies based on class or kinship.[19]

Female substitutes became national heroines not only for their martial skills but for their willingness to sacrifice themselves for their country. Only a few displayed the kind of contempt for traditional womanhood evident in Vietnamese portrayals of Lady Trieu, a nineteen-year-old girl who led a revolt against Chinese rule in 248 C.E. According to one account, she "went into battle astride an elephant . . . throwing her yard-long breasts over her shoulders." When people asked why she did not marry, she answered, "I wish to ride a strong wind and tame fierce waves, kill sharks in the Eastern Sea, force back the Chinese armies, and throw off the chains of slavery; how could I possibly accept to be some man's servant?"[20]

In seventeenth- and eighteenth-century Europe hundreds of women dressed up like men and joined regular armies. Disdain for marriage and a desire for independence may well have been a motivation. Recent studies suggest, however, that most were working-class women stuck in low-paying jobs. In England a few adventurous women were already disguising themselves as men in order to work as "labourers, butchers, cooks, porters, shipwrights, plasterers, ploughmen, stone-cutters, bricklayers, coachmen, pedlars, servants and East India Company recruits." Those who enlisted in the military took greater risks, but they were also more likely to be celebrated if they succeeded. Popular culture loved nothing quite so much as a ballad or broadside about a female warrior.[21]

A Massachusetts woman, Deborah Sampson, who served in the Continental Army during the American Revolution, fits this pattern. Born into a poor family, she was bound out as an indentured servant, then worked in a variety of jobs before attempting to enlist. The first time she tried, she failed, and her Baptist congregation expelled her for this transgression against womanly propriety. But she persisted, inspired perhaps by the story of Hannah Snell, a British woman whose story was widely known in America. Toward the end of the war, the Revolutionary army was desperate for sol-

diers. Since recruits tended to be teenage boys, some of whom did
not yet have beards, and since Deborah was taller than average and
clever at imitating male behavior, she passed. She served with distinction until a serious illness exposed her secret. Instead of being
drummed out in disgrace, she received an honorable discharge.
The poet Philip Freneau later praised her as a "gallant Amazon," an
identity she embraced in her quest for a government pension.[22]

A more curious example is the case of Catalina de Erauso, who
escaped from a Basque convent in 1607 dressed in male clothing,
and shipped off to the West Indies, where she lived the life of a
picaresque soldier and rogue for almost twenty years before she
was captured in a fight in Lima, Peru. When she confessed that she
was truly a woman, the Archbishop of Lima absolved her of her
sins and returned her to Europe, where she received a special dis-
pensation from the pope to continue living as a man. She was saved
by her intact virginity. In Spain, she skillfully played on her reputation as a marvel, then returned to anonymity in the colonies.[23]

Miracles stretched gender boundaries. Joan of Arc was called by
dreams and visions, as was a Pawnee woman who was so successful
in stealing enemy ponies that her tribe changed her name from
White Woman to Woman Who Goes As A Warrior.[24] Other North
American accounts tell of a mysterious man-woman who lived
among the Kutenai of northern Idaho in the nineteenth century.
Raised female, she adopted male garb after fleeing her marriage to
an English trader. Calling herself *qánqon kámek klaúla* (Sitting-in-
the-water-Grizzly), she became a powerful warrior and shaman
who mated with women, led raids against the Blackfeet, and proph-
esied the outcome of battles. In her last battle, enemy warriors
laughed when they ripped off her breechcloth, then trembled with
fear as one after another her wounds healed themselves. Only when
they opened her chest and cut off a piece of her heart did she die.
Though she lay in the open, birds and animals refused to touch her
body.[25]

Doña Beatriz Kimpa Vita, who led a popular uprising in the Kongo in the early eighteenth century, had her first vision when she was eight years old. When she was twenty, she fell gravely ill. In her illness a man dressed in the habit of a monk came to her. He said he had tried for a long time to heal the Kongo of its civil wars. Now, he had found a way. As he spoke he entered her head. When she awoke, she told her friends and family that she had been reincarnated as Saint Anthony, one of many saints venerated in local festivals that combined Christian and Kongolese traditions.[26] Over the next two years she led a powerful movement that promised to end suffering and restore peace. She taught that the Virgin Mary and her mother were both Kongolese, and that Jesus had been born in the long-abandoned capital of São Salvador. As common people rallied to her cause, she led a band of rebels who secured and restored the old capital and attempted to reconstitute a once united kingdom. But two years after her crusade began, it came crashing down when she became pregnant and enemy troops discovered her giving birth in a cornfield. Like Joan of Arc, she was burned as a heretic.[27]

State sponsorship, like miracles, can also alter gender norms. *Wall Street Journal* correspondent Geraldine Brooks tells the fascinating story of the creation of a women's army corps in the United Arab Emirates during the first Gulf War. When Saddam Hussein threatened neighboring Kuwait, the UAE considered enlisting women in order to expand its small army. In a conservative Muslim country that seemed impossible until Sheikh Zayed gave Hessa al-Khaledi, the Emirates' first woman civil engineer, the job of persuading women to enlist. She appealed to history. Potential recruits learned that the Prophet Muhammad's own aunt was the first Muslim woman to kill a man in battle. The state reinforced the lesson by naming the new women's military academy for Khawla bint Al-Muhammad, who rode beside the Prophet in battle. These and other stories made a new practice seem traditional. In a society where women were rarely seen outside their own families, the government couldn't ask male officers to train female recruits, so the United States Army sent ten female officers to help the Emirates set up their training regime. By 1996, they no longer needed the Americans. Women dressed in shape-concealing tunics, with their hair modestly tucked under tight-fitting black cotton scarves, served among peacekeeping troops in Kosovo.[28]

The most dramatic example of state sponsorship—the establishment of an elite corps of women warriors by the kingdom of Dahomey (present-day Benin)—originated much earlier. European observers reported the corps's existence as early as 1727. A century later, women made up almost half of the nation's army. There was nothing mysterious about their success. With few exceptions, the government followed the same practices used by other countries to create elite male units. They recruited girls young, trained them long and hard, rewarded them for good performance, and honored battlefield success. The result was predictable. Although women were never the majority of Dahomey's army, they constituted its best and most prestigious force.[29]

The women's army developed during a period when Dahomey's kings were involved in the international slave trade. Since males brought a better price in the Atlantic market, they reserved captive females for the palace guard. When slavery declined, the monarchy perpetuated the system by taking children from peasant families as tribute.[30] Building on indigenous myths about joint male/female rule, they described female soldiers as *ahosi*, or "wives of the king." But though this symbolic marriage brought some privileges, it did not bring freedom. Oral narratives recall girls jumping into wells rather than enter the palace. Once inside, most had no choice but to accept their situation. Many, however, thrived on the rigorous training and grew proud of doing things that village women could not. "Let the men harvest the manioc!" they sang.[31]

Their reputation for ferocity helped to terrorize neighboring societies, but it also played into European stereotypes about African savagery. By the 1870s, the *New York Times* could describe them as a regiment "more terrible than any beneath the sun."[32] They supposedly rushed into battle with teeth filed to spearpoints. In hand-to-hand combat, one even bit off a man's nose.[33] When the French finally succeeded in conquering the kingdom, clever businessmen recruited former *ahosi* to participate in ethnographic displays at European and American expositions.[34] Between 1890 and 1924, they appeared in St. Petersburg, Berlin, Hamburg, Frankfurt, Darmstadt, Zurich, Prague, Paris, Lyons, London, Brussels, Chicago, San Francisco, Atlanta, Buffalo, and St. Louis.[35]

Promotional materials depicted them as both sexually enticing and dangerous, much like the Amazons of ancient myth. Promoters in Chicago pointed to scars on the women's bodies as proof that they fought "to kill or be killed." A surviving French lithograph depicts a bare-breasted Dahomean brandishing two decapitated heads. A pamphlet distributed at London's Crystal Palace claimed that in processions through the Exposition grounds, they "approached the frenzy that borders on blood-shedding, but were restrained from actual violence." Other writers emphasized their sexuality, their dovelike eyes and rounded breasts. A German writer described an imagined visitor gliding his hand "with sensual curiosity across their soft skin." In contrast, for the Russian novelist Boris Pasternak, who recalled watching them perform at the Zoological Gardens in Moscow in 1901, they represented "serried suffering."[36]

An Amazon is more than a female soldier. She is an object of fantasy, longing, inspiration, and fear. *History isn't just what happens in the past. It is what later generations choose to make of it.*

The story of the Chinese heroine Mulan is a perfect example. As far as we know, she was born around the year 618 in the Anhui province in southeast China. When her father was summoned for military service to help repel northern invaders, she took his place. Dressed in men's clothing, she stayed in the army for twelve long years, then returned home and took up her life as a dutiful daughter. When the Emperor learned of her story, he wanted her to enter his service. Mulan committed suicide rather than obey his command. Over the years, her story was told and retold, appearing in popular poetry, in drama, and in political propaganda. One of the earliest versions, a folk poem dating from shortly after the actual events, stresses Mulan's ability to imitate her male peers. "When a pair of rabbits romp together, how can one know if they are male or female?" it asks. Later versions emphasize the Confucian virtue of filial piety: Mulan went to war to save her ailing father.[37]

The legend took on new layers of meaning when it emerged in the United States in 1976 in Maxine Hong Kingston's semifictional memoir *The Woman Warrior*. In this genre-defying book Kingston wove together her own girlhood memories with her immigrant mother's tales about China. In the mother's stories, the possibilities for women are both glorious and bleak. "No Name Woman" is forced to give birth in a pigpen when she gets pregnant out of wedlock. But in other tales swordswomen rage across China avenging wrongs. In Kingston's retelling, Mulan fights side by side with a male lover, her baby's umbilical cord tied to her flagpole. Kingston suggests that hero stories gave her mother the capacity to endure her difficult life. In the process they gave Kingston the power to become a writer. Like Ts'ai Yen, an ancient warrior-poet captured by barbarians, she learned to sing in a foreign tongue.[38]

By the time Disney took up Mulan's story twenty years later, China's complex heroine had become a fetching tomboy who runs away to escape the porcelain-doll deportment expected of young girls. With her trusty horse and her magical dragon, she wins love as well as fame on the battlefield, returning home as a strong yet perfectly feminine young lady. As one reviewer wrote, "Mulan is a character any woman can be proud to have her daughter emulate."[39]

For thirteen centuries writers have been making the same claim, though the characteristics that they have wished their daughters to emulate have shifted. The same has been true of the marvelous creatures the Greeks called Amazons.

Greek Stories Told and Retold

When Abby Kleinbaum taught her first class in women's history at Manhattan Community College in the spring of 1972, her students wanted to know if women had ever been powerful. Ten years later, she responded with a well-researched and still useful survey of the Amazon motif in European literature from the Greeks to the moderns. Her conclusion surely disappointed students eager to find evidence of female autonomy and power. Kleinbaum argued that in Western literature the Amazon was "an image of a superlative female that men constructed to flatter themselves." Winning an Amazon, through love or war, made a man a hero. If a woman was an exemplary warrior, then the skills of the man who defeated her appeared all the greater. If she was both beautiful and resistant to male advances, then the man who won her heart and bed was irresistible.[40] Kleinbaum's argument recalls Virginia Woolf's observation in *A Room of One's Own*, "Women have served all these centuries as looking-glasses possessing the magic and delicious power of reflecting the figure of man at twice its natural size."[41]

Obviously a motif that developed over at least ten centuries of Greek and Roman history and that appeared in papyrus fragments, red and black pottery, funerary monuments, painting, and architecture, and in epic, satire, lyric poetry, romance, tragedy, comedy, and oratory, cannot be reduced to a single meaning.[42] But it is just as obvious that stories about Amazons had something to do with the way Greeks thought about differences between the sexes. Here it helps to pay less attention to what Greek writers thought about women and more attention to what Greek society demanded of men.[43]

In the oldest Greek texts, the Amazon appears not in detailed narratives, but in an epithet—*Amazones antianeirai*, a curious combination of Greek and foreign syllables that connoted a strange people who were both warriors and women. In the context of heroic epic, the epithet was disturbing because it undercut a powerful norm—that prowess in battle belonged to men alone. Since a hero was only as worthy as his opponent, a creature who was truly *antianeirai*, or equivalent to men, was worth fighting. But if this same creature was also a woman, she destabilized the very concept of male heroism. The threat was not just to male authority but to maleness itself. An Amazon was a hybrid—a monster, which is why she had to be conquered.[44]

As the nature of Greek warfare changed, so did attitudes toward Amazons. As elite males discovered nonmilitant ways to prove their mettle, and as warfare was turned over to citizen armies and eventually to hired troops, Amazons became less monstrous and more human. Some writers even began to imagine them as potential lovers. In the fourth century C.E., a poet named Quintus rewrote an old story about Achilles's victory over the Amazon queen Penthesilea. After fierce combat, Achilles eventually kills her, but when he bends down to strip her of her armor, her beauty shines through the grime and gore, filling him with remorse, "for she was / Flawless, a very daughter of the Gods." In a response that would have been impossible for an epic hero, he laments her death, wishing that he had "borne her home, his queenly bride." Achilles's longing for Penthesilea became a symbol of redemptive love. In Roman sarcophagus decorations, for example, the two often appeared together.[45]

By the time Christine wrote there were already multiple representations of Penthesilea. A medieval Norman writer, Benoît de Sainte-More, placed her in an imagined kingdom of Feminie, a place of rare spices and exquisite herbs.[46] Boccaccio acknowledged her martial prowess, but only as a means of chiding slothful knights. If even a woman could learn to fight, he argued, then weak men could make up for their own natural deficiencies through practice. His brief account says nothing about Achilles's attraction for Penthesilea, though it perpetuated a legend that the Amazon queen came to Troy because she wanted the Trojan leader Hector to father her child.[47]

Christine transformed Boccaccio's story. In her account, Penthesilea combines male valor with female chastity. She does not want to mate with Hector. She wants to become like him, for "it is normal for someone to love one's peer freely." When she discovers that the Trojan leader is dead, she vows vengeance, fighting so valiantly that no man, not even Hector himself, can match her. Only when she is cut off from her own troops and surrounded by the entire Greek army does she succumb. In Christine's telling, Penthesilea is doubly heroic because she "never condescended to couple with a man, remaining a virgin her whole life."[48]

Penthesilea's story took on new meanings in the sixteenth century as an astonishing number of women ascended to the thrones of Europe. On tapestries and in paintings and engravings, she appeared alongside Joan of Arc in representations of the "Nine Worthies," female counterparts to male heroes of antiquity.[49] In England, Penthesilea was the one Amazon unequivocally praised during the reign of Elizabeth I. At a masque performed at the court of King James, the poet Ben Jonson placed Penthesilea at the head of a procession of queens. In Jonson's words, she was the consummate heroine, a woman who "is nowhere named, but with the Preface of Honour, and Vertue; and is always advanced in the head of the worthiest Women." Worthiness presumably included a willingness to expose her body. Drawings of Penthesilea's costume by the

Inigo Jones, "Penthesilea," from Ben Jonson,
The Masque of Queenes

renowned architect Inigo Jones show a see-through bodice that
revealed both nipples and navel.[50]

When the German poet Heinrich von Kleist took up the story
two centuries later, a chaste Penthesilea, even a tamed Penthesilea,
was the norm. Kleist changed that. In a verse drama composed in
1808, he scandalized contemporaries by transforming the Amazon
queen into the leader of a lustful band bent on kidnapping fair
youths who would father their children in an orgy of uncommitted
love. As in Quintus's story, the plot centers on the love Achilles

feels for the woman he has killed, but this time the outcome is different. "Moaning with grief," he lifts Penthesilea in his arms and "woos her back to life!"[51]

At that point, a new and even more ferocious struggle begins. Penthesilea's friends encourage her to believe that it is she who has overcome Achilles. Calmed by his love, she reveals the terrible origins of the Amazon kingdom. She tells him that when her people, the Scythians, were defeated in war, women were forced to share the "loathsome beds" of their husbands' and fathers' killers. In revenge they fashioned daggers from their own ornaments, hiding them in their hearths, until they were able to rise up as a group and throw off their conquerors. Vowing never again to be subject to men, they cut off their own right breasts. Achilles is horrified to discover that Penthesilea too has mutilated herself, but she reassures him that all her love is now concentrated in her left breast, near her heart.

In the very moment of declaring their love, the two warriors begin a struggle for dominance. Penthesilea vows to carry Achilles home to Amazonia and house him in tents of purple. He vows to carry her to Athens and make her his bride. When she discovers she is actually Achilles's prisoner, she becomes enraged and sends him away. Thinking he can only recover her love by letting her defeat him in battle, he arranges a sham contest, approaching her armed only with a spear. Humiliated by the ruse, she shoots him in the neck with an arrow, then joins her dogs in an attack on his flesh. Drunk with fury, she sinks her teeth into his breast. When she comes to herself, she hardly realizes what has happened. Dazed and with blood "dripping from her mouth and hands," she asks, "Did I kiss him to death?" Then she takes her own life.[52]

Critics continue to argue over the significance of Kleist's play. Was it an anguished response to the horrors of the French Revolution? A prescient portrayal of feminist angst? Or a projection of the author's own disordered psyche? (Kleist shot himself in 1811 in a suicide pact with a female friend.) Understandably, the play was never produced during the poet's lifetime. When it was finally premiered in Berlin in 1878, the audience mistook it for a comedy. It didn't fare much better in the 1970s, when several directors tried their hand at a revival. In Stuttgart, the Amazons wore earth-brown bikinis, and Achilles's friend Ulysses appeared in sunglasses and a G-string. In a 1977 London adaptation, Penthesilea warmed up her troops in a track suit. By the 1980s, however, German feminists had begun to explore the drama's radical potential. Focusing on Penthesilea's description of the tragic origins of the Amazon kingdom, some celebrated the heroine's assertion of sexual and political autonomy. Others saw the self-mutilation of the Amazons as a tragic replaying of the very violence once perpetrated against them.[53]

Twentieth-century attempts to revive Kleist's play return the story of Penthesilea to its origins. In the oldest Greek myths, Amazons were monsters, hybrids. Only gradually did they acquire the qualities that made them fit partners for heroes. Yet the most positive representations of their kingdom, as in Christine's *City of Women* or pageants enacted in the English court, were also celebrations of state power. The American poet Joel Agee, who has written a new English translation of Kleist's play, argues that the German poet understood that. Despite its revolutionary uniqueness, Kleist's Amazon kingdom is just another state. Like the Greek state, or the French and Prussian states that Kleist knew, it is hostile to freedom and ignorant of love. The French feminist Hélène Cixous makes a similar point. For one brief moment in the play, she argues, Achilles and Penthesilea find grace, but in the end both succumb to "masculine martial values" grounded in national pride. Neither can imagine a world without winners and losers.[54]

In reimaging old Greek stories, each generation reveals its own hopes and fears. In the United States, philosopher and radical feminist Mary Daly began calling herself an Amazon as early as 1978.

Arguing that European witch-hunting, Chinese foot-binding, Hindu widow-burning, African genital mutilation, Nazi medicine, and American gynecology all originated in a male desire to destroy female power, she urged readers to take up "the Sacred Double Axes of Amazons," turning misogynist slander against the perpetrators. For her the war against men was both symbolic and real. She wasn't interested in replicating male values but in rediscovering the loving communities of women hidden beneath old stereotypes. If men called them witches, feminists should embrace the label in order to give it new meaning. They should demand "brooms of their own."[55]

Gloria Steinem took a more playful approach. Using *Ms.* magazine as her platform, she transformed the comic book heroine Wonder Woman into a feminist icon.

The original Wonder Woman was the invention of William Moulton Marston, an eccentric Harvard-trained psychologist who in the midst of World War II wanted to create a positive model for girls. "Frankly," he wrote, "Wonder Woman is psychological propaganda for the new type of woman who should, I believe, rule the world. There isn't love enough in the male organism to run this planet peacefully. Woman's body contains twice as many love-generating organs and endocrine mechanisms as the male. What woman lacks is the dominance or self-assertive power to put over and enforce her love desires. I have given Wonder Woman this dominant force but have kept her loving, tender, maternal and feminine in every other way."[56]

He built his plot on the Greek story of Hippolyta, an Amazon maiden defeated and imprisoned by Hercules. In Christine's version of the same story, the Amazon queen negotiates peace with Hercules by allowing Hippolyta to remain with the Greeks and marry Theseus.[57] In Marston's version, the goddess Aphrodite intervenes and allows the entire Amazon kingdom to escape to a place called Pleasure Island where the woman warriors survive for thousands of years, until a badly wounded American intelligence officer is washed up on their shore. Princess Diana, the daughter of Hippolyta, heals him with her magical powers, then carries him back to his homeland. When he comes to, she refuses to reveal her identity. "I'm just—a woman," she says. "My Wonder Woman," he responds. Like Superman, Wonder Woman ends up in America disguised as an ordinary person, a nurse named Diana Prince.[58]

Wonder Woman entranced an entire generation of American girls with her bullet-deflecting bracelets, her magic lasso, and her comic sidekick Etta Candy. For all its magic, the stories touched on familiar female dilemmas. In an early episode, Diana Prince chides Etta for eating so much candy, warning her that if she gets too fat she won't be able to get a man. "Who wants to?" Etta replies. "When you've got a man, there's nothing you can do with him—but candy you can *eat!*" Etta insisted that a woman could be perfectly happy without a man. That was precisely what worried her critics. In the 1950s, one psychologist claimed that Wonder Woman's band of followers, students at the fictional Holladay College, were the "holiday girls, the gay party girls, the gay girls." Whether or not he understood the sexual implications of "gay," he believed they were lesbians in disguise. Today readers may wonder if the recurring bondage theme in the stories says more about Marston's fantasies. He was without question an unconventional man—the father of four children, two born to his wife and two to his assistant, who was the presumed model for Wonder Woman. According to the testimony of the children, they all lived happily together in one house.[59]

Like other women warriors, Wonder Woman changed over the years. By the 1960s, she had lost her magic bracelets and much of her power. In 1972, to the astonishment of the general public, she burst onto the cover of the first issue of *Ms.* magazine. Steinem, the editor, was determined to revive the heroine of her youth and to restore what was for her the most important theme of the old

Cover, *Ms.* magazine, July 1972

comics: that women had the capacity to rescue themselves. The cover implied that they might also have the power to rescue their nation. It shows an immense Wonder Woman striding across the earth with her landmark American eagle on her breast, crushing fighter planes with one hand and with the other holding an Asian city in the loop of her golden lasso. A banner across the top screams WONDER WOMAN FOR PRESIDENT. In 1973, a male writer for the comic phoned Steinem to say, "Okay, she's got her Amazon power back. She talks to the Amazons on Paradise Island. She even has a Black Amazon sister named Nubia. Now will you leave me alone?"[60]

The revival could not be stopped. Following fast on her debut in television and film, America's Amazon leaped out of the comics and into the shopping mall, as manufacturers produced action dolls, night lights, novelty telephones, electric toothbrushes, Pez dispensers and even scissors with Wonder Woman's legs as moving handles. Today there are Wonder Woman lunch boxes packed with gourmet cookies. Critic Lillian Robinson asks, "Where is the feminism in all this?"[61] The answer is surely not in the objects but in the fantasies they may or may not inspire.

Hunting Amazons in the Amazon

Amazon Bookstore is a worker-owned cooperative founded in Minneapolis in 1971. Its website identifies it as "the oldest feminist independent bookstore in North America." In 1999, it sued the online giant Amazon.com for copyright infringement, claiming that telephone calls destined for the mega-business were disrupting its own. The lawsuit shows how tricky the word *amazon* can be. In depositions, lawyers for the online corporation insinuated that the Minneapolis store, which took its name from the old Greek myths, was run by lesbians and really couldn't have anything to do with their company, which got its name from a very large river in South America. What the Amazon.com lawyers didn't say—or know—was that the river was named by Spanish explorers lost somewhere in the Brazilian jungle who thought they had stumbled on the women warriors described in the old Greek myths.[62]

Most scholars believe the name of the river comes from the narrative of Father Gaspar de Carvajal, who accompanied the Spanish explorer Francisco de Orellana during his 1541 expedition into the Brazilian interior. Carvajal not only reported seeing women wielding arrows, he included an elaborate description, purportedly supplied by a villager captured along the river, of a kingdom ruled by women who lived in stone houses and worshipped in great buildings "lined with heavy wooden ceilings covered with paint of various colors." He said these female rulers rode on the backs of camels and wore crowns of gold "as wide as two fingers."[63] Fifty years later, Sir Walter Raleigh used similar testimony from Indians near the Atlantic coast to confirm Carvajal's claim that somewhere in the interior there was a kingdom of women rich in gold.[64]

The desire to find—and conquer—these strange beings reinforced an already dominant theme in the literature of conquest, the representation of the lands themselves as "virgin." In a famous passage from his book *The Discoverie of the Large, Rich, and Bewtiful Empyre of Guiana*, Raleigh wrote:

> *Guiana* is a Countrye that hath yet her Maydenhead, never sackt, turned, nor wrought, the face of the earth hath not beene torne, nor the vertue and salt of the soyle spent by manurance, the graves have not beene opened for gold, the mines not broken with sledges, nor their Images puld down out of their temples. It hath never been entered by any armie of strength, and never conquered or possessed by any Christian Prince.[65]

For this would-be conqueror, America, like a desirable woman, was ripe for the taking. The violence of his verbs—"sackt," "torne," "spent," "opened"—made clear the close kinship of colonial conquest to rape. Lands, like women, could be "conquered" and "possessed." Failure to discover the mythical kingdom only reinforced the fascination.[66]

Today, the supposedly unspoiled areas of the Americas still inspire dreams. While corporations seek exotic woods, precious metals, and cheap labor, tourists flock to treetop hotels in the rain forest or to Isla Mujeres, seeking a simplicity and authenticity they believe has been lost from modern life.[67] Their imaginations are fed by rumors that a "chiefdom of Amazons" still exists at the mouth of the river, and that "the Amazons too will return." Scholars ask whether these beliefs have been borrowed from European stories, or come instead from somewhere deep within indigenous culture.[68]

In the 1980s, New Yorker writer Alex Shoumatoff decided to find out. He was fascinated with curious green stones known as muiraquitãs found in the Nhamundá-Trombetas-Tapajós region of Brazil. Often carved in the shape of frogs, these tiny amulets were linked to stories about women who lived without men "on a sacred lake called the Mirror of the Moon." According to one story, "At a certain month's full moon, once a year, men from a neighboring tribe come to the lake by canoe. When the visit has ended, the women present their lovers with the male offspring from the previous year's reunion, and with muiraquitãs, which they have obtained from an aquatic spirit called the Mother of the Muiraquitãs. The stones bring the men good luck in hunting."[69]

Shoumatoff thinks stories about women warriors derive from a seemingly universal fact—that, though "men are politically and economically dominant" in virtually every known society, some women reject their inferior status; "there are some women who emphatically do not like men and have no desire to be with them."[70] He was curious to know if Indians living in the area Carvajal visited might still tell such stories. Joined by a Belgian friend, he set off on a mission to find *muiraquitãs,* Amazons, and the lake known as the Mirror of the Moon. After many misadventures, he found the lake, which turned out to be a pond, "murky, and full of leaves." Unfortunately, none of the Indians he met was able to recall any stories about women who lived without men. The pond survived, such as it was. Was the myth extinct?[71]

Unexpectedly, late in the afternoon of his last day in the rain forest, Shoumatoff got his story. In a Kaxuiana Indian compound, a man named Kauka "began to speak in a melodious storytelling voice" as the women and girls of the compound "sat on a log at the edge of the lagoon . . . singing softly while combing each other's hair." Kauka said that long ago his father had told him a story about five women who awoke one night, "clutched hot peppers to their breasts and started to dance in a circle" until they rose from the ground and began to fly. When their husbands awoke, the women pelted them with the peppers, and then flew away to the top of the hill beside the Mirror of the Moon.[72]

The women left one girl child behind. When the abandoned husbands found her hiding under a basket, they cut her in pieces, giving her ears and vagina to the shaman, then distributing the other pieces among themselves. The next day, all of the pieces except the shaman's had grown into a woman. Determined to get his own woman, the shaman led a thousand men to the top of the hill where the wives had escaped. "Each woman lay down on her bed with her breasts pointing in the air and lifted her *tanga* and said, 'Supper is ready.'" But this was only a tease. When one man squatted over the most beautiful woman and attempted to make love, the others fell on him and killed him. Terrified, the remaining men climbed onto an airplane and flew away! Yes, Kauka said, it really was an airplane, though it flew "like a vulture gliding in the air." The surviving men became the founders of all the Indian nations.[73]

As Kauka spoke, several of the women came to the edge of the shelter, "nursing their babies in the gathering darkness and listening." Kauka told Shoumatoff that though women sang Kaxuiana songs to their children, "they don't tell the stories. . . . Only I know this story. Nobody else can tell it any more."[74] He did not say what happened to the wives who flew to the top of the mountain. Perhaps the women sitting quietly in the darkness knew that secret, but they weren't talking.

Further up the Amazon, in an area called Rondonia near the Bolivian border, the Brazilian anthropologist Betty Mindlin has spent years gathering stories. She says outsiders sometimes ask her whether there is "more equality between men and women, more possibility for harmony," in indigenous societies than in the modern world. She doubts it. Despite the lack of private property, the acceptance of nudity, and the strong ties of kinship and community, Rondonia is no lost Eden. The tales told in the rain forest show that "violence, repression, conflict, war, taboos, and rigid rules for behavior also exist in indigenous life." She has collected some of these stories in a book called *Barbecued Husbands and Other Stories from the Amazon*. She describes it as "an anthology of indigenous myths about love." But it is also a book about violence, food, rage, and the afterlife.[75]

The title story, told in a language called Macurap by both a female and a male storyteller, opens with little girls happily catching tadpoles in a fish-filled lake. Suddenly, an ugly old woman floats to the surface and tells the girls that they are spoiling the music and body paint used by the creatures of the lake. Then she begins to sing a song "so beautiful that the girls could hardly breathe." She tells the girls to fetch their mothers, who come running to see what is happening. Soon the mothers too are seduced by the music. When the old woman sees that they are enjoying themselves, she says, "Tomorrow you must come again to sing the frog song with me. But before you come, you must kill one of your husbands—one each day—so we can eat them while we sing. Now that's real food, not our little fish and tadpoles." The women are shocked, but as they listen to the music, they lose their fear. Each day they kill one husband, telling the others that the missing men have gone hunting.

The women sing and dance and eat roasted husbands until the remaining men send a young man to spy on them. When he discovers what is happening, the other men surround the dancing women and girls and kill them all. Overcoming the lure of her music, they also manage to kill the old woman. But when they return to their village, there is no one to prepare their food or sweep their houses. Although they take turns doing the women's work, when they chew maize to prepare a fermented drink called *chicha,* it tastes terrible. Fortunately, two little girls have escaped the massacre. Only one man, a chief, knows of their presence. He hides them until they are grown, then secretly lets them begin to make *chicha.* It tastes so good that when the men drink it, they exclaim, "There must be a woman around here somewhere!" The two girls come out of hiding, and the population begins to grow again.[76]

Like the story Shoumatoff heard on the lower Amazon, this one begins with a women's rebellion and ends with men restoring the village with the help of a girl or girls left behind. Neither story fully explains the women's rage. In the Macurap story, the music of the old woman represents a terrible, seemingly irresistible temptation and danger, but in both stories, the women's fury seems to come from something deep inside. It expresses itself in the joy of dancing with one another beyond the sight or control of men. But in both stories this enchantment leads only to violence. In the Macurap version it also leads to the massacre of the women. Only the innocence of the little girls and the gentleness of the chief who protects them restores balance to the village. The story reaffirms the orderliness of a world in which men hunt and women tend fields and make *chicha.*[77]

Mindlin got the story about barbecued husbands from two storytellers, Uberika Sapé, an elderly woman who was the first to share the mythology of her people with outsiders, and a leathery-skinned man named Iaxui Miton Pedro Mutum.[78] Mutum told another, quite different story about resistance to male control. In it, a male hunter deep in the forest discovers a beautiful woman who excels him in her skill with a bow. Instead of trying to conquer her, he succumbs to her graces, joining her and her sisters in a village inhabited entirely by women, except for one old man, the woman's father, who is frequently away. Eventually, the beautiful woman gives birth to a son, an enchanted child who grows as much in a few days as human children do in years.

The hunter is happy with his new life until he grows homesick for his mother and goes back to his old village for a visit. There a man called the Stubborn One forces him to reveal the secret of the women who live without men. The Stubborn One goes off to find them for himself. The women receive him politely, lure him to sleep, then kill and eat him. When the hunter returns, he finds a barren field where the women's village had been and buzzing bees in place of his son. Mutum ended the story with an explicit moral: "Because of the meddling of the Stubborn One, people lost the teaching of the women without men: the knowledge these women would have revealed to their husband as he grew more and more accustomed to them, as their children became his companions: the secrets of the leaves, of abundant hunting and fishing."[79]

This story, too, is about sex and power, but though it includes an episode of cannibalism, it conveys longing rather than fear. Although the woman found in the woods has mastered the male art of hunting, she is not a rival but a potential companion. When the hunter follows her to her village, he enters a paradisiacal, almost infantile state, where all his needs are met by a woman who is not only beautiful and loving but more skilled in almost everything than he. Instead of trying to overcome her, he joyfully submits to her power. Perhaps that is because the story isn't really about female prowess but about male competition. As long as the hunter has the women's village to himself, the dream persists. When the Stubborn One enters the story, everything comes crashing down.

It is impossible to know whether European explorers heard similar stories from people they encountered along the river they named the Amazon. The Macurap storytellers Mindlin worked with were born in the early twentieth century. By the time the Swiss anthropologist Franz Caspar visited their village in 1948, some were already working on rubber plantations in conditions of semi-slavery. Like other indigenous groups, they had been devastated by disease, but unlike some they managed to hold on to their land. After 1984, when the Brazilian government formally gave them control of their territory, they "forcibly but nonviolently" removed non-indigenous rubber workers. Today Macurap teachers work to preserve native traditions and promote literacy both in their own language and in Portuguese.[80]

Among the Macurap, both men and women tell stories. Mindlin explains that as Sapé and Mutum spoke, a young mother named Ewiri Margarida, sitting with a child at her breast, recast their words into "a very beautiful Portuguese." Working with both the original Macurap and the Portuguese translation, Mindlin experimented with different ways of putting the stories into writing. Her objective was to re-create the enchantment she felt when she first heard them. For the London edition of *Barbecued Husbands*, another translator recast Mindlin's written Portuguese into English.[81]

Thus, stories told and retold in the rain forest took on new form as they were translated from one language to another, then reproduced in print. In the process, they moved from the intimacy of oral narrative to the firmness of a published text. The same thing happened centuries before to the Greek stories that became legends about Amazons. Over many years, they moved from formulas sung by singers of tales into written epic and then into drama and history. Taking visual form in pottery, Parthenon friezes, and Roman sarcophagi, they entered the art and literature of Western Europe, eventually emerging in the travelers' tales that gave the name *Amazon* to the region where Betty Mindlin sat listening to Macurap elders.

Mindlin believes the stories she gathered in the rain forest reveal universal dilemmas. She would agree that the details—the catching of tadpoles, the chewing of grain to make *chicha,* the shape of arrows and huts—are grounded in a particular culture, but in her view the fantasy of a world without men seems to come from something fundamental in human experience. Like myths about Amazons, Macurap tales test the boundaries of gender, asking how the world might look if women assumed male roles, assaulted male authority, or rejected male lovers.[82]

Historians are usually less interested in discovering universals than in tracing change over time. When we dig through the accumulated refuse of the past, we want to know whether a detail comes from the first or the tenth layer in the excavation and how it relates to other things buried beside it. Historians like to see evidence close up. Things that look the same from a distance often reveal surprising differences when seen side by side. An Athenian warrior is not a Macurap hunter. A tadpole is not a camel. A lake in the forest is not a kingdom of gold.

Still the human need to push against the boundaries of gender does seem universal. Stories from the Amazon dance between myth and history.

Gender and War

In a recent study, political scientist Joshua Goldstein compiled data on the sex breakdown in attributes presumed essential to success in combat. He concluded that men are actually more dominant in the military than biological distinctions would predict. Public perception to the contrary, no one has yet found a gene for war.

Researchers have been able to find some distinctions between men and women, but, even in areas that seem obvious, like size and strength, there is often more variation within the sexes than between them. Although men are on average taller than women, the tallest woman in a given group may tower over the average man. The same thing is true for speed. Among the 30,427 runners who completed the 1997 New York Marathon, the median woman was 11 percent slower than the median man, but the majority of men finished well behind the fastest women, and the majority of women finished well ahead of the slowest men. The same is true for other qualities associated with war, like risk-taking or aggression. In the production of war, Goldstein argues, culture works overtime. Men fight because it is manly to do so, and in fighting they reinforce the connection between manhood and war.[83]

Hence, in some settings, gender itself is a weapon. Destroy a man's manhood, and you destroy his will to resist. In the spring of 2004, the Associated Press carried a story about an Iraqi prisoner of war who was forced to remove his clothes when interrogated by American marines. Earlier he had been subjected to torture by Saddam Hussein's secret police. He told a reporter that he preferred being jabbed with electric prods, beaten, and hung from the ceiling with his hands tied behind his back to being stripped of his clothing in front of American soldiers. "It's OK if they beat me. Beatings don't hurt us; it's just a blow. But no one would want their manhood to be shattered. They wanted us to feel as though we were women, the way women feel, and this is the worst insult, to feel like a woman."[84]

That, at least, was the way his speech was represented in the American press. But the United States, too, was dealing with the conundrums of gender. Early in the war, television audiences were treated to competing images of two soldiers—Jessica Lynch, portrayed as a wholesome blonde rescued from the specter of Iraqi abuse, and Lynndie England, depicted as a sadistic prison guard taunting Muslim men. "If Jessica Lynch was the pure alabaster Joan of Arc," one web blogger wrote, "Lynndie England represents her exact opposite, a cigarette-dangling, wisecracking dame in desert-camo dungarees, and the Pentagon's worst nightmare."[85] Here it was again—the old struggle between good Amazons and bad Amazons, women to be celebrated and women to be vanquished. But as the story of Jessica Lynch unfolded, even the good Amazon began to flicker and fade.

Initial reports said that Lynch went down fighting, that when the Humvee in which she was riding was attacked, she had fought furiously. Later stories revealed that she had offered no resistance at all, that she was part of a supply team who never should have seen combat and had been caught in a firefight because of faulty directions and confusing orders. Of the five soldiers in her Humvee, she was the only one who survived. Although she was beaten and perhaps raped, she was saved by Iraqi physicians who cared for her when she was brought under military guard to a civilian hospital being used as a cover for the resistance. By the time an American unit broke into the hospital and conducted the dramatic rescue recorded by military videographers, the Iraqis had already left.[86]

For reporters covering the war, "Remember Jessica Lynch" became a mantra for checking the facts before printing a story. Jessica Lynch was no Rambo. She was a former beauty queen who followed her brother into the army because that seemed like the best way out of a depressed West Virginia town ironically named Palestine. When the first rescuer burst into her hospital room, he took off his helmet and said, "We're United States soldiers and we're here to protect you and take you home." Numb with pain and shaking with relief and fear, she could only answer, "I'm an American soldier, too." She was a soldier, but she didn't like it when people treated her as a hero. "I'm not a hero," she said. "If it makes people feel good to say it, then I'm glad. But I'm not. I'm just a survivor. When I think about it, it keeps me awake at night."[87]

In the United States, press coverage of the war played on contrasting visions of Western and Muslim women—one group supposedly free to undertake any work a man might do, the other constrained by Islamic law and *burqas*. Yet Muslims also produced Amazons, women who confused interpreters by behaving as both combatants and women.

When Wafri (or Wafa) Idris, a twenty-eight-year-old college-educated Palestinian woman, blew herself up in a Jerusalem shopping center, some Muslim commentators questioned whether a woman could legitimately participate in "holy war." Others transformed her into both a Muslim and a feminist heroine. "Wafri Idris elevated the value of the Arab woman, and, in one moment, and with enviable courage, put an end to the unending debate about equality between men and women," an Egyptian editor wrote. Some, playing to Western sensibilities, invoked Joan of Arc. The head of psychiatry at an Egyptian hospital compared her to the Virgin Mary. "From Mary's womb issued a child who eliminated oppression, while the body of Wafa became shrapnel that eliminated despair and roused hope," he wrote. A columnist for an Egyptian daily picked up the theme, using her example to chide other women. "She bore in her belly the fetus of a rare heroism. What are the women of velvet chatting in the parlors next to the act of Wafa Idris?"[88]

These commentators may or may not have known that Idris was childless. After a late-term miscarriage, doctors told her she would never bear a child. When her husband wanted to take another wife, she resisted, and he divorced her. Idris put her life back together by training as a medic, volunteering with the Red Crescent Society, the Palestinian affiliate of the International Red Cross. She raised doves, doted on her siblings' children, and once, while helping to retrieve the wounded from a battle with Israelis, was hit by rubber bullets. Some said she sought martyrdom; others that she was devoted to saving life, not taking it. When interviewed by a reporter, her mother expressed pride in her daughter's sacrifice. "I wish every man, every woman, would do the same, be a bomber," she said. Then she broke down crying. "I have lost a daughter."[89]

Over the centuries, in many cultures, female combatants have demonstrated bravery, devotion to kin and country, and self-reliance. They have embodied miracles, ratified female aspirations, terrified their nation's enemies, and broken their mothers' hearts. Their stories matter because they force us to confront the fictions that divide the world into two kinds of people, and that use gender to glorify war and to justify the power of men over women and of some states and nations over others.

In films, poems, parades, and pageants, and in spontaneous demonstrations at the edges of barbed-wire barriers or monuments, people honor the sacrifices of their nation's defenders. But curiously, over time, the memory of women warriors often transcends whatever cause they served. The Greek historian Herodotus identified the Amazons with the Scythians, but few if any of those who later adopted his stories knew or cared about Scythian history. Who remembers today the name of the king Joan of Arc championed? In 1900, English suffragists marched under her banner without recalling that when she was alive, she despised the English. During World War II, both the German Reich and the French Resistance employed her image.[90] Amazons are free for the taking. In the recent wars in the Balkans combatants on both sides celebrated their female fighters as Amazons reborn.[91] Amazon stories exist outside time and space inside the hope of female power. They yearn toward justice, yet acknowledge a terrible violence at the heart of history.

In the rain forest, writers collect Amazon tales. On the steppes, archaeologists dig for bones. In libraries and archives, scholars reconstruct the histories of long-forgotten wars. They wonder where the fury comes from and why it will not go away.

Chapter Three

ॐ

SHAKESPEARE'S DAUGHTERS

𝒱irginia Woolf went to the British Museum to find out why women were poor. She soon gave up. There were too many experts, too many opinions, and too little real information. So she did what researchers often do when they are stumped. She narrowed her question. She decided "to ask the historian, who records not opinions but facts, to describe under what conditions women lived, not through the ages, but in England, say in the time of Elizabeth." She wanted practical information: "how they were educated; whether they were taught to write; whether they had sitting rooms to themselves; how many woman had children before they were twenty-one." But the historian she turned to, Professor George Trevelyan, disappointed her. His new and highly acclaimed history of England contained only a few grim sentences on women. Woolf learned from his book that wife-beating was a recognized right, and that daughters who resisted their parents' choice of a husband were "locked up, beaten and flung about the room," but little else. Apparently, nothing more was known about women before the eighteenth century.[1]

Since history had failed her, Woolf turned to fiction. She created her own description of women writers in the age of Elizabeth, by giving William Shakespeare a sister. In Woolf's fantasy, Judith, like her brother, had a gift for language, but when he went to school to study the classics, she stayed at home to do the mending. When he went to London to try out the stage, she hid in the apple loft to scribble a few pages, "but she was careful to hide them or set fire to them." When she refused to marry a neighbor's son, her father beat her severely. "Then he ceased to scold her. He begged her instead not to hurt him, not to shame him in this matter of her marriage." Torn between duty to her family and the "force of her own gift," she ran away to London, where she attracted the attention of a gentleman actor who seduced and then abandoned her. Pregnant, she killed herself in despair. For Woolf, the moral of the story was clear: there were no female writers in William Shakespeare's time because women were not free to develop their gifts. "For it needs little skill in psychology to be sure that a highly gifted girl who had tried to use her gift for poetry would have been so thwarted and hindered by other people, so tortured and pulled asunder by her own contrary instincts, that she must have lost her health and sanity to a certainty."[2]

Woolf's larger point is irrefutable. No woman could have lived the life of William Shakespeare. But though Woolf had no way of knowing it and Professor Trevelyan didn't notice, there were women writers in Shakespeare's time. The last decade of the poet's life was an especially fruitful period. Between 1611 and 1621, Elizabeth Cary published the first original drama by an English woman, Aemilia Lanyer the first country house poem, Mary Wroth the first prose fiction, and Rachel Speght the first signed polemic.[3] Today works like theirs are studied in colleges and universities, not only because they are "firsts," but because they are complex and interesting on their own terms.[4]

Thanks to decades of research, historians can also now answer Woolf's specific queries about education and marriage in the age of Elizabeth. For common people, England was still a mostly oral society. Although literacy was rising, in some counties fewer than

15 percent of women and only half of the men could sign their own names.[5] For aristocratic women, however, the sixteenth century was an age of educational reform. There was even a flurry of interest in women's history. In 1521, Bryan Ansley, an official in the court of Henry VIII, translated and published Christine de Pizan's *Book of the City of Ladies*. Henry's daughters must have had copies. A six-panel set of tapestries called the "Citie of Ladies" was among the treasures he passed on to Elizabeth.[6]

Contrary to the old myths, most women beneath the aristocracy married in their mid-twenties rather than their teens. Their husbands were a few years older. Couples married late because their economic contributions mattered and because it took time to accumulate the goods needed to set up a household.[7] Woolf was right, however, in thinking that a discontented girl might head for London. The city's population tripled between 1580 and 1640 as thousands of young people left farms and villages. Girls worked as scullery maids, button-makers, silk-winders, and spinners. They served in tradesmen's houses or managed stalls in public markets. But only the desperate applied to theaters. As one contemporary expressed it, "There are no women that keep playhouse doors but are whores."[8]

In such a setting, well-behaved women seldom made history. Their names appeared on parish registers when they married or died, but otherwise they left few marks on surviving records. In contrast, girls who gave birth out of wedlock, testified against powerful men, or used their remarkable gifts to vilify their neighbors often made memorable appearances in court. They did not act on the London stage, but they performed in the theater of ordinary life.[9]

The invisibility of women who conformed to the expectations of their neighbors is apparent in Shakespeare's own family. Joan Shakespeare, the only one of William's four sisters to survive to adulthood, married a Stratford hatter, raised four children, and died at the age of seventy-six, leaving no record beyond a brief mention in her brother's will. We know no more about the poet's own daughters. Susanna, the elder, married at the age of twenty-four, gave birth to several children, and died in her sixties. Judith, the second daughter, lived a wife for fifty years and died silently, though her husband was occasionally in trouble with the law. Judith and Susanna may have been happy or unhappy, gifted or ordinary. There is no way of knowing.[10]

Their names, however, provide a symbolic link to stories retold in Christine's *Book of the City of Ladies,* stories about biblical heroines whose encounters with evil men cast light on the dramas played out in English courts and on the lives and works of gifted women. Together, the names, the stories, the legal records of other English women, and the literary works of their contemporaries provide an unexpected portrait of Shakespeare's literal and symbolic daughters.

Susanna and Judith

In the Christian Bible, Susanna is a victim of sexual intimidation, Judith a model of righteous vengeance. In Shakespeare's time, literate people could have read the stories directly, though not in the new King James Bible, which eliminated the section of the Christian Bible called the "Apocrypha" to designate books not a part of the Hebrew canon. But with or without King James, both stories were too well known to disappear. They appeared in sermons, ballads, and folklore, and of course in women's names. Elite families preserved them in embroideries and engravings, or in oil paintings, such as those of the Italian artist Artemesia Gentileschi, whose portrayal of *Susanna and the Elders* was in the English royal collection in 1637. Some people may even have had access to the 1521 edition of *The Book of the City of Ladies,* which told both stories very much as they appeared in the Bible.[11]

In Christine's account, Susanna is relaxing in her garden one day when "two old men, false priests," accost her and demand sexual favors. When she refuses, they threaten to turn her in to authorities and say they had found her with a lover. Susanna says it is better to die in the flesh than to lose one's soul. The men make good on their threat. She is taken before the authorities, and condemned to die. But as she is "being led to her execution, with a great procession of people in tears following her," the prophet Daniel, still a babe in his mother's arms, miraculously begins to speak, telling the crowd that the false priests have deceived them. The people listen. The false priests confess and are executed. Susanna is freed. "God . . . ," Christine assures her readers, "always provides for those dear to Him."[12]

Judith was the instrument of a different kind of miracle. In Christine's telling, when enemy troops under a general called Holofernes are besieging a Jewish city, Judith quietly enters the enemy camp. When Holofernes discovers her presence, he lusts after her "with a great craving." Judith is not afraid. She encourages his attentions, all the while praying to God in her heart. On her third day in camp, she tells Holofernes to send all his servants away and she will come to his tent at midnight. Finding him in a drunken stupor, she tiptoes into the tent, takes his sword, and cuts off his head. Then, gathering her bloody trophy into her apron, she slips out of the enemy camp and returns to her people. In the morning, when Holofernes's army see their leader's head displayed on the city walls, they abandon the siege. Israel is saved.[13]

As a name for girls, *Susanna* was more common than *Judith*. But both names grew in popularity over the course of the sixteenth century. By 1600, *Susanna* was one of the top ten names for girls in many English parishes, and *Judith*, which wasn't even in the top fifty in 1540, had risen to twenty-third.[14] In naming their daughters, William and Anne Shakespeare were following a trend. Some parents may have been thinking of the Bible stories, while others may simply have named their daughters after close friends or family, as the Shakespeares did.

The overarching moral of the two stories—that God will aid and protect virtuous women—reinforces a traditional emphasis on female chastity. But the plots of the stories potentially undermine the lesson. Susanna's story warns that even chaste women face sexual danger and that respectable men lie. Unlike the victim of Woolf's fable, Susanna resists seduction, but in the short run, that doesn't do her much good. It is her word against that of the evil elders, and they prevail. Susanna is a heroine because she would rather die than succumb to men's propositions. Although the ostensible moral is that God will protect the innocent, the operable theme is that earthly systems often fail. Even though the crowd believes Susanna and mourns her condemnation, they are helpless to challenge authority until the prophet Daniel miraculously intervenes.

The story of Judith argues the opposite, that a clever woman may use sexual attraction to destroy a man. Judith prevails because she isn't afraid to use her own power. Unlike Woolf's Judith, the biblical Judith destroys her enemy rather than herself. For ordinary women, the lessons these stories taught were powerful but contradictory. A woman should be both chaste and alluring, both innocent and bold.

The same dilemmas appear in raw form in the records of England's courts.

Stories Told in the Court

Woolf was surely correct when she wrote, "Chastity had then, it has even now, a religious importance in a woman's life."[15] But it had a legal significance as well. Fornication and bastardy were public offenses. Although women, who often carried the evidence in their bellies, were easy targets, men too faced the constraints of the law. A man who bedded a woman was supposed to wed her, as William

Shakespeare did when at the age of eighteen he married Anne Hathaway, a woman eight years his senior who was pregnant with his child. Susanna Shakespeare, born six months after the wedding, was actually its cause.[16] Neither the pregnancy nor its outcome was unusual. Although a quarter of English brides were pregnant at marriage, very few babies—roughly 2–3 percent—were born to unwed mothers. In most cases, a combination of social pressure and the threat of legal action forced people to marry. When they didn't, the law insisted that the man responsible for a pregnancy pay for a woman's delivery and the maintenance of her child. In case of conflict, state-sponsored church courts determined guilt or innocence.[17]

Contemporaries called England's ecclesiastical courts "bawdy courts," and for good reason. Much of their business concerned sexual transgressions or sexual slanders. Courts had a dual obligation: to fix responsibility for child support and to punish flagrant violations of the moral order. Morality was the issue in the case of Thomas Quiney, a Stratford man who in 1616 married Shakespeare's daughter Judith. Shortly after the wedding, a single woman named Margaret Wheeler accused Quiney of fathering her child. Since both she and the baby died shortly after delivery, there was no need to provide maintenance. The Stratford court nevertheless summoned Quiney to answer charges of "carnal copulation" and sentenced him to stand in a white sheet before the congregation on three successive Sundays. To avoid further public humiliation— a whipping or public shaming in the marketplace—he paid a fine.[18]

Two years later, another Stratford case touched close to the Shakespeare family. William and Anne had named their twins after close friends, Judith and Hamnet Sadler, who became the children's godparents. In 1618, the parish register noted that Sadler's daughter, who was also named Judith, had given birth to a son out of wedlock. Since the court records are incomplete, we don't know whether or not she was tried for this offense, but four years later, she again gave birth. Though the child died, the court summoned her to answer a charge of "incontinence," along with a man named William Smith. At the next session, Smith brought three witnesses, one man and two women, who testified that Judith Sadler did "upon her knees swear and protest that the said William Smith did not ever at any time have any carnal knowledge of her body . . . and did acknowledge that she had done him great wrong in raising such a fame; and did there with tears protest that she was heartily sorry that she had done him that injury; and that one Gardiner was the true father of her child." At this point, the little drama ends, offering no further information on Judith or her reputed partner in crime.[19]

Taken together, however, the two cases demonstrate community concern with sexual behavior. Men as well as women could be shamed by an untoward pregnancy. Still, the consequences for women were greater, which is why so many of them appear as plaintiffs and witnesses as well as defendants. Ecclesiastical courts were in some sense women's courts. Although judges and juries were male, females played an essential part not only in cases of sexual transgression but in actions for sexual defamation and slander. In London, three-quarters of the plaintiffs and more than half of the defendants were female.[20] Where depositions survive, the voices of women come through with astonishing power.

Court documents are not transparent records of fact. People's stories were shaped by the legal system. If a conviction required proof of force, witnesses would emphasize pain and bodily injury. If a suit involved a plea for damages, plaintiffs would emphasize loss of income or reduced value in the marriage market. Forced to describe their sexual lives before a male clerk, some women surely censored their own language; conversely, clerks probably substituted legal terms like "carnal copulation" for colloquial expressions like "had me." Still, historians have been able to use such sources to break the silence around the lives of ordinary women.

Cases of rape or attempted rape produced the most harrowing stories. Katherine Irish was typical in emphasizing male violence and her own inability to resist. She testified that while she was guiding a man home from her master's house, he "took me by the neck . . . and held me so fast that I was not able to speak." She added that as she fled, she was "forced to leave the lantern I lighted him home by in the place where he did struggle with me." The lantern abandoned in the field became a silent witness both to her terror and to her dutiful behavior as a maidservant. She didn't merely forget the lantern, she was *forced* to leave it behind.²¹ Jane Bringley's pail functioned in the same way. Bringley told the court that she was accosted on her way home from milking. Thrown violently to the ground, she was brutally raped, but when her assailant fled, she resumed her duties. "[He] being done he rose up from me and went away . . . and I did take up my milk and went home."²² Lacing their stories with workaday details, the two women demonstrated the unpredictable nature of the crime, and assured their judges that they had done nothing to entice their assailant.

A woman who didn't cry for help and who didn't attempt to fight back made herself culpable. Then as now, defendants usually insisted that sex was consensual or, worse, that the woman had actually solicited intercourse. When a woman cried "rape," most men answered "whore," making her reputation rather than his behavior the issue. Courts in this era felt free to document a victim's prior sexual history and that of her family and friends as well. The person with the most convincing story or the most credible witnesses won.

Fourteen-year-old Sara Kempe testified that Joshua Taylor came into the house when she was alone, put his hand in his codpiece and said, "Sweetheart, take up thy clothes." When she refused, he "took me and laid me upon a bench and took up my clothes and did do me, bidding me not to cry out, whereupon I did not cry out." Later when she was so sore and bruised that she could not urinate, she told her mother what had happened and the mother called the authorities. Even though Sara failed to cry out, her age and medical testimony helped to convict her rapist.[23]

That wasn't always enough. Although juries were usually responsive when a child was involved, one jury acquitted a man of raping an eight-year-old girl, even though a surgeon testified that she had indeed been molested, because her parents were "of no good Repute, and that no Complaint was made of it in a long time after it was done, and several Witnesses for the prisoner, made it out to be only a design to get money of the Prisoner."[24] In the case of Sara Kempe, her mother's quick action and her family's sound reputation ensured conviction. For the other girl, there was no such protection.

Then as now, juries worried about false accusers, unrighteous Judiths who lured men into bed. There probably were women who behaved that way. Records from London's Bridewell Court document what one historian calls a "subculture of semi-professional sexual extortion." A woman or her accomplice would entice a man into a compromising situation, then sue him. Prostitutes focused on former clients, hoping for hush money.[25] Michael Drayton, an Elizabethan poet known for his love sonnets and meditations on English history, may have been the victim of such a scam. In March of 1627 he was summoned by London's Consistory Court because of "suspicion of incontinency with Mary Peters, wife of John Peters, as the fame goeth." A witness claimed to have seen Peters with her clothing pulled up past her navel while Drayton inspected her "privie parts." Although Drayton admitted visiting Peters, he denied the charges and was acquitted after the case turned into a fight between Peters and her landlady over who had brought the most shame to the house. Drayton's reputation—or perhaps his social status—protected him.[26]

If court records expose not-so-well-behaved women, they also confirm literary stereotypes about masters who preyed on their maidservants. A London cook supposedly told his maid, "Thou art my servant and I may do with thee what I please." Another man, defending his own behavior, alluded to the sexual habits of the aristocracy when he told the court "he was as well able to keep a whore in his house as his neighbours and that it was the fashion now a days and that the best sort of gentlemen now in the country keep a whore in their houses."[27]

One of the most outrageous offenders was a man named Francis Carewe who, in one of many actions against him, admitted that he "had had a hundred harlots and couldn't support all their babies." He seems to have met his match in a feisty woman named Elizabeth Foxegale, who had negotiated a private settlement after becoming pregnant by Carewe, then kept coming back for more money. The court tried to settle the case by awarding her ten shillings damages in addition to child maintenance and at the same time cautioning her "not to molest or trouble Mr Carowe any more." She responded by demanding twenty shillings instead of ten. She got it.[28]

Slander trials show that in boardinghouses and neighborhoods, women were the chosen enforcers of sexual propriety. Their targets were often other women. In London, three-quarters of all defamation cases were brought by women, and in half of those cases both plaintiffs and defendants were female. The slander of choice was "whore." Even when the dispute was about some other issue—space, control of resources, or management of servants and children—the accusation took sexual form. "Thou art a whore and an errant whore and a common carted whore and thou art my husband's whore," one woman screamed at another. In neighborhood conflicts, words like these were often understood as insults merely, not as descriptions of actual behavior, but their use reinforced a tendency to define a woman's value through her body.[29]

Accusers didn't rely solely on courts to punish offenders. They used their own voices and bodies to shame, expose, and banish the women they disdained. Sometimes they resorted to violence, scratching a rival's nose to give her a "whore's mark," in imitation of the slit nose, a form of punishment actually used to punish sexual offenders in some places. But mostly, they engaged in an elaborate kind of street theater. Seeing a child in the street, an artful neighbor picked it up and said, "Thou art a pretty child," then in a knowing voice said for all to hear that the child's mother "did not stand in a white sheet for nothing," an allusion to the penance for fornication imposed by church courts.[30]

Even when directed at men, sexual slanders were often about other women. If a wife was a "whore," her husband was a "cuckold." A "cuckold," as everyone knew, was a man whose wife was unfaithful. Hence, he was shamed, not by his own behavior, but by hers. Such accusations were not so much about sex as about authority. A man became a cuckold because he could not rule his own household. But strangely, a woman who did not allow her husband to rule was herself to blame. In 1595, Anne Webb accused Margery Dunne of being a "hackney queen," a "hackney jade," a "common, ridden jade," and a "codpiece queen." Then she leveled a double whammy, claiming that Dunne wanted to be a husband rather than a wife, a man rather than a woman. "Thou monster thou, put off thy long petticoat, put on a pair of britches, put off the white kerchief and put on a flat cap, for thou hast a snaffle [bridle] for thy husband to make him lie upon the boards all night and thy self upon two or three feather beds." Another woman, trying to keep a prisoner in Bridewell from getting bail, insisted that the woman was a whore and her mother a bawd. Then she offered her own solution to the problem of disorderly women. "If I were a man and had a wife I would set her in a garden to weed or pull up thistles rather than she should ride into the country with apprentices or keep boys company."[31]

In court, outspoken women were as likely to enforce as to challenge gender roles. The sexual economy demanded responsibility on both sides, but the stakes were different. For men, sex was ultimately about economic responsibility. A man was supposed to support his own children, but for him to do that he needed to know who they were. Unless a man could be certain his wife was chaste, he had no way of knowing if every child in his house was his own. Hence the exalted celebrations of chastity and the raucous accusations of whoredom and cuckoldry repeated on stage and in court. The celebration of chastity exposed the weak underbelly of patriarchy—that no man could be absolutely certain his children *were* his own. Women had the opposite problem. An unmarried woman who was pregnant had no way of disputing a charge of fornication. Since it was men who made and administered the laws, even a woman as righteous as Susanna could not know that she would be listened to if a man forced himself upon her. On both sides of the bed, a reputation for chastity mattered.

But to define the issue as a simple contest between male and female interests is to ignore the many other variables that determined success or failure in court. The complexity of English enforcement of sexual norms is more easily seen in detailed accounts of two sensational cases—one a case of out-of-wedlock birth that almost became a trial for witchcraft, the other a case of defamation in which the defendant lost in part because what she said was true. The stories of Agnes Bowker and Margaret Knowsley demonstrate the overpowering concern for maintaining social order that animated local elites.

Two Remarkable Stories

In depositions, Agnes Bowker portrayed herself as a vulnerable maidservant, seduced and abandoned. As in Woolf's fable about Judith Shakespeare, she tried to commit suicide when she found that she was pregnant. In her case, however, providential intervention twice prevented her taking her own life. She first went into the woods intending to hang herself with her own sash. When it broke, she tried drowning, but neighbors pulled her out of the waist-high pond. Thwarted in her attempts to destroy herself, she ran away, wandering from town to town until, on the sixteenth day of January 1569, between the hours of six and seven at night, she was delivered, not of a child, but of a strange creature that looked for all the world like a skinless, shriveled cat. Her midwife pronounced it a monster.

The first warning that something was wrong came when one of the attending women examined Agnes in labor and felt something inside the birth canal prick her finger. Frightened, the attendants began to leave the room. The midwife begged them to stay, reassuring them by addressing whatever it was emerging from Agnes's body: "In the name of the father and the son and of the holy ghost: Come safe and go safe and do no harm." But when she saw the thing, she cried out, "now in the name of God what have we here?"[32]

The town fathers dissected the supposed monster and said it was surely a cat. It even had bacon in its craw. Sober dames questioned the mother closely. Was this a trick? Had she in fact given birth earlier and disposed of the baby? In response, Agnes spun out a dark and wondrous story. When first in labor, she had claimed that a fellow servant was the father of her child. Now she explained that the real cause of her woe was an adulterous schoolmaster named Hugh Brady who had solicited her when she worked in his house. Although his wife had sent her away to London, when she returned, he found her and tricked her into selling herself to the Devil. Brady's wickedness knew no bounds. One day when she was on an errand to fetch meal, he came riding by. Reining in his horse, "he gave her sixpence and bade her come to St Mary's church." In the very porch of the church, he "had his carnal pleasure upon her." Later strange creatures came to her, one in the form of a bear. When she knew she was with child, she consulted a stranger, a

Dutch woman, who asked the cause of her sadness. The woman told her, "Thou art neither with man child nor woman child, but with a Mooncalf, and that thou shall know shortly."[33]

In the 1560s, monsters were serious business. In that decade alone, no fewer than eight pamphlets appeared describing strange creatures born to English women. Some attributed these apparitions to the wickedness of the mother. Others argued that disordered wombs reflected social disorder. The English had plenty to worry about. Queen Elizabeth was ill and no one knew who might succeed her. France and Spain threatened war. Economic depression followed outbreaks of plague.[34]

Agnes Bowker's delivery divided her community. Some saw a portent, others only a mystery. The attending women said Agnes really did give birth to a cat, though on closer questioning, some admitted that the light was dim. A local earl, leaving nothing to chance, performed his own experiment, killing and skinning a cat and comparing it with the creature that had supposedly emerged from Agnes's womb. He wrote up the results, complete with a life-size drawing in red ink of the presumed monster, and sent the whole package off to the bishop of London. After two weeks, the bishop responded that Agnes's story "appeareth plainly to be a counterfeit matter; but yet we cannot extort confessions of the manner of doings." In other words, he didn't believe that Agnes had given birth to a cat, but he didn't see any point in torturing her or her attendants to get at the truth.[35]

It is hard not to conclude that Agnes Bowker and her midwife were in collusion, perhaps to mask an infanticide. But if so, why did so many of their neighbors let them get away with it? In another town—or another decade—the stories Agnes told might have triggered an accusation of witchcraft. But in this community, the leading citizens seemed reluctant to launch an inquisition that might disturb the peace of the town. They approached the matter scientifically, less concerned with enforcing their own beliefs than in reassuring themselves that the whole thing was the product of female fantasy. In her own way, Agnes Bowker was a gifted woman. For a time she held the whole country's rapt attention. When her part was over, she walked offstage and was never heard from again.

Things did not work out so well for Margaret Knowsley. The testimony in Knowsley's case runs to over nine thousand words and includes depositions from twenty-eight witnesses, twenty of whom were women. But though some neighbors testified in her behalf, and though her charges against her master were no doubt true, she could not overcome the barriers of class. Common people were not without weapons against the powerful, but when a servant stood up against her master, she needed an impeccable reputation and strong allies.[36] Knowsley had neither.

Although she was a wife and mother, she was forced to work as a housekeeper in the homes of her betters. Her master, Stephen Jerome, was an educated man with degrees from Cambridge, and the newly installed pastor in the parish of Nantwich. Knowsley claimed that during the summer and autumn of 1625, while she was going about her chores, he propositioned her, saying that "he had an inward burning in his body" that required "the use of a woman." He said that if she would yield to him she would get her reward. When she refused, he attempted to rape her, but succeeded only in ejaculating over her clothes.[37]

Knowsley initially told her story only to close friends, begging them not to talk of it. But of course they did. Soon the whole town was in an uproar, divided for and against the minister. Terrified of being caught in a fight between powerful factions, Knowsley recanted, claiming that she had never told such a story, that she wouldn't for the world abuse the reputation of such a gentleman. It was too late. Jerome sued for slander. When Knowsley's husband was unable to post bond, she went to jail, even though she had small children at home and, as court documents note, "one sucking on her breast." Jail revived her memory—and her anger. She sent the court a 2,500-word petition affirming all the allegations and more. Her defiant document sealed her fate. According to the law, words did not need to be false to be slanderous. By putting her accusations into writing, no doubt with the help of one or more of Jerome's enemies, Knowsley made herself liable to a charge of sedition. She had challenged public authority.

Her charges received unexpected confirmation when Nantwich aldermen learned that Jerome had been dismissed from a prior position for "notoriously scandalous" behavior. He had solicited the favors of a married woman, had promised to amend his behavior, and then had attempted the same thing six months later.[38] But this information did not help Knowsley. She had destroyed the presumed peace of Nantwich. In June 1627, the court decided it was "high time to give exemplary punishment unto such lewd members whereby discensions and heartburning have sprung up and increased between divers gents and others of good rank within the town." Because Knowsley's behavior "did savour little of grace or repentance," the court sentenced her to be whipped through the town at the cart's tail on three successive market days, and to stand for two hours in the open market in a cage with papers pinned on her body that said she had unjustly slandered "Mr Jerome a preacher of Gods word."[39]

The case might have turned out differently if Knowsley's husband had initiated an action against Jerome before the stories spread. But even if Knowsley had possessed the resources to pursue a court action, a countersuit would still have been possible. Jerome had not, as she herself admitted, succeeded in his solicitations. By the time the case came to trial, the issue had become not his behavior, but her words. Should she have been silent, like Susanna?

In the seventeenth century, as today, people loved to see the powerful get their comeuppance. Then, as now, that seldom happened. Laws were harsh, but enforcement varied widely from town to town. Some neighborhoods, fraught with conflict over religion, politics, or distribution of land, probed the dark corners of people's lives. In other places, common people united to protect errant folk from the eyes of authority. Whether or not a person was prosecuted depended on who was paying attention and why.

Three Gifted Women

Court records give us some sense of what might have happened to Shakespeare's imagined sister had she run off to London and become pregnant by a gentleman actor. But court records can't tell us what it would have taken for a talented woman in Shakespeare's time to fulfill her gifts. The stories of Aemilia Lanyer, Elizabeth Cary, and Artemisia Gentileschi give us some hint.

Like Woolf's Judith, Cary was betrothed while still in her teens. Lanyer became pregnant out of wedlock. Gentileschi was raped and then seduced. None of them died in despair. Cary and Lanyer became serious writers, Gentileschi an even more successful painter. Their stories suggest the circumstances under which a woman born in the sixteenth century might become an artist. Although all three had both talent and pluck, that was not enough. They were apparently less pliable than other girls of their class, less susceptible to conventional molding, but they were also less pampered and protected. They had fathers who attempted to further their interests, yet pushed them into situations where they not only were forced to live by their wits but had access to the kind of training they needed. They had another advantage as well. Although none was born into an aristocratic family, all three had powerful patrons. Lanyer came of age in the shadow of Elizabeth's court and was encouraged by aristocratic women linked to Anne of Denmark, the wife of James I. Cary and Gentileschi were sustained by a circle around Henrietta Maria, the Catholic wife of Charles I. Both kings had famously independent spouses, women known both for their lavish patronage of the arts and for religious deviance.

Like the stories told in the "bawdy court," the lives of Lanyer, Cary, and Gentileschi reflect the power of reputation, the temptations of rebellion, and the dangers and opportunities of sexual intrigue. But they also take us into a world where talent and connections might lead to artistic achievement.

AEMILIA LANYER

Aemilia Lanyer was born Aemilia Bassano in London in 1569. Her father, Baptiso Bassano, was a native of Venice who had come to England in 1538 as a musician in the service of an English nobleman. Within a few years, he was playing at the court of Henry VIII. By the time Aemilia was born, he was one of Queen Elizabeth's court musicians. Aemilia's mother, Margaret Johnson, may also have come from a family of musicians, but little is known about her.[40]

Lanyer's life would be as unknown as her mother's but for two circumstances—in 1597 she consulted an eccentric London astrologer named Simon Forman who kept detailed case notes of their meetings, and in 1611 she published a remarkable volume of poetry, *Salve Deus Rex Judaeorum*, a poetic setting of the birth, death, and crucifixion of Jesus that managed at the same time to be a celebration of learned women.[41] The evidence of the two sources is radically different, though complementary. Forman's notebooks detail Lanyer's ailments, her ambitions, and her encounters with men. The poems both document and demonstrate her development as a writer.

Lanyer was twenty-eight years old when she consulted Forman. She told him that when she was eighteen, she had become the mistress of Elizabeth's lord chamberlain, Henry Carey, a man forty-five years her senior. Her affair with the lord chamberlain was managed, according to the norms of the time, with impeccable good taste. When she became pregnant in 1592, she hastily married Alphonso Lanyer, a court musician of Huguenot descent. Carey may have provided the dowry.[42]

By the time she visited Forman, she said that her husband had squandered her small inheritance and gone to war. She wanted to know if he was likely to achieve knighthood. Forman knew how to please a potential client. He cast her horoscope and predicted that her husband would be knighted, and that she would "be a Lady or attain to some further dignity." But he also predicted that her financial problems would continue. Then he tried to seduce her. According to his diary, she led him on, though in the end resisted. He later plotted the whole experience in one of his astrological charts, referring to himself in third person and using his personal euphemism, "halek," for sexual intercourse. His report claimed that "he went and supped with her and stayed all night, and she was familiar & friendly to him in all things. But only she would not halek. Yet he told all parts of her body willingly & kissed her often but she would not do in any wise." Like many men faced with rejection, he dismissed his hoped-for lover as a "whore."[43]

Lanyer's husband did not achieve knighthood. She did not become a lady. But in 1611, at the age of forty-two, she became a published poet. She had obviously spent the previous decade cultivating patrons rather than lovers. She also appears to have experienced a religious conversion. *Salve Deus Rex Judaeorum* contains dedications to nine women, beginning with a 160-line poem to Queen Anne that subtly alludes to a theatrical extravaganza produced at Whitehall in 1609, with texts by the poet Ben Jonson and costumes and scenery by the architect Inigo Jones. *The Masque of Queenes* ended with Anne and her ladies-in-waiting carried in three triumphant chariots, one drawn by eagles, one by griffins, and one by lions, each preceded by torchbearers and fearsome hags bound in chains. Whether Lanyer witnessed the masque or only heard about it, we do not know.[44]

Most of the dedications are serious poems in their own right. Like Christine, Lanyer mixed classical and biblical allusions, celebrating pagan heroines like the Scythian Amazons alongside biblical paragons like Judith and Susanna. But the real heroines of the book are her contemporaries, learned women who choose virtue over vanity.[45] In Lanyer's view, Lady Margaret Clifford, who may have been responsible for the author's own conversion, surpassed even the heroines of the Bible: "For that one head that Judeth bare away, / Thou tak'st from Sinne a hundred heads a day." Lanyer praises Clifford for rejecting physical beauty as the measure of female worth. A beautiful complexion, perfect features, and graceful proportions may be pleasing to the sight, but "All these do draw but dangers and disgrace."[46] Lanyer might have been recalling her own life when she wrote, "That pride of Nature which adornes the faire . . . Is but the thred, that weaves their web of Care."[47]

One literary historian judges Lanyer "a credible peer" of her male contemporaries Ben Jonson and John Donne. Like them, she made her way by courting her social superiors. Because her patrons were women, she felt free to defend female worth, asking why women should be "by more faultie Men so much defam'd?"[48] In a prose invocation to the *Salve*, she challenged those, including persons of her own sex, who believed old slanders against the female sex.[49] In the poem itself, she devoted almost a hundred lines to a speech by Pilate's wife, who defends Eve against those who would blame her for introducing evil into the world. "If Eve did erre, it was for knowledge sake." Those who use Eve's guilt as an excuse for their own tyranny are guiltier still: "If one weake woman simply did offend, / This sinne of yours, hath no excuse, nor end."[50]

Little is known about Lanyer's life after her book appeared, though scattered documents in a lawsuit over the lease of a house tell us that in 1617 she set up a school in a well-to-do district of London "for the education of noblemen and gentlemen's children." When she died in 1645, parish records list her as a "pensioner," a term that at the time meant a person with a retirement income. Perhaps through teaching, perhaps through appeals to well-placed patrons, she eventually achieved financial security if not wealth. That she also achieved lasting "dignity" can be attributed to her poetry—and to the scholars who three centuries later rediscovered her work and her life.

ELIZABETH CARY

Religion, access to the court, and poetry also played important roles in the life of Elizabeth Cary, though her story unfolded in a radically different way. She was a privileged girl, a child prodigy who taught herself French, Spanish, Italian, Latin, and Hebrew. According to her daughter, she also learned from a "Transylvanian, his language, but never finding any use of it, forgot it entirely."[51] Not surprisingly, she attracted attention. The poet Michael Drayton (the man who faced charges of "incontinence" at Bridewell) dedicated three poems to her, writing "Sweete is the French tongue, more sweet the Italian, but most sweet are they both if spoken by your admired selfe."[52]

Cary wasn't beaten and flung about the room, but she suffered at least one of the trials Woolf gave Judith Shakespeare: She was betrothed before she was out of her teens.[53] She and Henry Cary had barely spoken to each other before they married. Fortunately, Elizabeth had plenty of time to adjust to her new state. Henry was frequently away serving in Queen Elizabeth's wars. Elizabeth improved her time by joining with a circle of aristocrats who shared her interests. She wrote two plays—so-called closet dramas meant to be read rather than performed. *The Tragedie of Mariam, The Faire Queene of Jewry*, was published in 1613, the title page attributing it to "that learned, virtuous, and truly noble Ladie, E.C."[54]

The title character is an outspoken woman who talks back to a tyrannical husband and pays with her life. Like the biblical Susanna, Cary's heroine is falsely accused of adultery, but God does not rescue her. Nor is Mariam able to use her beauty to destroy tyranny. As a tragic heroine, she is both noble and flawed. In the last act, she repents her own folly in relying on her sexual allure to preserve her life in a treacherous court. She learns that death comes even to beautiful women and that when their mothers fall from favor, children also suffer. The chorus offers an unconvincing moral—that had Mariam shown more humility, she might have prevailed. The play itself exposes the relationship between domestic and public tyranny that Cary explores elsewhere in her writing. A complex work, it demonstrates Cary's fascination with Jewish history and with theological issues related to Henry VIII's divorces.[55] It was not, however, a work destined for the stage.

Cary's own life was filled with drama. By 1625, she had given birth to eleven children. In that year, she left her husband in Ireland, where he was lord governor, and formally converted to Catholicism. She later claimed that the defining moment was the death of her oldest daughter in childbirth at a time when she was herself still breast-feeding her youngest child. Overcome by maternal love and grief, she was sustained by her daughter's dying vision of a beautiful woman arrayed in white standing at the end of her bed. Surely this was the Virgin Mary.[56] When Cary's conversion became public, her father disinherited her, her husband withdrew his support, and most of her friends abandoned her. Since her husband had custody of their minor children, Cary struggled to maintain relations with them. After his death, she managed to have her two youngest sons kidnapped and sent to France, "out of the danger of living amongst their Protestant friends."[57]

In doing so, Cary violated an explicit act of Parliament. When the Privy Council launched an inquiry, she was both evasive and clever. Reminding the Council that she was a lawyer's daughter, she said she didn't know where the boys were, that she had never interfered with their religious choices, and that if they had gone to France, port officials, not she, were responsible. Angry at her "uncertain and illusory answers," they threatened further investigation, though in the end seem to have let the matter drop.[58] She eventually saw six of her children convert to Catholicism, including three daughters who entered French convents.

For Cary, private piety was never enough. In 1630, she deliberately, in fact brazenly, courted public controversy by arranging to have published in France her own English translation of a Catholic polemic. Authorities immediately seized and burned all the copies they could find. Adding fuel to their fury was Cary's dedication to Henrietta Maria, the Catholic queen of Charles I.[59] Although Henrietta Maria could not rescue the book, she may well have intervened to protect Cary from further prosecution. Before long, however, the queen herself would need rescuing. As England careened into civil war, Protestant religious zealots imagined Catholic women in and out of the court as "whores of Babylon." As one Puritan partisan wrote, "The King was eclipsed by the Queen and she persuaded him that Darkness was Light, and that it was better to be Papist, than a Protestant."[60] By that time, however, Elizabeth Cary was dead though one of her daughters, safe in France, was writing the biography that would preserve her story. Today *The Tragedie of Mariam* is back in print.

ARTEMISIA GENTILESCHI

Like Lanyer, Artemisia Gentileschi was the daughter of a man who earned his livelihood in the arts. Like Cary, she was a child prodigy who dazzled contemporaries while still in her teens. Although her medium was painting rather than poetry, she, like them, dealt with issues of sexuality, rebellion, and piety.

Born into an artist's family, she was trained from an early age to fulfill her great gifts. Her father, Orazio Gentileschi, was her greatest champion, though in his zeal to promote her talent, he exposed her to sexual danger. In the Rome where Artemisia grew up, piety cohabited with prurience. The same artists who painted saints and Madonnas sometimes produced pornographic engravings. Artemisia's father was heavily influenced by his friend, the painter Caravaggio, a man who scandalized contemporaries by insisting on using live models even for religious subjects. His enemies claimed he had used a prostitute as a model for the Virgin Mary. Without question, he paid working-class women to pose. Although Artemisia knew that she should stay away from the studio when her father's friends were there, she found this difficult to do. Her mother was dead. Her father was away. She was responsible for instructing a male apprentice, and Luzia, the neighbor charged with watching over her, was unreliable.[61]

So it happened that early in 1612, Orazio brought charges at the papal court against Agostino Tassi, a friend and fellow artist, claiming that Tassi had "deflowered" his daughter. The voluminous records from the trial not only preserve the testimony of competing witnesses but offer a detailed account of the supposed assault in Artemisia's own words. She told the court that Tassi had been pursuing her for months. On the fateful day, he came into the studio where she was working at her easel. "Not so much painting, not so much painting," he cried as he pulled her away from her work. When she begged for help, Luzia left. Tassi grasped her arm and forced her to walk around, moving ever and ever closer to the bedroom door. When she complained that she felt ill, he retorted, "I have more of a fever than you do." Then he pushed her into the bedroom and shut the door.

Artemisia's testimony continued:

> He then threw me onto the edge of the bed, pushing me
> with a hand on my breast, and he put a knee between my
> thighs to prevent me from closing them. Lifting my clothes,
> which he had a great deal of trouble doing, he placed a hand
> with a handkerchief at my throat and on my mouth to keep
> me from screaming. He let go of my hands which he had
> been holding with his other hand, and, having previously
> put both knees between my legs with his penis [*membro*]
> pointed at my vagina [*natura*], he began to push it inside. I
> felt a strong burning and it hurt very much, but because he
> held my mouth I couldn't cry out.[62]

The precision of the description, with its emphasis on the exact
arrangement of hands, knees, skirts, and thighs, suggests the eye of
an artist, but its specificity was also shaped by the demands of the
law. Since the charge against Tassi was "forceful defloration," both
Artemisia's virginity and his violence were at issue. When court
officials asked if she had bled from the assault, she explained that
she was menstruating at the time and couldn't tell for sure, though
she thought that the blood was redder than usual.[63]

The next part of the story is more difficult for modern readers to
comprehend. Artemisia told the court that after Tassi had "done his
business," she pulled herself away from him, grabbed a knife, and
threatened to kill him. He merely laughed, opening his waistcoat to
invite the attack. Although she nicked his chest with the point of his
knife, he subdued her by promising to make the assault good with
marriage. "And with this good promise I felt calmer, and with this
promise he induced me later on to yield lovingly, many times, to his
desires." But when Tassi was unable to prove that his first wife was
dead, the agreement unraveled. Tassi didn't deny having had sexual

relations with Artemisia, but responded that the suit was meaningless because Artemisia was a promiscuous girl who was no longer a virgin when he met her. In the end, it was Artemisia's veracity that mattered.

The court tested her by using one of the milder forms of torture available under Roman law. As attendants pulled cords tighter and tighter around her fingers, she stood firm in her account. The verdict was a compromise between an unqualified conviction, which would have required Tassi to pay reparations to Orazio, and an acquittal, which would have confirmed Tassi's assault on Artemisia's character. The court banished Tassi from the city for five years, though it took another sentence for another crime to finally force him to leave.[64]

In the trial, Orazio said he did not learn about the assault until long after it happened. The court may not have accepted this explanation at face value. That he delayed pressing charges for almost a year suggests he may have been willing to accept the conventional remedy for any form of sex outside of marriage—that the man marry the woman. One witness suggests that negotiations for a marriage actually continued during the trial itself. That they failed surely had to do with uncertainty about the state of Tassi's first marriage. But by the time the trial was over, the bigger issue was the assault on Artemisia's character. The verdict helped to restore her own and her father's honor. Shortly after the trial ended, she married the younger brother of the man who had shepherded the case through the court.[65]

Neither marriage nor the birth of four children impeded Artemisia's success as an artist. Her husband gradually faded from the picture as her career flourished. She was the first woman admitted to the Academies in Florence and Rome. She received commissions from the Medicis, became a friend of Galileo, and produced paintings for many of Europe's rulers, including Philip IV of Spain and Charles I of England. In letters she played up this fame, bragging to one correspondent, "I have seen myself honored by all the kings and rulers of Europe to whom I have sent my works." Poets praised her, and so did her fellow artists. She was not only successful, she was famous.[66] Eventually, her father's association with Charles I and his queen, Henrietta Maria, brought her to England, where she remained for three years. The queen probably already knew of her work through commissions Artemisia received from her mother, Marie de Medicis.[67]

Scholars have made much of the fact that Artemisia's first dated painting was of Susanna and the Elders. Most visual representations of this story arranged the characters horizontally. The vertical arrangement of Gentileschi's painting allows the leering men to tower over the nude woman, visually weighing her down as she raises her hands in a futile effort to push them away.[68] Though the painting predates the alleged assault by Tassi, it may allude to his earlier harassment. Whatever the biographical content, it infuses a conventional subject with searing psychological meaning.[69]

Around the time of Tassi's trial, Artemisia completed a dramatic canvas showing Judith in the very act of murdering Holofernes. Some critics believe that the violence of the image reflects Artemisia's rage over Tassi's assault. As Judith grasps Holofernes by his hair, blood rains down on the bedsheets and splatters on her luxurious gown. That the force of this painting comes from Artemisia's own experience is plausible, though it is important to point out that the theme was an old one. Many painters, including Caravaggio, had portrayed Judith's story.[70] In the light of Tassi's trial, what is surprising about Artemisia's representation of Judith, both in this version and in others, is the bond she creates between Judith and the servant who assists her. If Artemisia felt any such bond with Luzia, she certainly hid it from the court. Her paintings are as much about trust between women as hatred of the tyrant Holofernes.

In Caravaggio's treatment of the same story, a sweetly innocent Judith is egged on by a fierce and witchlike old woman. In

Artemisia Gentileschi, *Susanna and the Elders*, ca. 1610

Artemisia's paintings, the women are virtually the same age, separated only by slight differences in clothing. In a later painting, the
bodies of the two women appear in profile, overlapping and close to
the picture plane, their heads turned as if listening for any hint of
discovery. Judith grasps an upright sword. The maid holds
Holofernes's severed head, now a ghastly gray, in a basket, poised
on her hip like laundry. In another painting of the same event,
Judith, her face half lit by a flickering candle, turns toward the door
of the tent, sword in hand, while the servant gathers up the severed
head in a bloody rag. There is an unspoken intimacy in these pic-

Artemisia Gentileschi, *Judith Beheading Holofernes,* ca. 1612–1613

tures, a common understanding that appears to be the source of their power.[71]

Artemisia Gentileschi, like many artists in her era, created strong images of powerful women. But she also painted sweet Madonnas, transcendent saints, and several compelling tributes to the art of painting. She was a professional artist who knew how to court and keep patrons. The same can be said of her contemporaries, Aemilia Lanyer and Elizabeth Cary. In different ways, they all negotiated the boundary between invisibility and scandal, and in the process made history.

Virginia Woolf's Fable

Virginia Woolf despaired over the absence of women writers in Shakespeare's time. Why was it, she asked, that "no woman wrote a word of that extraordinary literature when every other man, it seemed, was capable of song or sonnet."[72] Today the questions are different. Why was it that Woolf knew nothing about the women writers who were contemporaries of Shakespeare? Why did Professor Trevelyan dismiss women's lives with a few grim sentences? The records were there, but no one had bothered to look. Woolf's fable is a reminder of a central theme of this book: that history is made in libraries as well as in streets. Because Woolf went looking for forgotten women, others eventually joined the search.

As far as we know, William Shakespeare did not have a wonderfully gifted sister. If he had, she would probably have been smart enough to stay away from the London stage. For women, the barriers to public achievement were high, but they were not impenetrable. With a strong will and powerful patrons, Shakespeare's sister might have developed her gifts. But ironically, these same qualities, differently applied, might have led to a favorable marriage, a comfortable existence, and invisibility. That is surely what happened to Anne Hathaway. Unmarried and pregnant at twenty-six, she used whatever resources she had available to her, including a small inheritance, to achieve a formal union with a man who was about to rise in the world. The marriage may or may not have been compatible, but it survived, as did Hathaway and her daughters Judith and Susanna. We do not know whether Shakespeare's wife and daughters were content with their lives. Because they were well-behaved, they did not make history.

⤲

Chapter Four

SLAVES IN THE ATTIC

On a bright autumn day in 1839, Elizabeth Cady and her sisters were singing in the parlor of the large country house owned by their cousin, the abolitionist Gerrit Smith. Suddenly, Smith walked in and with a mysterious air summoned them to the top of the house. Pledging them to secrecy, he opened the door to a little-used room. There sat a beautiful young woman—a runaway slave.

"Harriet," Smith said, "I have brought all my young cousins to see you. I want you to make good abolitionists of them by telling them the history of your life—what you have seen and suffered in slavery." For the next two hours the girls listened, weeping, as Harriet told of being sold for her beauty in a New Orleans market. The details were too horrible to repeat, except in whispers. The tension deepened when at twilight they saw her slip out of the house into a waiting carriage wearing a Quaker bonnet. A few days later, they were relieved to hear that she had made her way safely to Canada.[1]

Writing about this event half a century later, Stanton did not use Harriet Powell's full name. Perhaps she had forgotten it. Perhaps she deliberately left it out. Whatever the reason, her omission adds to the mythical power of the story. Without a full name, one runaway can stand in for every slave who ever fled a master. Powell's story can evoke other Harriets, other attics:

Harriet Jacobs, for example, who in 1861, under the pseudonym "Linda Brent," wrote about hiding in a cramped space above her grandmother's shed for seven long years rather than submit to the sexual propositions of her master.

Or Harriet Tubman, the brave "general" of the Underground Railroad, who helped dozens of other slaves escape.

Or Harriet Beecher Stowe, the white writer who filled *Uncle Tom's Cabin* with beautiful quadroons and dramatic escapes, and who in the grim last section of the novel told a dark tale about a mysterious female slave hiding in the attic on a plantation owned by the evil Simon Legree.

All these Harriets made history, though not in Stanton's memoir.[2] In her telling, the encounter in the attic had less to do with the history of slavery than with her own evolution from naïve schoolgirl to public advocate for women's rights. That was the autumn she fell in love with Henry Stanton, who as an agent for the radical American Anti-Slavery Society was a frequent visitor to Smith's house. On a walk through the woods, Henry had "made one of those charming revelations of human feeling which brave knights have always found eloquent words to utter, and to which fair ladies have always listened with mingled emotions of pleasure and astonishment." Although Elizabeth was smitten, she feared her father would never consent to her marrying an abolitionist. "So I lingered at Peterboro to prolong the dream of happiness and postpone the conflict I feared to meet." For her, as for Harriet, Smith's house became an oasis.[3]

Harriet's escape foreshadowed Elizabeth's own. Seven months later, pressed into action by Henry's imminent departure for London as a delegate to the World Anti-Slavery Convention, she braved her father's displeasure and "without the slightest preparation for a wedding or a voyage," married him.[4] The runaway in the attic had introduced her to the horrors of slavery. The female abolitionists she met in London introduced her to feminism. When convention leaders refused to admit women as delegates, they collected in the gallery, pondering the insincerity of men "who, while eloquently defending the natural rights of slaves, denied freedom of speech to one-half the people of their own race."[5]

For Stanton, slavery became a metaphor for the female condition.[6] Years later, in a speech at Waterloo, New York, she accused men in all parts of the world of enslaving women, "from the Mahometan who forbids pigs, dogs, women and other impure animals to enter a mosque, and does not allow a fool, madman or woman to proclaim the hour of prayer,—from the German who complacently smokes his meerschaum while his wife, yoked with the ox, draws the plough through its furrow,—from the delectable gentleman who thinks an inferior style of conversation adapted to women—to the legislator who considers her incapable of saying what laws shall govern her." Women everywhere were subject to men. "I am a slave, a favoured slave," she exclaimed, quoting a line given to a harem girl in Lord Byron's poem "The Corsair."[7]

At one level, the rhetoric was nonsensical. Stanton was not a slave. Nor, whatever his deficiencies as a husband, was Henry a sultan. But the language was well chosen. For a white woman to declare herself a slave was the ultimate misbehavior. It was one thing to reach out to a poor suffering creature like Harriet. It was another to identify with her degradation. In Stanton's lifetime, nearly everyone assumed that middle-class white women were among the most privileged and pampered creatures on earth. They were the mothers, the muses, and the lovers of men, the caregivers of children, and the hope of the weary. Stanton cut through that sentimental view. To be a perpetual dependent was to be a slave, regardless of how comfortable one's position. At Seneca Falls in 1848, she and her collaborators gave up the deference due to them as fair ladies and demanded "all the rights and privileges which belong to them as citizens of the United States."[8]

For Stanton, the antislavery movement was a way station

on the road to something bigger. That is the way it has been treated in many histories of the women's suffrage movement. Recent accounts do better. They help explain how Harriet Powell ended up in Smith's attic and where she went when she left there, and they show the complex interplay between sentimental literature, evangelical religion, abolitionism, and women's rights. Stanton's story looks different when placed alongside the lives of Harriet Powell and her namesakes. The biographies of the four Harriets—Powell, Jacobs, Stowe, and Tubman—take slaves out of the attic.

Three Runaways and a Novelist

In Stanton's memoir, HARRIET POWELL appears from nowhere. In reality, her escape was managed by a powerful network that linked wealthy patrons like Gerrit Smith with free blacks who risked social ostracism, violence, and even death to help others gain their liberty.[9] Powell had come to upstate New York from Mississippi as a nursemaid in the family of John Davenport, who had booked them into the best hotel in Syracuse. Powell was terrified that she might be sold when they returned to Mississippi. Somehow she communicated her anxieties to a black waiter who, with the help of antislavery allies, arranged for her escape. On October 7, while her master and mistress were attending a party, she left their child asleep in its room and slipped out of the hotel into a carriage, where two respectable white citizens were waiting with her disguise—a man's cloak and hat. They delivered her to a farmer in a neighboring town, changing carriages along the way to avoid detection. Eventually she reached Smith's house in Peterboro.[10]

Outraged to discover his slave missing, Davenport offered a $200 reward for information leading to her recovery. He described her as a young woman "of a full and well proportioned form" and "so fair that she would generally be taken for white," adding that a discerning person would recognize certain African traits, such as "a prominent mouth with depressed nostrils, and receding forehead." She had worn a black print dress, small rings in her ears, and three gold rings on her fingers. She had left her bonnet behind.[11]

The local abolitionist newspaper, *The Friend of Man*, hooted at the spectacle of a supposed gentleman advertising as property a woman who might have passed for white. "Some of the anti-abolition gentry at Syracuse, begin to think it rather too bad to enslave handsome white ladies, with gold rings on their fingers," the editor wrote.[12] In December, the paper reprinted a piece from the *Toronto Free Press* dated "Jubilee 12, 1839" which parodied Davenport's advertisement. "Found on the Canadian shore, a young woman who says her name is Harriet Powell," it began, adding, "When found, her head dress consisted of a Freedom Bonnet, and a Liberty Cap."[13]

All the abolitionist accounts of Harriet's rescue emphasized her physical attractiveness and her fear of being sold. One paper said that in Mississippi "a man of bad character" had tried to purchase her. A Toronto writer was more explicit: "From her admissions and style of dress, I suppose she came from the seraglio of some 'Patriarch.' "[14] There was some foundation for such stereotypes. In slave markets, color defined a person's capacity for work. Dark-skinned slaves, female as well as male, were deemed healthier, stronger, and more likely to perform well in the fields. Light-skinned women, often described as "delicate," supposedly made better seamstresses, house servants—or concubines.[15] In the New Orleans market especially, there was no ambiguity about the "fancy trade." Men openly bid for light-skinned women, often paying three times the median price for young women who fulfilled their fantasies. Flirting with propriety, they listed their purchases as seamstresses or cooks, then unabashedly flaunted them as mistresses. Not they, but those who questioned their behavior, were guilty of indiscretion.[16]

But there was also a literary quality to the stories abolitionists told. Rescued from slavery, Powell became the captive instead of a centuries-old story that originated in lurid "tales from the harem." To be worthy of rescue, escaped slaves needed to be well-behaved. That is why all the stories about her emphasized her refinement. Although she was ignorant of religion (an indictment of her master), her manners were graceful, her voice soft. Even better, she was duly grateful for the help she received: "the trickling tear told that her heart felt far more than her tongue could utter."[17]

In April, *The Friend of Man* printed a letter that Powell purportedly dictated to the Canadian woman in whose home she was then living.

> Dear Sir—I am sure you will be happy to learn that I am well and quite contented in my present situation. I am still in Kingston, and living with Mr. and Mrs. Hale, where I have an opportunity of attending the Methodist Chapel every Sunday. I am very much obliged to all my kind friends who assisted me in gaining my liberty; and I think, not all the money in the United States could induce me to return to slavery. I am most anxious to hear something of my dear mother and sister; Mrs. Hale wrote to Mr. Gerrit Smith for me, some time ago, but we have not received any answer. I should be most thankful to receive any intelligence. Please give my love to all my friends, and accept the same yourself from,
>
>   Your obliged,
>   HARRIET POWELL[18]

There is no reason to doubt Harriet's concern for her mother and sister. Davenport, like other slave owners, counted on family bonds to keep slaves, especially female slaves, from fleeing.

How Harriet felt about life in Ontario we do not know, though *The Friend of Man* soon reported that she had married Mr. Henry

Kelly, "a respectable colored man, in good pecuniary circumstances." Canadian records show that in the next fifteen years, she
gave birth to eight children, three of whom died in infancy. Little
else is known about her life except that she died in Kingston,
Ontario, in 1861.[19] Crossing the border into liberty, she moved out
of history.

The year Harriet Powell escaped from a Syracuse hotel, HARRIET
BEECHER STOWE published her first piece in *Godey's Lady's Book.*
Her earlier publications had all been in religious periodicals or local
papers. *Godey's* was different. An immensely successful magazine
with a national readership, it touted itself as "a proud monument
reared to the Ladies of America as a testimony of their own worth."
Stowe knew her own worth. Despite marriage and the birth of four
children, she was determined to become a writer. In 1839, she was
living in Cincinnati, Ohio, where her husband, Calvin, was a
teacher at Lane Seminary, an evangelical school presided over by
her father, Lyman Beecher. Harriet had also been a teacher, helping
her older sister Catherine run girls' schools both in their native
Connecticut and in Ohio. Now that she was a matron with young
children, that sort of work was more difficult. Calvin agreed that
she should become "a *literary woman.*" For him, it was "written in
the book of fate."[20]

"If I am to write, I must have a room to myself, which shall be
my room," Harriet insisted. She began by converting one of the
rooms in their house into a study with a glass door into the nursery. Then she set about finding a servant.[21] Her sketch in *Godey's*
turned that quest into comedy. Posing as a newly married woman
in a western town, she told a rollicking tale about the deficiencies
of household servants: A snuff-faced old woman claimed to be a
cook but could not recognize a tin oven. A capable woman "with a
temper like a steel trap" stayed a week, "then went off in a fit of
spite." Even worse was the "rosy, good-natured, merry lass, who
broke the crockery, burnt the dinner, tore the clothes in ironing,

and knocked down every thing that stood in her way about the house." When she forgot to replace the stopper on a barrel of molasses, the contents "ran soberly out into the cellar bottom all night, till by morning it was in a state of *universal emancipation*." The sketch ended with a plaintive cry: "What shall we do? Shall we go for slavery, or shall we give up houses, have no furniture to take care of—keep merely a bag of meal, a porridge pot, and a pudding stick, and sit in our tent door in real patriarchal independence?"[22]

Although Stowe would never have revealed her secret in *Godey's,* a periodical that firmly avoided politics of any kind, her seemingly offhand allusions to "universal emancipation" and "slavery" hinted at turmoil in Cincinnati more intense than troubles over household help. In 1833, two upstart students at Lane, one of whom was Henry Stanton, staged an eighteen-day conference to debate the slavery issue. When Lane students voted overwhelmingly in favor of immediate abolition, the school's trustees imposed a ban on political debate. The trustees were outraged not only by the speeches but by the abolitionists' "disreputable" habit of fraternizing with free blacks. Stanton and his collaborator, Theodore Weld, were thrown out of Lane. Harriet's father and husband were left to repair the damage.[23]

Cincinnati was a resoundingly pro-slavery town. When a radical antislavery printer arrived in 1837, a mob organized by the town's political and economic leaders broke into his shop, pied his type, and threw his press in the river. Horrified at this assault on free speech, Harriet, who had been subdued by a girlhood bout with public petitioning, began to listen with more sympathy to the arguments of abolitionists. Under the pseudonym "Franklin," she sent a letter to her brother's newspaper arguing that an attack on one press undermined the free speech of all Americans. In pieces written under her own name, however, she studiously avoided politics.[24]

It took a family tragedy and the Compromise of 1850 to change that. Shortly after Harriet's sixth child, a healthy, happy baby boy, died of cholera, Calvin accepted a professorship at Bowdoin College in Maine.[25] Back in New England, Harriet launched her great antislavery novel *Uncle Tom's Cabin,* a book that urged readers who had lost a child to identify with the suffering of slave mothers. First published in installments in a moderate antislavery journal, it appeared in book form in March 1852, selling 10,000 copies in the first week and 300,000 by the end of the year, rapidly becoming the runaway best-seller of the nineteenth century.[26]

Southern apologists insisted that the novel's tales of woe were largely inventions. Stowe responded with a *Key to Uncle Tom's Cabin,* a compilation of trial records and slave narratives that matched episodes and characters in her book with factual accounts. Her critics were hardly mollified, asking how a supposed lady could immerse herself in such degrading and incendiary stuff. One Southern writer, William Gilmore Simms, exclaimed, "Mrs. Stowe betrays a malignity so remarkable that the petticoat lifts of itself, and we see the hoof of the beast under the table."[27]

Stowe's *Key* offers unexpected insight into that comic sketch in *Godey's.* In it she explains that she modeled the beautiful and well-behaved character Eliza on a runaway she had once employed in Cincinnati. Because the girl's mistress had voluntarily brought her to Cincinnati, the Stowes considered her free. When the girl's master tried to take her back, Calvin and one of the Beecher brothers "drove about ten miles on a solitary road, crossed the creek at a very dangerous fording, and presented themselves at midnight, at the house of John Van Zandt, a noble-minded Kentuckian," the model for the Quaker Von Tromp in the book. Stowe concludes, "The reader may be interested to know that the poor girl never was re-taken; that she married well in Cincinnati, is a very respectable woman, and the mother of a large family of children."[28]

Stowe had more trouble documenting the gothic tale that ends her book, the story of a half-crazed slave named Cassy who escapes by hiding in her master's attic. Although "delicately bred," Cassy is seduced and then abandoned by a white lawyer. When her young son flees to her arms as he is about to be sold, she seizes a bowie knife and, in a moment of madness, kills him rather than see him consigned to a lifetime of bondage. Without faith, without hope, she is nevertheless determined to rescue a gentle, fifteen-year-old, Bible-reading slave named Emmeline from the loathsome Simon Legree, whom she hates as the devil.

Cassy's plan is ingenious. She and Emmeline will walk away from the plantation in broad daylight, deliberately attracting the attention of field hands who, for a drink of spirits, will gladly betray them. While Legree and his posse are gathering hounds to pursue them, they will circle back to the empty house and hide in the attic. Legree will never look for them there. The plan works. By day, Cassy and Emmeline hide under the eaves in the shelter of "an immense box, in which some heavy pieces of furniture had once been brought." At night, Cassy moves mysteriously about the house in a white shroud, terrifying the superstitious Legree, who in his drunken mania thinks she is a ghost. At the height of the haunting, Cassy and Emmeline slip away to freedom.[29]

When she wrote her *Key to Uncle Tom's Cabin*, Stowe had no evidence that an actual slave had ever fled to an attic. She had not yet heard of HARRIET JACOBS.

The year Harriet Powell hid in Gerrit Smith's attic, Jacobs ended her fourth year huddled in a cramped crawl space above her grand-mother's shed. She eventually spent seven years in this truncated attic, occasionally climbing down through a secret trapdoor to exercise her stiff limbs, but mostly lying as quietly as she could to avoid detection. Through a tiny hole in the wall, she could see her own children at play.

Jacobs's grandmother, Molly Horniblow, was descended from slaves emancipated during the Revolution, then captured and returned to slavery in North Carolina after the war. Horniblow eventually purchased her own freedom, but was unable to emancipate her children or grandchildren, though her little house became their refuge.[30] Like her mother and grandmother before her, Jacobs became a household servant. But this position exposed her to the sexual propositions of her imperious master, Dr. James Norcrom. He tried tenderness, then terror, though he stopped short of rape. When he refused to let her marry a fellow slave, she accepted the attentions of a young white lawyer, hoping Norcrom would lose interest in her once she became another man's mistress.[31] She had two children by her white lover, but her love for them exposed her to a new danger. Norcrom promised that if she would cut off all communication with her children's father, he would set her up in her own cottage where she and they could live together. Her labor would be light, only a little sewing, and eventually she would be free. When she refused, he banished her to his plantation and threatened to take the children from her grandmother and break them in to fieldwork. Hoping that if she was out of the way, he would ignore her children, Jacobs fled, hiding in the woods and then in the home of a sympathetic neighbor.

Like Harriet Powell's master, Norcrom advertised for her return, describing her as a "light mulatto, 21 years of age," whose thick black hair curled naturally but could be "easily combed straight." In her master's eyes, she was attractive though somewhat vain. "Being a good seamstress, she has been accustomed to dress well, has a variety of very fine clothes, made in the prevailing fashion, and will probably appear, if abroad, tricked out in gay and fashionable finery."[32]

When Norcrom put the children up for auction, their father arranged for a visiting slave trader to buy them on his behalf and return them to Jacobs's grandmother. Meanwhile, Jacobs had settled on a daring ruse. She would let the world believe she had fled to the North, but would hide instead in the crawl space above a storage shed attached to her grandmother's house. There she could watch over her children while waiting for a better chance to escape. She would stay in this space for seven long years.[33]

In 1842, as slave patrols searched for another slave hidden in the neighborhood, she learned that friends had bribed a visiting ship's captain to carry both of them to the North. This was the moment Jacobs had been waiting for. Her brother John was already in Boston, having been "decoyed away by abolitionists" when he went to Washington, D.C., as a servant to Jacobs's former lover, who had been elected to Congress. Her daughter, Louisa Matilda, was also safely in New York as a servant to the congressman's sister. Jacobs too found her way to New York, where she became a nursemaid in the family of a white editor.[34]

As the first installments of *Uncle Tom's Cabin* were appearing, Jacobs watched in fear as "slave catchers" appeared in New York City ready to test the provisions of the recently enacted Fugitive Slave Act.[35] A Quaker abolitionist suggested that she publish her life story. But how could she do it? She was no writer. Perhaps Mrs. Stowe would take it on. She asked her friend to send the great writer an outline of her story, but before she could receive a response she had another idea. Reading in the newspapers that Stowe was about to leave for an extended tour of England, Jacobs asked her employer to write to her asking if she would be willing to take Louisa Matilda with her. With the help of her abolitionist uncle, the girl had received a good education at a female seminary in upstate New York. She could corroborate Stowe's fictions with a true firsthand account of life in slavery. Her mother would even be willing to pay her expenses with her own earnings.[36]

Stowe declined the offer. She claimed that adding another person to her party would be too much trouble. In any case, if Louisa Matilda's "situation as a Slave should be known it would subject her to much petting and patronizing which would be more pleasing to a young Girl than useful and the English was very apt to do it and she was very much opposed to it with this class of people." She might, however, be willing to include Jacobs's story in the next edition of her book—that is, if Jacobs's employer could verify its details. Jacobs was outraged. Although she sent Stowe a polite note, she vented her anger in a letter to a Quaker friend, "Mrs. Stowe thinks petting is more than my race can bear well what a pity we poor blacks cant have the firmness and stability of character that you white people have."[37]

Stowe's rejection gave Jacobs the courage to tell her own story. She began with an anonymous letter to the *New York Tribune,* and then, encouraged by the response, began a longer narrative. The white abolitionist Lydia Maria Child agreed to edit it for publication. But even while properly insisting that "this narrative is no fiction," Jacobs could not bring herself to use her own name. The book appeared in 1861 under the pseudonym "Linda Brent." One difficulty she felt obliged to confront was that, although abolitionists routinely accused slave owners of sexual exploitation, her own story involved a voluntary liaison with a white man.[38] She attempted to deflect the censure of white readers by explaining her circumstances. "I was a poor slave girl, only fifteen years old," she wrote. Shifting into third person, she continued, "to be an object of interest to a man who is not married, and who is not her master, is agreeable to the pride and feelings of a slave, if her miserable situation has left her any pride or sentiment."[39] Although she could not choose her master, she could choose her lover.

In 1839, as Harriet Powell hid in Gerrit Smith's house and Harriet Jacobs huddled in an attic in North Carolina, HARRIET TUBMAN hoisted barrels of flour into carts on a wharf in Maryland. She was not a well-behaved slave. Dark-skinned and feisty, she seemed designed for hard labor.

While still a child she had been hired out as a nursemaid. Her job was to keep the baby quiet. Whenever it cried in the night, her mistress reached for a whip. After one flogging, Harriet lunged forward and bit her mistress's knee. After another, she hid in the pig-pen for days, fighting off an old sow for food scraps until hunger sent her back to the house. Her toughness soon ended her employment as a house slave. She worked in the fields, on the wharves, and for a time alongside her enslaved father, cutting and preparing timber. One day, when she was in her teens, a heavy lead weight thrown at another slave hit her in the head, leaving her bedridden for months, and subject for the rest of her life to "spells." After the accident, her master tried to sell her, but could not find a buyer.[40] In her mid-twenties, long after other slaves began childbearing, she married John Tubman, a free black. The couple had no children.[41]

Contemporary descriptions of Tubman employ terms quite different from those used for the other Harriets. Jacobs was known for "intelligence" and "decorum," Tubman for "quaint simplicity." Powell could pass for white; Tubman was "coal-black."[42] But celebrations of her life were also more extravagant. Over time, she became known as a Black Joan of Arc, a Florence Nightingale, and an American Moses.[43] Perhaps her darkness, her labor-hardened body, and her illiteracy allowed her a level of "misbehavior" unavailable to the other Harriets.

She escaped from Maryland in 1849, and a year later undertook her first rescue mission, focusing at first on her own relatives, although John Tubman declined to join her. Nobody knows how many people she led north. Some say she made nineteen trips and rescued more than three hundred slaves. Recent biographies suggest ten or twelve trips, resulting in freedom for sixty to seventy fugitives—still a substantial contribution for a woman who risked her own life and liberty every time she set out to guide others along the escape route from Maryland to Pennsylvania, and then through upstate New York and across the Niagara Falls suspension bridge into St. Catharines in Canada West (now Ontario).[44]

Although Tubman could neither read nor write, she controlled her own story through the power of her voice. She mesmerized her listeners, throwing her whole body into her performance, sometimes singing in a rich, deep voice. A historian who heard her tell about her Civil War adventures was fascinated by the poetry of her prose. "And then we saw the lightning," she said, "and that was the guns; and then we heard the thunder, and that was the big guns; and then we heard the rain falling, and that was drops of blood falling; and when we came to get in the crops, it was dead men that we reaped." Others were amused by her wily sense of humor. One of her favorite stories was about a fugitive slave who was so terrified of being recaptured that when the train passed over the suspension bridge from the United States into Canada, he didn't even look at Niagara Falls. "Only one more journey for me now, and that is to Heaven!" he exclaimed. "Well, you old fool, you," Tubman chortled, "you might have looked at the Falls first, and then gone to Heaven afterwards."[45]

But while Tubman could charm an audience, she was, despite her reputation, neither simple nor unsophisticated. She was a brilliant strategist in the woods or on a stage. She was also a radical. Like her sometime patron Gerrit Smith, she embraced the militant millennialism of John Brown. Although her biographers differ on the extent of her involvement in the planning for his ill-fated attack on the arsenal at Harpers Ferry, there is no question but that she helped raise funds for his support and may have begun to recruit troops for his campaign. For reasons that are not entirely clear, she did not participate directly in the assault. Perhaps if she had, it would not have ended in disaster.[46] During the Civil War, she played a major role in a raid on the Combahee River in South Carolina where newly commissioned black troops managed to liberate almost eight hundred slaves. Tubman and her scouts guided Federal boats up the channel and persuaded frightened slaves to come aboard.[47]

To Tubman, the whole thing seemed a miracle like the Israelites crossing the Red Sea, but there was nothing pious about Tubman's descriptions. There were "pigs squealing, chickens screaming, young ones squealing." She laughed when she told about a woman who named one pig for a Confederate general and another for the Confederate president Jefferson Davis.[48] After the raid, Tubman dictated a letter to the editor of a Boston antislavery paper. "Don't you think we colored people are entitled to some credit for that exploit?" Then she asked if someone might send her a Bloomer costume because she had torn the long skirt of her dress while loading slaves on ships. Tubman's reference to the much-lampooned feminist costume exemplifies her sense of humor but it also shows her close connection to reform circles in Boston and Rochester in the years before the war.[49]

The frontispiece to a biography of Tubman published in 1869 portrays her as she may have looked during the war. Dressed in a common striped skirt, she wears a man's warm coat and a plaid turban. She carries a large bag over one arm and with both hands grasps the barrel of her rifle. She may or may not have carried a gun during the years she was rescuing slaves, but without question she had a reputation for toughness. William Sill, who interviewed her for his massive documentary history of the Underground Railroad, reported that when conducting runaways, she had a "very short and pointed rule or law of her own, which implied death to any who talked of giving out or going back."[50] And yet, she was in other ways a remarkably traditional woman. More than one account mentions her skill as a quilter. One says that when the refugees were hiding in the woods by day, "she pulled out her patchwork, and sewed together little bits, perhaps not more than an inch square, which were afterwards made into comforters for the fugitives in Canada."[51] (There is no evidence, however, that quilts hanging on clotheslines guided Tubman or any other runaway on a journey to freedom.)

Harriet Powell, Harriet Jacobs, and Harriet Tubman all con-

HARRIET TUBMAN.

Frontispiece, Sarah Bradford, *Scenes in the
Life of Harriet Tubman,* 1869

tributed to nineteenth-century feminism. Powell's contribution was
of course that interview in the attic of Gerrit Smith's house, but
Tubman and Jacobs also played supporting roles in the movement
that Elizabeth Cady Stanton held dear. Their major work, however,
was with newly freed slaves. In the fall of 1863, Jacobs offered a
prayer for Northern victory and the emancipation of all slaves at a
meeting of the Women's National Loyal League at which Stanton

presided. A year later, Jacobs was elected to the League's executive committee.⁵² Before the end of the war, she and Louisa Matilda went south, working to ensure that blacks had "something to say" about the organization of schools in areas under Union control. In Alexandria, Virginia, she brought old-time black residents together with refugee slaves to break up "this aristocratic notion" that the freedmen were inferior.⁵³

Jacobs continued her work with relief agencies after the war, even traveling to London to raise funds for an orphanage and home for the aged in Savannah. When renewed violence made work in Georgia impossible, she returned to the North, opening boarding-houses in Cambridge, Massachusetts, and then in Washington, D.C. Like other free blacks, she struggled to maintain her liveli-hood in the last decades of the nineteenth century as racial cate-gories hardened, but she did not give up her quest for equality for African Americans or for women. A year before her death in 1898, she participated in the organizing meetings of the National Associ-ation of Colored Women.⁵⁴

Tubman also devoted herself to freed slaves. After the Comba-hee raid, she worked in the refugee camps established by the Union Army on the Sea Islands of South Carolina. Volunteering as a nurse and assistant, she earned her own livelihood by cooking, washing, and selling root beer and provisions. After the war, frustrated by her inability to collect back pay, Tubman returned to Auburn, New York, where with the help of Gerrit Smith and others, she had ear-lier established a home.⁵⁵ When she learned that her first husband was dead, she married Nelson Davis, a black veteran twenty years her junior, who had been boarding at her house. Soon, however, he fell prey to tuberculosis, leaving her with the responsibility of pro-viding for a large extended family and the impoverished friends she seemed to attract. She worked her small farm, raised hogs for extra cash, and sometimes showed up at women's suffrage meetings to share her droll stories about the war. Proceeds from her autobiography went to her charitable enterprises, which included a home for aged blacks. She named its main building John Brown Hall. Tubman died in Auburn in 1913.[56]

By escaping, Harriet Powell, Harriet Jacobs, and Harriet Tubman, like the fictional heroines of Harriet Stowe's novel, stood apart from the nearly four million slaves who remained in bondage in the United States on the eve of the Civil War. Although the details of their lives differed, the overall argument of their stories was the same: Slavery violated the most cherished norms of womanhood. If a well-behaved woman was domestic, slave women were forced to labor beside men in the fields. If a well-behaved woman was religious, slave owners denied their slaves even the rudiments of Christian instruction. If a well-behaved woman was maternal, slave owners denied slave mothers access to their own children. If a well-behaved woman was chaste, slave owners constantly threatened their slaves with sexual violation. When slaves rebelled—running away, engaging in an illicit liaison, or even, in the case of Stowe's Cassy, killing their own children—the guilt rested on the heads of their masters.

But what if the rebel was a white woman, a wife and mother with a well-functioning cookstove and a pew in church? Could a white woman borrow the right to rebel?

Why White Women Called Themselves Slaves

Stanton was not the first white American to declare herself a slave. During the American Revolution, property-owning white men claimed that Britain's Parliament had enslaved them by levying taxes without their consent. As the radical pamphleteer Thomas Paine expressed it, *"if being bound in that manner, is not slavery, then is there not such a thing as slavery upon earth."*[57] The idea was not as far-fetched as it seems. English common law defined liberty as a right to the undisturbed possession of property. Without question,

Parliament was disturbing American notions of who had the right to deprive them of property. That real slaves were toiling in American fields did not undercut the argument; perhaps it even enhanced it. Slave owners like Thomas Jefferson or George Washington knew exactly what it meant to be a slave. Slaves had no claim on their own persons or labor. Whatever they produced belonged to their master.

Although chattel slavery was under attack at the end of the eighteenth century, it belonged to a long and some thought honorable tradition. Slaves were among a crowd of dependents subject to household authority. When people today talk about assaults on the "traditional family," they demonstrate the limits of historical memory. The medieval historian David Herlihy has explained that the English word *family* comes from the Latin *familia,* which in its earliest uses connoted "a band of slaves." The Latin word for father, *pater,* has an equally complex derivation. It originally meant someone in authority, not a biological parent.[58]

The concept of the family as an authoritarian conglomerate of unrelated persons persisted in early modern Europe. A fascinating passage in the work of the sixteenth-century French jurist Jean Bodin begins with a question: How many persons does it take to make a family? Bodin answers that it takes a master and at least three other persons, whether they be his children, slaves, servants, or free dependents who have voluntarily submitted to his authority. Then, almost as an afterthought, he acknowledges that a family must also include a wife:

> But for as much as Families, Colleges, Companies, Cities, and Commonweals, yea, and mankind it selfe would perish and come to an end were it not by marriages . . . preserved and continued, it followeth well that a family cannot be in all points perfect and accomplished without a

wife. So that by this account it cometh to passe, there must be five persons at least to make up an whole and entire family.

A wife wasn't a slave or a servant, but neither was she a companion or partner. Her job was to reproduce, her duty to obey. Bodin fell back on medieval notions of women as more lustful than men, when he said that in commanding a husband to rule over his wife, God was also signifying the importance of the soul ruling the body and reason mastering "concupiscence," or fleshly desire.[59]

By the time of the American Revolution, the Enlightenment emphasis on progress, benevolence, and education had undercut authoritarianism generally, yet older ideas about household authority persisted. The same men who declared that all men were created equal wrote slavery into the Constitution. Nor did most show any inclination to question the authority of husbands and fathers in the family.

The contradiction between revolutionary political ideas and conservative notions of household governance appears in the famous exchange between Abigail Adams and her husband, John, when in 1776 she urged him to "Remember the Ladies" in the new code of laws that she supposed Congress was about to enact. "Do not put such unlimited power into the hands of the husbands," she wrote, applying to marriage the same critique of absolute power that her husband had used to justify resistance to Britain. "Remember, all Men would be tyrants if they could. If perticular care and attention is not paid to the Laidies we are determined to foment a Rebelion, and will not hold ourselves bound by any Laws in which we have no voice, or Representation." She was teasing about the rebellion, but not about the need for new laws. She knew that under the strictures of common law a wife could be subject to the arbitrary will of a tyrannical or incompetent husband.[60]

John responded, "As to your extraordinary Code of Laws, I

cannot but laugh." His laughter betrayed a genuine fear. He knew that one of the criticisms of the revolutionary movement was that an assault on monarchy would disrupt an entire social order. "We have been told that our Struggle has loosened the bands of Government everywhere. That children and Apprentices were disobedient—that schools and Colleges were grown turbulent—that Indians slighted their Guardians and Negroes grew insolent to their Masters. But your Letter was the first Intimation that another Tribe more numerous and powerful than all the rest were grown discontented." Adams's list is telling. By grouping wives with children, apprentices, Negroes, and Indians he assigned a traditional household heirarchy.[61]

But he didn't stop there. He had read the sentimental literature. He knew that in the kingdom of the heart, a wife was herself a monarch. He also knew how to tease. "Depend upon it, We know better than to repeal our Masculine systems. We have only the Name of Masters, and rather than give up this, which would completely subject Us to the Despotism of the Petticoat, I hope General Washington, and all our brave Heroes would fight." Abigail was wise enough not to push her point.[62] The argument ended in a draw because the two of them were using competing ideas about the position of women within the family. Abigail argued by analogy to politics. She was interested in legal authority. In contrast, John appealed to influence, the informal power that people exercise in face-to-face relations. In her view, the logic of formal politics had some relevance for the household. In his, the two domains operated by different rules. His approach had some support among political philosophers. As the French thinker Montesquieu expressed it, "Women have never been wont to lay claim to equality, for they have so many other unusual advantages that for them equality of power is always a situation for the worse."[63] If men ruled by right of law, women wielded power through personal—and sexual—attraction.

Yet in the United States (and a few years later in France) the crisis of revolution exposed the contradictions in these two positions. If the war required women to act, could they do so on their own or only as adjuncts to men? Esther Reed, the author of a broadside published anonymously in Philadelphia in 1780, tried to have it both ways. Reed, the wife of Pennsylvania's governor, and her friend Deborah Bache (Benjamin Franklin's daughter) had organized a Ladies Society to provide shirts for soldiers. In rousing prose, she urged American women to follow "those heroines of antiquity"—Deborah, Judith, and Esther—who had acted valiantly in defense of their country. She even invoked the memory of France's Joan of Arc, reminding readers that it was "the Maid of Orleans who drove from the kingdom of France the ancestors of those same British, whose odious yoke we have just shaken off." Then Reed backpedaled, assuring those who might be "disposed to censure" that the Ladies were only offering their gratitude to the men who were the real defenders of their country. Her words linked liberty with domesticity and female sovereignty with sweetness. "Born for Liberty, disdaining to bear the irons of a tyrannic Government," American women were nevertheless "content to reign by sweetness and justice." Offering fealty to their brave defenders, they might help to break the chains of their nation's "slavery," but were apparently unaware of their own.[64]

For African American women the stakes were higher. In the North, so-called "freedom suits" began even before the war. One of the earliest was instituted in Salem, Massachusetts, by Jenny Slew. Although one court said she couldn't sue because she was a slave and another because she was a wife, she persisted and in 1766 won her freedom.[65] As the black poet Phillis Wheatley exclaimed in her 1773 letter to the Mohegan leader Samson Occum, "in every human Breast, God has implanted a Principle, which we call Love of Freedom." She didn't think it would take a philosopher to discover that the American "Cry for Liberty" didn't fit very well with "the exercise of oppressive Power over others."[66]

During the war, nearly four thousand slaves fled to the British lines in the hope of emancipation. Thomas Jefferson's slave "Black Sall" was among them.[67] After the war, runaways headed to the few Northern states that had already banished slavery. One of the most famous fugitives was Ona Judge, who served Martha Washington as parlor maid in the presidential mansion in Philadelphia until 1796, when she slipped out into the night and fled on a friendly vessel. The president was convinced Judge had been seduced by some scoundrel. In his opinion, nothing else could explain her astonishing disloyalty. When an agent tracked her down in New Hampshire, Judge told him that though she loved the president and his lady, she loved freedom more. The agent reported that he saw no prospect of her returning voluntarily and feared that any attempt to return her forcibly, "like a felon to punishment," might result in a public outcry, since the prevailing sentiment in New Hampshire was for "universal Freedom."[68]

At the time, the cry for "universal freedom" rang loudest not in the United States, but in Britain, where slavery was associated with sugar production in the West Indies. In 1792, British abolitionists launched a massive boycott of slave-grown sugar. Although the boycott was organized by men, it appealed to women, not only as consumers but as feeling persons. William Cowper's "The Negro's Complaint" speaks in the voice of a slave:

> *Why did all-creating Nature*
> *Make the plant for which we toil?*
> *Sighs must fan it, Tears must water,*
> *Sweat of ours must dress the soil.*

Other writers claimed that in sweetening their tea with sugar, ladies were actually consuming the flesh of slaves.[69]

In her *Vindication of the Rights of Woman*, which appeared in England at the height of the boycott, Mary Wollstonecraft turned

the image inside out by attacking the false propriety—the sweetness—that kept women from acting as independent beings. "Is one
half of the human species, like the poor African slaves, to be subjected to prejudice which brutalizes them . . . only to sweeten the
cup of man?" she asked. "Is this not indirectly to deny woman reason?"[70] She feared the very influence that Adams and other men
invoked as a substitute for political power. "When I call women
slaves, I mean in a political and civil sense," she wrote, "for, indirectly, they obtain too much power."[71]

In revolutionary Paris, an actress and political pamphleteer
named Olympe de Gouges developed a similar argument. "This
sex, too weak and too long oppressed, is ready to throw off the yoke
of a shameful slavery," she wrote. Like Wollstonecraft, she
believed that women had the same capacity for reason and civic
engagement as men. Her *Declaration of the Rights of Woman and
Citizen* picked up where the *Declaration of the Rights of Man and Citizen* left off. She disdained the notion, common then among French
intellectuals, that women were "inactive" citizens. "I am a woman,"
she wrote, "and I have served my country as a great man."[72]

In 1792, the Library Company of Philadelphia hung a painting
in its headquarters titled *Liberty Displaying the Arts and Sciences*. In
it, a rosy-cheeked white woman in a fashionable white dress sits on
her pedestal like a schoolmarm. She *is* a schoolmarm. There is a
globe on her right, a pile of books at her left, and on the floor beside
her are an easel, brushes, and a lyre. If it weren't for the cap-
crowned pole leaning lightly on her right shoulder, she might be a
teacher in one of the newly opened academies in the early American republic, except that the students gathered around her on the
ground represent slaves. A boy in a red coat leans forward, his head
resting wearily on one hand, while behind him a mother holds a
young child whose arms stretch hopefully forward.

When Samuel Jennings, an expatriate American artist living in
London, first proposed contributing a painting to the library's new

Samuel Jennings, *Liberty Displaying the Arts and Sciences,* 1792

building, he suggested a portrayal of Minerva, the goddess of wisdom. The gentlemen of the Library Company, however, demurred. They wanted nothing less than "the figure of Liberty (with her Cap and proper Insignia)" surrounded with "Groups of Negroes sitting on the Earth, or in some attitude expressive of Ease & Joy."[73]

The gentlemen of the Library Company were proposing a radical transformation of an already familiar image. In the eighteenth century, artists on both sides of the Atlantic portrayed Liberty as a white woman holding a floppy cap perched on the end of a pole. Liberty's symbols derived from an ancient Roman ceremony in which a slave about to be freed was touched with a rod (the *vindicata*) and given a soft hat (the *pileus*). During the American Revolution, Liberty appeared on maps and newspaper mastheads, in political cartoons, and in the earliest designs for the Great Seal of

Frontispiece, "Rights of Women Presented to
Liberty," *Lady's Magazine and Repository of Entertaining
Knowledge*, Philadelphia, September 1792

the United States. In the 1790s, she recrossed the Atlantic to
become the icon of the French Revolution.[74]

In each setting, her role was to liberate white men. The Library
Company picture changed that. Its composition alludes to a then
famous image, produced in England in the 1780s by the pottery
manufacturer Josiah Wedgwood, which shows a kneeling African
imploring the viewer, "Am I not a man and a brother?"[75] The slaves
in Jennings's picture are both active petitioners and deferential subjects. Liberty, the painting suggests, is a kind and gentle goddess.
She will listen to their plea.

This was not the only unexpected representation of Liberty to
appear in Philadelphia in 1792. In September the frontispiece to
the *Lady's Magazine and Repository of Entertaining Knowledge*

portrayed a female figure offering the goddess a petition labeled "Rights of Women." Long excerpts from Mary Wollstonecraft's *Vindication of the Rights of Woman* appeared inside. Women trained only to please men could not be virtuous, one excerpt argued. "They may be convenient slaves, but slavery will have its constant effect, degrading the master and the abject dependant."[76]

Thus a quarter of a century before Elizabeth Cady Stanton was born, feminists were connecting slavery with the position of women. But the link remained metaphorical. The female petitioner in the *Lady's Magazine* and the white goddess in Jennings's painting had not yet joined forces. On both sides of the Atlantic, the nascent crusade for women's rights ended almost as quickly as it began. In France, Olympe de Gouges went to the guillotine for siding with the wrong political faction. In Britain and the United States, revelations about Mary Wollstonecraft's personal life besmirched her arguments. In the short run, the ideas expressed by John Adams proved more powerful than his wife's imagined rebellion. Middle-class Americans agreed that a wife should rule in the parlor, but if she engaged in direct political activity, she disrupted a God-given division of labor. Like Liberty, a well-behaved woman belonged on a pedestal.

In the 1830s that began to change.

How Good Behavior Led to Rebellion

There would have been no women's rights movement in the United States if middle-class women had not been so well-behaved. Energized by the religious revivalism that swept through the nation in the early years of the Republic, they joined missionary societies and sewing circles to relieve the poor, convert the heathen, and preserve the world from sin and sorrow. They asked nothing for themselves, yet in their separate female societies, they wrote constitutions, elected officers, managed funds, and hired and fired employees. But

with so much work to do and so few hands to do it, it was often hard
to define the limits of their sphere. If a woman really was destined
to influence men for good, where did her duty stop?[77]

That question troubled Catharine Beecher (Harriet Beecher
Stowe's older sister), who in 1823 established the Hartford (Connecticut) Female Seminary. When Beecher learned, sometime in
1829, about plans to remove Cherokees from the state of Georgia,
she felt called to do something about it. Righteous women had long
been involved in missionary work among American Indians. How
could they turn their backs now? She thought of the biblical story of
Esther, who in a time of trouble risked her life to petition the king.
Surely American women could do as much. Working through the
evangelical press, Beecher and her friend, the poet Lydia Sigourney,
sent an unsigned circular to "the benevolent ladies of the United
States" asking them to petition Congress on behalf of the Indians.[78]
Eighteen-year-old Harriet, an assistant in her sister's school, was
ecstatic. "Last night we teachers sat up till eleven o'clock finishing
our Cherokee letters," she wrote, adding that "the excitement, I
hope, is but just begun." The excitement, however, was too much
for Catharine. When conservative ministers and expansionist politicians mocked her campaign, she decided she had misread the Bible.
Esther had indeed petitioned the king, but since the king was her
own husband, she had in fact confined her activities to the domestic
sphere. Perhaps American women should follow her example.[79]

Women in the growing antislavery movement were not so easily
silenced. By 1833, they had the example of English women—many
of whom were fellow Quakers, Methodists, and Baptists—who
within ten days gathered 187,137 female signatures on a "huge
featherbed of a petition" that supportive male relatives presented to
Parliament.[80] Their crusade was enhanced by publicity surround-
ing the publication in 1831 of the *Narrative of Mary Prince,* the first
autobiographical account by a female runaway. A former slave in
Bermuda who had been brought to Britain by her master, Prince

enlisted sympathetic women in the British antislavery movement to prevent him from carrying her back to the West Indies. Her editors assured readers that the story of her excruciating labor in the salt works and her brutal treatment by her master came from her own lips. Lest anyone mistrust the account, they testified that Prince's body still bore the marks of the whip. Their efforts and those of other female abolitionists helped to bring about an act of Parliament that in 1838 ended slavery in the British West Indies.[81]

In the United States, however, where slavery was a much more important part of the economy, petitioning brought a different result. Members of Congress were so annoyed that they passed an infamous "gag rule" which effectively tabled all antislavery petitions sent to them, even those that deferentially addressed recipients as "Fathers and Rulers of Our Country."[82] But the more Congress ignored them, the more earnest the antislavery ladies became. In Bangor, Maine, a female society vowed to gather the signature of every female in the state over the age of fourteen, all the while insisting that they had nothing to do with the "turmoil and strife" of politics. These women claimed the right to define good behavior for themselves. The real sin, they said, was failing to act.[83]

A writer who identified herself only as "A Female Petitioner" satirized the argument that women stepped out of their proper sphere by taking up the topic of slavery. The same people who condemned women for abolitionist agitation praised their fund-raising activities for missionary societies and other charities. "A chart of 'the appropriate sphere of woman,' then is laid down thus: for Burmah, China, and Arabia, Africa and the islands of the sea, you may feel deep interest, and exert yourselves to support missionaries. For the exercise of domestic charity, you have home missions to sustain, tracts to distribute from house to house, Bibles to circulate, the 'oppressed' seamen to succor, the blind to assist, and the sick to visit. But the dark spot of slavery must not be assailed; that is a private affair altogether."[84]

Addressing audiences that included men as well as women, Angelina Grimké, a South Carolina slave owner–turned–abolitionist, argued that without the right of petition women were "mere slaves known only through their masters." From May to November 1837, Grimké addressed more than forty thousand persons in eighty-eight meetings in sixty-seven towns. Of forty-four petitions sent to Congress from Massachusetts in that year, thirty-four, or 77 percent, were from places she and her sister Sarah had visited.[85]

In a letter to the Grimkés, Catharine Beecher countered that "Woman is to win every thing by peace and love; by making herself so much respected, esteemed and loved, that to yield to her opinions and to gratify her wishes, will be the free-will offering of the heart." By courting controversy, activists lost "the sacred protection of religion, all the generous promptings of chivalry, all the poetry of romantic gallantry." If petitions "will be deemed obtrusive, indecorous, and unwise, by those to whom they are addressed," what good could they possibly do?[86]

Angelina Grimké shot back. "When I look at human beings as moral beings, all distinction in sex sinks to insignificance and nothingness; for I believe it regulates rights and responsibilities no more than the color of the skin or the eyes." She believed that "whatever it is morally right for man to do, it is morally right for woman to do," and that "until this important principle of equality is recognized and carried out into practice, . . . vain will be the efforts of the church to do anything effectual for the permanent reformation of the world."[87]

For proslavery writers, differences between males and females were analogous to differences between the races. They pointed out that the Bible discussed the responsibilities of masters and slaves in the very same passages where it considered the rights of parents and children, husbands and wives. All human beings had rights, but those rights were framed by the position each person occupied in a God-given social order. Hence, a husband had "the rights of a husband . . . a father the rights of a father; and a slave, only the rights of a slave."[88] South Carolinians were sickened by the behavior of the Grimkés. How could women from their own state behave in such an unseemly way? When a woman goes about "haranguing promiscuous assemblies of men," one pastor warned, "she is stepping forth from her rightful sphere and becomes disgusting and unlovely." A female writer dismissed the sisters as "petticoated despisers of their sex," "would-be men," and "moral monsters."[89]

The Grimkés were dangerous because they were so earnest. They were not sexually promiscuous, profligate spenders, gossipy neighbors, or slovenly housewives. They were pious and self-denying women who walked around in chaste Quaker bonnets. But like other well-behaved women they chose to obey God rather than man. The notoriety created by their public speaking obscures their real transgression. Quaker women had been speaking in public for more than a century. It was the political import of their cause that raised a furor.

Without political rights, what could a well-behaved woman do for an enslaved woman? She could influence her husband and brothers, refuse to purchase slave-grown cotton or sugar, and purchase tracts, newspapers, and books. But if her activities became too insistent, too *public,* she opened herself to physical danger as well as ridicule. This was especially true for those societies that included African American members.

In the fall of 1835, a mob broke into a meeting of the Boston Female Antislavery Society. The officers stunned the interlopers by continuing to conduct their business as though nothing had happened. When the city's mayor insisted that for their own safety they adjourn, the women locked arms, two by two, black and white women together, and walked safely into the street.[90] This incident turned out to be a rehearsal for a far more virulent attack in Philadelphia in 1838. When the mob threatened, the women managed to get out of the meeting using the same strategy, but that night the crowd came back and burned their new building to the ground. The women resumed their meeting the next day at the schoolroom of Sarah Pugh, an African American teacher. White leaders announced to the press that they planned to "expand, not contract their social relations with their black friends."[91]

It was a similar assault on free speech that made Gerrit Smith an abolitionist. In 1835, outraged at vigilante efforts to stop an anti-slavery meeting in a Rochester, New York, church, he became an earnest and public advocate for immediate abolition. He not only contributed to the rescue of runaways, he bragged about it in local newspapers—to the dismay of Judge Daniel Cady, who said he might as well write directly to slave owners inviting them to sue him.[92] In upstate New York, abolitionist sentiment was nourished by the religious revivalism that gave the region the name "Burned-Over District." Although most religionists were more concerned with their own salvation than with the emancipation of slaves, radicalism in religion sometimes led to radicalism in politics, as it had for Gerrit Smith.

Henry Stanton was an even earlier convert from faith to activism. Inspired by the preaching of Charles Grandison Finney—the same revivalist whose sermons had sent Elizabeth Cady into a deep depression when she was a student at Troy Female Seminary—he abandoned the study of law to enter the ministry, then abandoned the ministry to become a full-time anti-slavery agent. Along the way, he and his friend Theodore Weld staged that famous debate at Lane Seminary in Cincinnati. By the time Elizabeth met him, he was a polished and experienced public speaker, who also knew how to outrun mobs. He was also well acquainted with the debates between female reformers. When Theodore Weld married Angelina Grimké in 1838, Henry and Gerrit Smith were both present. (It may have been the Welds' example, rather than any innate feminism on Elizabeth's part, that led the Stantons to remove the word "obey" from the ceremony when they married in 1840.) Henry may have known Catharine Beecher as well, since she was living in her father's household and running her own school in Cincinnati when he and Weld were there.[93]

All of this formed an essential but unacknowledged background to the stories Stanton told in *Eighty Years and More*. But there is yet another history submerged in her sprightly memoir, another connection between her life and slavery.

Declarations of Independence

In *Eighty Years and More*, Stanton described a demonstration organized by her friend Susan B. Anthony in Philadelphia on the hundredth anniversary of American independence. On July 4, 1876, Anthony and three companions interrupted the all-male program at Independence Hall by walking down the aisle and presenting a women's "Declaration of Rights" that Stanton had helped to write. Distributing printed copies as they walked out of the room, they assembled outside, under a blazing sun, where Anthony read their Declaration to the assembled crowd. "Our faith is firm and unwavering in the broad principles of human rights proclaimed in 1776," she declared. "Yet we cannot forget, even in this glad hour, that while all men of every race, and clime, and condition, have been invested with the full rights of citizenship under our hospitable flag, all women still suffer the degradation of disfranchisement." She closed by invoking that century-old letter of Abigail Adams: "We will not hold ourselves bound to obey laws in which we have no voice or representation."[94]

As at Seneca Falls, Stanton and her collaborators drew their inspiration from the original Declaration of Independence. "Ours contained as many counts, and quite as important as those against King George in 1776," she later wrote. Women were taxed without representation. They were denied the right to a trial by a jury of their peers. They were denied equal protection under the laws. The

1876 Declaration also included several allusions to the Fourteenth
Amendment, which, while broadening the definition of citizenship
to include freed slaves, for the first time introduced the word *male*
into the Constitution. Stanton had actually fought against passage
of the amendment, because she considered it a betrayal of women
leaders who had devoted their energies to winning the war, only to
have their demands ignored in the effort to guarantee the rights of
freed slaves. "Woman's wealth, thought and labor have cemented
the stones of every monument man has reared to liberty," the Declaration proclaimed. "We ask of our rulers at this hour, no special
favors, no special privileges, no special legislation. We ask justice,
we ask equality, we ask that all the civil and political rights that
belong to citizens of the United States, be guaranteed to us and our
daughters forever."[95]

Stanton had a complex attitude toward the Fourth of July. On the
one hand, it symbolized her deepest political values, but on the
other it represented women's exclusion. *Eighty Years and More* suggests that for her it carried still deeper and unacknowledged meanings. Stanton claimed to have inherited her rebellious spirit from her
maternal grandfather, James Livingston. What she didn't say in her
memoir or anywhere else was that slaves were also a Livingston
inheritance. The federal census of 1790 for Johnstown credits Livingston's household with three slaves. In *Eighty Years and More*,
Stanton recalled with affection and a bit of condescension these
three men, "Abraham, Peter, and Jacob, who acted as menservants
in our youth." (The term *menservants*, of course, was a euphemism.)
She remembered their banjo-playing and dancing and the enjoy-
ment they took in the children's games. Quoting a minstrel song,
she said, "They are all at rest now with 'Old Uncle Ned in the place
where the good niggers go.' " As late as 1820, her own father's
household included one male slave.[96] This was no doubt Peter
Teabout, the man she wrote about with such affection in her memoir. Born in Albany sometime before 1784, he was too old to qualify

under New York's Gradual Emancipation Act of 1799, which offered eventual freedom to those born of slave mothers after July 4, 1799. Peter's freedom came under the state's Universal Emancipation Act, which freed all slaves within its borders on July 4, 1827, the year Stanton turned twelve.[97]

Peter is very much present in her recollections of July 4 celebrations in Johnstown, which she associated with both liberty and license. She wrote, "The festivities were numerous and protracted, beginning then, as now, at midnight with bonfires and cannon; while the day was ushered in with the ringing of bells, tremendous cannonading, and a continuous popping of fire-crackers and torpedoes. . . . On these occasions Peter was in his element, and showed us whatever he considered worth seeing; but I cannot say that I enjoyed very much either 'general training' or the Fourth of July, for, in addition to my fear of cannon and torpedoes, my sympathies were deeply touched by the sadness of our cook, whose drunken father always cut antics in the streets on gala days, the central figure in all the sports of the boys, much to the mortification of his worthy daughter."[98]

Strangely, Stanton was able to connect "Independence Day" with the humiliation of her family's cook but not with the emancipation of her family's slave. In her portrayal, Peter's love of Independence Day is part of his general love of fun. But surely it meant more to him than that. (In some parts of New York, free blacks celebrated two holidays, July 4 as the anniversary of the nation's independence, and July 5, as Emancipation Day. Elsewhere, July 4 carried both meanings.[99] Perhaps Stanton obscured the record of her family's slaveholding because it embarrassed her. Or maybe Peter Teabout just didn't seem like a slave to her, because he represented all that was happiest about her childhood. The omission is nevertheless both surprising and telling.

For Stanton, gender was always more important than race. Although she acknowledged the struggle for black emancipation in the years following the Civil War, for her the searing issue was not race but the betrayal of Republican leaders who refused to add female suffrage to the constitutional amendment giving freedmen the vote. Women had sacrificed their own cause to help win the war. Now, the very men who had once praised them as "wise, loyal, and clear-sighted" considered them impertinent for demanding the vote. "And thus it ever is," Stanton wrote, "so long as woman labors to second man's endeavors and exalt his sex above her own, her virtues pass unquestioned; but when she dares to demand rights and privileges for herself, her motives, manners, dress, personal appearance, and character are subjects for ridicule and detraction." In Stanton's bitter words, male leaders rejected the broad principle of natural rights by opening "the constitutional door just wide enough to let the black man pass in."[100]

The irony was that by 1898, when Stanton published her memoir, black men, too, had largely lost the right to vote. She seems not to have noticed. Nowhere in her autobiography did she confront the nation's retreat from its commitments to freed slaves. True, she was hardly alone in that. A decade after the war, Northern leaders were more interested in reconciliation with the white power structures of the South than in fulfilling promises to freed slaves. Northern blacks had also lost ground. Emancipated slaves like Jacobs, who had worked side by side with white reformers during the war, found it harder and harder to find employment. Eventually history, too, forgot them. By 1900, even Tubman, a minor celebrity in the years immediately following the war, had disappeared from public consciousness except in black classrooms and churches.[101]

In the twentieth century, America rediscovered its slave heroines. Harriet Tubman came first. In the 1940s, Earl Conrad, a journalist and labor activist, published a biography that laid the groundwork for her recovery.[102] The civil rights movement of the 1960s made her a household name. Among schoolchildren, the story of her guiding people to freedom by following the North Star may have supplanted the old story of George Washington chopping down the cherry tree. But most Americans preferred not to notice her militancy. In Maryland, a proposed outdoor mural based on the 1869 engraving aroused so much controversy it was never completed. Painter Mike Alewitz told a reporter for National Public Radio, "We live in a country that is surrounded by images of people with weapons, but one black woman with a rifle, one black woman, and it scares the authorities in an unbelievable way." (Tubman kept her rifle in an Alewitz mural in the Frederick Douglass Library at the University of Maryland, Eastern Shore.)[103]

Incidents in the Life of a Slave Girl was rediscovered in the 1970s as teachers of women's history began searching for narratives by black women, but Harriet Jacobs remained anonymous until literary scholar Jean Yellin rediscovered the person behind the narrative. Scouring the publications and private papers of nineteenth-century reformers, Yellin was "amazed to realize that Jacobs had achieved some celebrity as the author of *Incidents,* and that it was only later that her identity was forgotten." Yellin was even more surprised to discover that Jacobs had "used her celebrity among northern reformers to win support for her relief mission among the black war refugees." Today, Jacobs's autobiography is a standard text in courses on nineteenth-century American history and literature, and has been translated and published in German, Portuguese, French, and Japanese. A scholarly edition of her letters and papers is under way.[104]

Thanks to the work of historians and librarians in the United States and Canada, the beautiful runaway hidden in Gerrit Smith's attic also has a presence beyond her brief appearance in Stanton's memoir. Harriet Powell lost her reputation for good behavior as well as her bonnet when she fled that Syracuse hotel, but as *The Friend of Man* reported, she acquired something better—a "Liberty Cap." By stealing herself, she made a mark on history.

Chapter Five

༄

A BOOK OF DAYS

*Y*irginia Woolf called her "Anon." She was a poet who never signed her name. Maybe she didn't sign her name because she didn't know how to write. Or maybe she was too well-behaved to call attention to herself. She made up songs as she rocked her baby to sleep. She knitted socks and hemmed sheets and washed dirty cups in the scullery. She was a loyal sister and a good friend. Or a beautiful woman who gave pleasant parties. She was a caring nurse, an able secretary, or a stiff old lady crossing a London street in clothes that smelled of camphor. "All these infinitely obscure lives remain to be recorded," Woolf wrote.[1]

With the rebirth of feminism in the 1970s, lots of people became interested in Anon. Community groups and filmmakers organized oral history projects. Quilt researchers set up documentation centers in shopping malls, and public school teachers sent children home to interview their grandmothers. In Sonoma County, California, in 1978, the local women's commission dedicated a weeklong celebration to women's history. The idea spread. In 1981, Representative Barbara Mikulski, a feminist Democrat from Maryland, and Senator Orrin Hatch, a conservative Republican from Utah, sponsored a Joint Congressional Resolution establishing the first National Women's History Week.[2] The national organizers emphasized ordinary as well as famous women. The official poster for 1983, for example, featured the worn hands of an American Indian woman twining a basket.

That same year, Sally Fox launched a project that became a personal passion. She got the idea as she was packing her bags for Paris. Her husband, Maury, a professor at the Massachusetts Institute of Technology, had a one-semester appointment abroad. She was willing to take time off from her own work as a picture researcher to go with him, but she worried that she would become bored without an agenda of her own.

"I need a goal," Fox told a friend at lunch. "I can be a tourist for one or two weeks, maybe three, but then I need to get dressed and go to work."

Without saying a word, her friend went into another room and came back with a thirty-year-old greeting card, a souvenir from France's national library, the Bibliothèque Nationale. On the front was a picture of an earnest woman in a red dress sculpting a marble effigy of someone who looked very much like her except for her posture. The marble woman lay as if in sleep, or death, her wavy hair flowing unbounded to her waist, her arms folded quietly across her body.

Fox was captivated by this five-hundred-year-old image of one woman memorializing another. She had found her project. Once she and Maury were settled in Paris, she went to the manuscript reading room of the Bibliothèque Nationale to look for more images of medieval women. She didn't want halos. She wanted real people going about their lives.

Because there was no entry for "women" in the picture catalog, she sifted through thousands of black-and-white photographs looking for leads. Then, one by one, she called up the original manuscripts, determined to discover even in sacred and allegorical works a visual record of forgotten women. She was driven by

Sculptor, from Giovanni Boccaccio,
Les Livres des clères et nobles femmes, fifteenth century

delight in the pictures themselves, but also by a passion to redress a grievance. She had been around the block. She knew how the world relied on yet ignored women's work. Gradually, in the illuminated pages of thirteenth- and fourteenth-century manuscripts she began to find evidence of a female presence even in centuries when most women seemed mute.

The semester in Paris ended, but her mission had just begun. At home in the United States, she searched in academic libraries and major museums. Her research eventually took her to London and Oxford, then to Belgium, the Netherlands, Germany, Austria, Italy, and Spain.[3] The result would not be a scholarly monograph but a lavishly illustrated daybook, the kind sold in museum gift shops or quality bookstores.

The Medieval Woman: An Illuminated Book of Days appeared in 1985. Small enough to fit into a handbag or a briefcase, it alternated richly colored pictures with blank spaces for filling in landmark events, six entries to a page. At a time when women in the United States were moving into a whole range of supposedly "non-traditional" occupations, the pictures were entrancing. They remain so today. Here are infinitely obscure lives lavishly, brilliantly illustrated.

The title page shows a muscular woman shearing sheep. On the leaf opposite, a woman in a red scarf lifts a blacksmith's hammer. Inside is a woman miner with her pick. Elaborately coiffed ladies lean on fantastically shaped lecterns reading books while others defend a castle with a crossbow. Female workers feed chickens, fry bread, stir gruel, hackle flax, and dry noodles on long wooden racks. These pictures came from manuscripts so valuable that only kings or nobles could own them, yet they invoke the smells and stains of kitchens, fields, and streets. One vignette shows all the steps in preparing and cooking tripe. Another reveals the secrets of making a bed. These medieval women do the predictable and the unpredictable. They sell leeks, jewelry, butter, and fish; transport salt, grain, and wood; gather cabbages and spinach; cultivate silkworms; manufacture clothing and nets; and, in one astonishing miniature, deliver a baby by cesarean section.[4]

In the year Fox's book appeared, the *New York Times* published a story about Denise Rutledge, a four-foot-eight-inch-tall teenage mother from Brooklyn, who built an eight-foot-high sheet-rock wall in a vocational training class, then demolished it with a hammer and carefully reconstructed it. "I figured if a man could do it, I could do it, too," she said.[5] Fox's book made such a feat seem like old news. In the picture for July 19–24, for example, a white-hatted woman in blue holds a trowel while her female companion lifts a heavy block onto an unfinished structure. The caption reads, "Masons Constructing the City Wall." Alas, the credit line undercuts the comparison. Although few people in 1985 would have rec-

Christine and Lady Reason, *Collected Works of
Christine de Pizan: Cité des Dames,* fifteenth century

ognized the source, the picture of the female masons comes from a
fifteenth-century edition of *The Book of the City of Ladies.* The
woman with the trowel is Christine de Pizan. Her helper is Lady
Reason. They are laying the first stones for an imaginary city of
women.[6]

In the context of recent scholarship, the images Fox gathered
seem less literal but even richer and more intriguing. They invite us
to attend to the symbolic as well as the practical implications of
women's work. They ask us to think about continuity as well as
change. And they expose some of the ways in which Anon. made
history.

Golden Ages

In many eras, people have yearned for a time beyond memory when life was simpler or more satisfying. For Christine de Pizan that "golden age" was in antiquity. For nineteenth-century Romantics, it was in the Middle Ages, seen as a time of chivalry and religious faith. Some early-twentieth-century feminists—contemporaries of Virginia Woolf—also found aspects of life in medieval Europe worthy of praise. Alice Clark, the author of an influential history published in 1919, thought that women had more economic power in centuries when the home was a workshop and every member contributed to its support. Capitalism, she believed, brought a decline in female status by turning middle-class women into house-wives and poor women into impoverished piece workers or factory operatives. By separating production from consumption, it produced the "angel in the house."[7]

A first look at the *Illuminated Book of Days* seems to support the notion that women's work was more varied in times past. The picture for June 19–24, for instance, shows a female miner hacking away at a stony ledge. Strewn around her on the ground are lumps of ore, some dark, some shining like jewels. But on the ground near her feet, three fat books give her secret away. She is one of twelve allegorical "ladies of rhetoric" in a fifteenth-century how-to book for poets. She is mining words, not rocks.[8]

It would be easy to dismiss this image, like the one of Christine as a mason, as pure fantasy. That would be a mistake. The picture is idealized, but not entirely false. Other sources tell us there actually were female miners in medieval Europe. In Saxony, they labored in open-pit silver mines. In England, they gathered and washed lead ore. In Austria, they mined salt. This low-paid, dirty work persisted for centuries. In Lancashire, England, women worked underground in coal mines until 1841, when reformers outlawed the practice.

Then they became "pit-brow lasses" screening and hauling coal. Hauling was women's work in other places as well. In 1870, one German miner claimed that when his wife died, he lost his horse.[9]

A historian who looks hard enough will find women somewhere in the world doing almost anything—even blacksmithing. For centuries, women labored at tiny backyard forges producing small metal objects—needles, pins, nails, screws, files, cutlery, and chain-links used in armor.[10] But that isn't what's going on in the beautiful illuminations of smithing in Fox's calendar. These represent Dame Nature restoring the world through copulation. In medieval allegory, a woman's body was the anvil, a man's penis the hammer. Fox's pictures of smithing come from *The Romance of the Rose*, a text that Christine despised for its sexual innuendoes and misogyny.[11] In these medieval images, as in most representations of women's work today, there is a mixture of meanings. (Think of Aunt Jemima pouring syrup or Betty Crocker stirring up a cake.)

The most compelling images in Fox's book are often the most difficult to interpret. In the picture for the week of July 7, a woman holding a curved knife stands by while a female attendant lifts a child from a mother's body. What is surprising about this picture is not the presence of a female surgeon (there were a few in medieval Europe), but the fact that the mother is still alive. Before the twentieth century, surgical delivery was almost invariably a desperate attempt to remove a still-living infant when its mother had died in labor. In the medieval imagination, an abdominal delivery required either divine or diabolic intervention. One miracle story described a woman "of the country of the Goths" who was pregnant for almost thirty months when the Virgin Mary intervened. "Miraculously the stomach of the poor woman opened contrary to nature and without the help of a doctor. The dead and already putrid child was extracted in pieces and the mother was completely healed." In contrast, woodcuts illustrating the birth of the Antichrist, the Satanic opposite of Jesus, show naked mothers with gaping wounds in their abdomens.

Birth of Julius Caesar, from Jean Bondel, *Histoires anciennes jusqu'à Cèsar,* c. 1375

Punished for their sexual sins with death, these mothers are unable to deliver the Devil's progeny in a normal way. In contrast, the picture in Fox's book is one of several honoring an unsupported legend about the birth of Julius Caesar. Somehow the adjective *cesarean,* "having to do with cutting," came to mean *Caesarean,* "having to do with Caesar," even though there is no evidence in ancient sources that there was anything unusual about Caesar's birth.[12]

It is a relief to know that some medieval illustrations were supposed to be factual. The picture of two women making pasta, for example, comes from a fourteenth-century edition of a "Book of

Preparing noodles, from *Tacuinum Sanitatis,* c. 1385

Health" (*Tacuinum Sanitatis*), a treatise attributed to a physician
named Ibn Butlan who studied in Baghdad in the eleventh century.
While one woman pats out dough, the other arranges long strands
on a tall wooden rack. The inscription supports the conclusion of
recent scholarship that pasta, like wheat, entered Europe from the
Middle East. "The dough—*trij* in Arabic—is rich in nourishment,"
it says, warning that such a food "should be . . . thoroughly and
carefully prepared." A sixteenth-century Venetian writer, Ortensio
Lano, claimed that a peasant woman named Libista invented ravioli
and a woman named Meluzza Comasca was the first to make

lasagne. He didn't attempt to name the woman who invented the first noodle. We can think of her as Anon.[13]

The picture that first took Fox to the Bibliothèque Nationale is one of two images in her book representing the Roman sculptor Marcia. According to Boccaccio, Marcia was so chaste that "whether she was painting or sculpting," she used only female models. Since in Roman times statues were usually "rendered as nude or half nude" she avoided male subjects because she would have had either "to portray the men in an unfinished state or, by adding all the details, to forget maidenly delicacy." In medieval illustrations, Marcia's female subjects are also fully clothed. What survived in later centuries, however, was not the image of chastity but the fact that she was a sculptor. In the Renaissance Marcia's story helped to validate the work of other female artists.[14]

In Italy, the first truly famous female sculptor was Properzia de' Rossi (1490–1530), who in the early part of her career performed the astonishing feat of carving the entire passion of Christ on a peach pit. (Some of her carved and silver-encrusted fruit stones survive.) She went on to create full-scale statues in the basilica at Bologna, including some that surely required the use of male models. Her biographer considered her a worthy successor to Marcia despite rumors that her portrayal of the biblical story of Potiphar's wife attempting to seduce the young Israelite servant Joseph reflected de' Rossi's own lust for a younger man. Though twice hauled into court for minor transgressions—once for throwing paint on a fellow artist—she inspired later generations of women in Bologna, a city that became a center of female artistic endeavor.[15]

In the eighteenth century, another Bolognese woman, Anna Morandi, was both an artist and a scientist. Married in 1740 to a fellow anatomical modeler, she gave birth to five sons before her husband's death in 1755. Unlike the legendary Marcia, she had no reservations about sculpting male bodies. Morandi illustrated her fifty-seven-page study with twenty-two detailed wax models of male anatomy. (These may have been the models that Lord Byron found "not the most decent" when he visited the anatomical museum in Bologna in 1817.) In a witty rejoinder to those who defined achievement by sex, she created a self-portrait in wax that shows her holding a wax model of the human brain. In a matching portrait, her husband clasps a heart.[16]

By the time Sally Fox published her *Book of Days* Marcia and her successors were largely forgotten. In New York in 1985 a group of female artists tried to change that. Calling themselves the Guerilla Girls, they picketed art shows and museums, punning on their name by appearing in public in gorilla masks. One of the posters they planted on New York subways pictured an Ingres nude with a gorilla head and asked: "Do women have to be naked to get into the Met Museum?" An explanatory note claimed that in the modern art section of the Met, 85 percent of the nudes and only 5 percent of the artists were female. Another poster targeted patrons of high-end galleries: "When racism & sexism are no longer fashionable, what will your art collection be worth?" These were women making history—though ironically they adopted the names of dead female artists to protect their own identities.[17]

Fox's *Book of Days* predicted the future as it illuminated the past.

Virtuous Women

The title of Fox's calendar alludes to the elaborately illustrated prayer books—"books of hours"—that in the thirteenth century began to structure daily worship for wealthy and pious laity. These typically had two parts: a sequence of seven prayers illustrated with gold-encrusted images of the Virgin Mary, and a calendar of saint's days and feast days illuminated with vignettes of seasonal labor.[18]

There are faint echoes of these expensive calendars in the printed almanacs that served common people in later centuries. Some eighteenth-century diarists, including the Maine midwife Martha Ballard, adopted the numbering system that the almanacs borrowed from books of hours, which listed the days of the month in one column and the days of the week in another, using a "dominical letter" for Sunday. Ballard's descriptions of daily work echo the seasonal vignettes in the old illuminations. As rural families had done for centuries, her family sheared sheep in the spring, slaughtered hogs in autumn, and huddled by the fire in winter. Like the medieval women in Fox's calendar, she and her daughters hackled flax, carded wool, and made butter and cheese, using tools that had changed little over the centuries.

Although it is not immediately apparent, Ballard's book also retained some of the religious character of the old books of hours. Her matter-of-fact entries were in some sense a personal accounting to God. Sometimes they even ended with a prayer. "May the Great parent support us thro life and may we be conformed to his will is the desire of me his undeserving hand maid," she wrote at the end of one very trying day.[19] By referring to herself as a "hand maid," Ballard inadvertently associated herself with one of the central scenes in the illuminated "Hours of the Virgin." At the Annunciation, the Virgin Mary responds to the Angel Gabriel, "Behold the handmaid of the Lord; be it done unto me according to thy word."[20] This was, of course, the same scripture that Christine appropriated when she responded to the call of Lady Reason.

Diaries like Ballard's fashioned life as a pilgrimage. That perspective persisted through the nineteenth century. Emily French, a divorced washerwoman who worked near the mines in Colorado in the 1890s, penned her credo in the opening entry of her diary: "Let me only in the fear of God put on these pages what shall transpire in my poor life. Poor truths are only of value. I seek not the applause of the people only that I may deserve the epitaph—She hath done what she could."[21] In an oral history conducted by volunteers in the little town of Warner, New Hampshire, in the 1980s, an elderly woman named Katherine Greenlaw put the same sentiment in a slightly different way: "It had to be done so I did it."[22] There was no heroism here, just an effort to hold life together under difficult circumstances. The meaning was in the doing.

The picture Fox used for June 1–6 shows laborers cutting and raking hay in the shadow of a great castle owned by the Duke of Berry, Christine's powerful and, some said, ruthless contemporary. To the duke and his illuminator, there were two kinds of people in the world—those who ruled and those who labored.[23] Another excerpt from those Warner, New Hampshire, interviews offers a counterpoint to the orderly image of haying in the Duke of Berry's beautiful book. Warner was no medieval fiefdom, but even in rural New England in the early twentieth century there were distinctions between those who did the work and those who merely imagined it. Dorothy Sawyer told an interviewer that after she was married, her husband cut hay for the town's richest woman. "You see, the girls and I worked in the hayfields just like the men," she recalled. "One day it was so hot and humid, we were all so miserable, but in those days we didn't quit, so we began to tease each other and fool around. Somebody went to the house to get some cold water, and [the rich woman] said, 'I just love to watch you. You are all having such a good time!' We did nearly quit then."[24]

Representations of work are seldom neutral. In any setting, a wise person will ask, "Where is this praise of my labor coming from? And whose interests does it serve?" In Judaeo-Christian culture, the most famous celebration of women's work is in Proverbs 31, the passage that honors a virtuous woman who seeks wool and flax, plants vineyards, makes clothing of scarlet, and provides bread for her family. Lady Reason drew upon this scripture in her instructions to Christine. "No matter how dark it is, the light from her labor will never go out," she said, paraphrasing Solomon.[25] The notion of women's work as both varied and never-ending is reflected as well in a Japanese warrior chronicle that describes a farmer's wife who weaves "linen garments for spring, summer, and autumn," makes "cotton robes for the New Year," "grinds the barley and plants the rice fields," and when needed, takes "her husband's place at the plough." No matter how difficult the task, she persists. "When the firewood refuses to burn she labors long over it because she will not serve meals that are not tasty."[26] It had to be done so she did it.

This is the kind of praise that wakes well-behaved women at dawn and keeps them moving till late at night. It is important to note, however, that neither the Japanese chronicle nor the biblical text describes "housework" as usually understood. The virtuous woman of Proverbs, like the industrious Japanese wife, works outdoors and in, and when necessary takes over the responsibilities of her husband. In some places, that vision of women's work persisted into the nineteenth century, but for many middle-class women it was replaced by a new, more exalted idea. Work became something that men did for pay. Women, in contrast, made homes. Advice-givers assured them that if they created a little bit of heaven in their domestic spaces their husbands would not stray. "With what fond longings does he turn toward that bright paradise, his home, and gaze upon that bright and central orb, whose genial light kindles with soft and heavenly radiance upon the scene of loveliness which invites him to rest," enthused one writer.[27] Language like this imposed a new burden on wives—to accomplish work without seeming to do it.

Elizabeth Cady Stanton despised those who waxed poetic about the "home as woman's sphere," while denying a wife even the right to move a stove without her husband's permission. In the early years of marriage, she enjoyed housekeeping. But as her family expanded, she discovered that keeping "half a dozen human beings in proper trim" was exhausting and lonely work. To make things worse, her children were constantly sick. "Now I understood as I never had before, how women could sit down and rest in the midst of general disorder."[28]

It wasn't housework that distressed Virginia Woolf. It was the battle with an ideal that she called The Angel in the House. Such a woman "excelled in the difficult arts of family life. She sacrificed herself daily. If there was chicken, she took the leg; if there was a draught she sat in it—in short she was so constituted that she never had a mind or a wish of her own, but preferred to sympathize always with the minds and wishes of others." In order to become a writer, Woolf had to kill the Angel. "My excuse, if I were to be had up in a court of law, would be that I acted in self-defence. Had I not killed her she would have killed me."[29]

On the frontier, in utopian societies, or in times of war, a vision of women as engines of productivity prevailed, though here too the theme was service to others. Listen to the Mormon prophet Brigham Young during a period when skilled workers were hard to find in Utah Territory: "We believe women are useful, not only to sweep houses, wash dishes, make beds, & raise babies, but they should stand behind the counter, study law or physic, or become good bookkeepers & be able to do the business in any counting house, and all this to enlarge their sphere of usefulness for the benefit of society at large. In following these things they but answer the design of their creation."[30] When Chairman Mao said "Women hold up half the sky," he was engaged in a similar effort. He wanted "iron-willed girls" and "red women companies" who would go into factories or fields to sustain China's collective economy.[31] During World War II, the United States government also urged women to leave their homes for the good of the nation. In those years, a new paragon—"Rosie the Riveter"—joined the panoply of virtuous women. A popular song spread the word: "She's making history, / Working for victory." When the men returned, of course, "Rosie" went back to the kitchen, the mop, and the typewriter.[32]

The work changed, but the celebration was consistent. *It had to be done so she did it.* Sometimes, however, the work stayed the same and the meaning changed. That is the case in the curious history of women and dairying.

Cows and Women Making History

The picture in Fox's book for the week of August 13 shows a woman milking a large red cow with a calf beside it. As streams of milk fall into a wooden tub, the calf turns its head toward its mother. There is an affecting realism in the grouping of animals and objects. The yoke, the wooden bucket with its slats and rings, the curve of the cow's tail, the reach of its tongue, all seem observed from life. Except for the clothing, this could be Martha Ballard doing her morning milking, or the speaker in the Robert Frost poem about going out to the pasture to fetch a little calf so young it tottered when its mother licked it.[33]

History warns against such easy identification. In its original context, this cow was more than a cow. She was a symbol of Jesus and his crucifixion. The picture comes from a thirteenth-century bestiary, a moralizing book about animals. The author of the explanatory text gives a Christian interpretation to a passage from the Hebrew Bible that refers to the ritual slaughter of "a red heifer without spot, wherein is no blemish, and upon which came no yoke." He says Jesus is the "red heifer, because His human form was made red by the blood of the passion." That a heifer is a female animal does not concern him. Since females signify weakness and males power, he concludes that Jesus was crucified in weakness, then resurrected in power.[34]

The notion of the red heifer as a symbol for Christ was a familiar one in medieval Europe. Carvings in the cathedral at Chartres are just one representation of the *vacca rufa,* or red heifer, prefiguring the crucifixion.[35] In the picture Fox chose, the illustrator muddled

Milking a cow, from *Bestiary* (MS. Bodley 764, f. 41v., English), c. 1225–1250

the symbolism by portraying a scene from daily life, picturing a full-grown cow (a heifer is by definition a young animal) and by placing a yoke on her neck. Maybe he couldn't read. Maybe he didn't think of animal sacrifice when he thought of a cow. Or maybe he had his own ideas about Christian symbolism. For a pious reader, the presence of the woman may have added to the power of the story. Just as she drew milk from a cow, a faithful Christian drew strength from Christ. The yoke on the cow could be a mark of mortality, suffering, and redemption. As Jesus said to his disciples, "Take my yoke upon you, and learn of me."[36]

The calf in the picture is still unyoked. Like an unbelieving Christian, it is hard to control. Notice how its neck and front leg protrude beyond the frame of the picture, though with her tongue, the mother cow draws it back. The woman might be unyoked too. The flounce of her skirt also extends beyond the border; the thin fabric clings seductively to her body. The more we probe this seemingly simple picture, the more complicated it becomes.

Now flash forward three hundred years. Here is another

portrayal of a woman and a cow, this one in words. It comes from the records of a German court. In 1623 on a farm in Obermarchtal, a village near the Danube, dancers are celebrating the harvest when an old woman moves toward the enclosure where dairy cattle are tethered. Seeing her movements, a girl in the crowd screams. The mistress of the house comes running. What is this old hag doing loitering near her cows? She has already caused the death of a horse and made the red bull sicken and die. What is she muttering or strewing in the hay? "You shitty witch," the housewife screams as the old woman runs away. Hauled into court, Ursula Götz confesses under torture. She is a witch, just as her neighbors suspect, but if the court is going to condemn her she is going to tell a good story. She confesses that she has killed over eighty animals, horses and pigs as well as cows. She has had sexual intercourse with the Devil, who has given her a black salve to harm people. She has sucked the blood of young children and used it to make her potions. Her confession convicts her, but it also wins a measure of mercy. She is not burned alive. The executioner beheads her first, then throws her body to the flames.[37]

Her story is not an isolated case. Between 1500 and 1700, about 100,000 persons were accused of witchcraft in Europe and North America. Forty to fifty thousand were executed. Eighty percent of these were women. A witch was the dark mirror of a good wife. She not only caused babies to die and men to become impotent, she stole wine from cellars, corn from barns, and milk from the udders of cows and sheep. In a world of scarcity, witches took food from their neighbors.[38] In New Haven, Connecticut, in 1653 an angry woman, who had been refused buttermilk at a neighbor's house, fixed her eye on a sucking calf. Soon it went wild, bolting into a corn patch and pawing up hills. When its owner tried to tie it down, it lifted a great post as if it were a feather.[39]

In Norfolk, England, about the same time, a frightened farmer told a court how strange things had befallen all his beasts. First, a large hog lost the ability to grunt and move about. When his wife tried to nurse it by feeding it some milk, it bit her hand. Worried that the hog was mad, the farmer sent his wife to the apothecaries to get a remedy, but the horse she was riding fell lame, swelled up like a bladder full of air, and died. Then terrible things happened to his calves. The leg of one turned straight upward. Others acquired a terrible stench, "their hair standing upright upon their backs and they shaking in such sort as I never saw." When the horrified farmer tried to end the curse by using counter-magic to burn a dead calf, he was himself taken with gripping pains. At that moment, the woman he suspected of causing his troubles came to the house, "whereupon I did earnestly chide her, and said I would beat her, and that day, I praise God, I was restored to my former health."[40]

A woman could become a witch by being poor and resentful or by seeming a bit too good at what she did. In the French Lorraine, a woman named Synnelle Adam became known as the "butter-maker" because she could get more cream from one cow than others could get from four. Some said her trick was collecting dew before dawn on May mornings. In court, she insisted that she was simply more careful than other people, though she did admit to using magical prayers to heal animals and people. In another case from the same area, a little girl admitted that her father put threads in the road for his neighbors' cattle to pass over, then took the threads home, warmed them by the fire, and rubbed them on the backs of his own animals. In that way, he drew away milk that belonged to others.[41]

Stories like this exploded into history, then faded away. For reasons no one can compress into a sentence, fear of magic diminished and the witch craze ended. But women continued to milk cows. Now, however, their work was idealized in poetry, painting, and in a whole array of new consumer goods. Perky milkmaids in striped stockings and flat-brimmed straw hats pranced across bed curtains and chimney tiles, and embellished tea sets and platters.

Sophisticated people imagined the life of the humble milkmaid as simpler and more authentic than their own. In the 1790s, English bluestockings were astonished to discover a village milk woman who was herself a poet. To please her readers, Anne Yearsley adopted the pseudonym Lactilla, though she seldom wrote about milk or cows. More commonly, writers looked on from a distance while other women did the milking. In 1803, Dorothy Wordsworth, the poet's younger sister, described a visit to a rural cottage in Scotland. Overhearing her rustic hostess "milking behind the chimney," Wordsworth said to herself that this fortunate family "lived nicely with their cow: she was meat, drink, and company."[42]

Meanwhile, far away in Maine, Martha Ballard filled her diary with the labor of dairying. "I have been Doing my house work and Nursing my Cow, her Bag amazeingly sweld," she wrote on a November day, and in June, "I have made a Chees Since 8 Even[ing]. It is now 10; it is in the press. How great my Toil." When a cow became too old to give milk, butchering brought the hard work of processing its thick fat or tallow into candles. Ballard tried out the fat over the fire, then tied homespun wicks in rows on long poles or sticks of the right size to allow dipping several at once into a kettle of hot fat. She dipped and cooled, dipped and cooled, building up layers of fat. "I made Candle wiks & Dipt 27 Dozn three times over," she wrote. Ballard's cows helped create her diary. "I rose, lit my Candle & wrote this," she noted.[43]

Ballard's Philadelphia contemporary Elizabeth Drinker did not keep a cow, but one day she recorded in her diary another woman's distressing adventure: "Our Milk Man's wife, two or 3 days ago, as she was rising from milking a Cow, had the side of her Belly torn by the Cows horn, 5 or 6 inches long, and so deep that the fat turn'd out, 'tis well 'twas no deeper as she is 6 or 7 months gone with Child."[44] Had Drinker kept her own cow, she probably would have hired someone else to do the milking. Advertisements in colonial newspapers show that dairy maids were much in demand. A

"Negro wench" who understood the business was "fit for a gentleman's country house." In the North, Irish servants were more plentiful. In 1764, a ship just arrived in New York from Ireland advertised both firkins of butter and "Dairy Maids."[45]

Dairying was an ancient art in the Emerald Isle. Some said that in earlier centuries Irish mothers washed their newborn babies in milk, and that, when an important person died, calves were taken away from their mothers so they would join in the wailing. An Englishwoman settled on an estate in Ireland in the early nineteenth century was jealous of a neighbor whose "County Antrim woman" had made a fortune for him. "She makes each cow rear two calves, sometimes three, and she expects besides five pounds of butter per week from each when but a little cream is wanted."[46] In Donegal, groups of women still lived together in summer in temporary huts, or "*buailes,*" where they herded cows and passed their time with storytelling, knitting, and churning.[47]

But in other places the ancient link between women and cows was weakening. With improved transportation, dairying expanded from a cottage industry to a commercial operation. Where that happened, men took over the milking. In some parts of England, farmers resisted the transition, referring to male milkers as "teat-pullers." But in the United States in the nineteenth century, native-born women rapidly abandoned their cows. To be seen in the barn was a sign of crudeness or poverty.[48]

That may help explain why in 1871 people blamed Catherine O'Leary for the great Chicago Fire. O'Leary was an Irish immigrant who with her husband owned a small property on Chicago's West Side. She added to the family income by managing a small dairy. Although the fire does seem to have begun in her barn, she told the fire commissioners that she and her husband and their five children were all in bed when it happened. She could not tell them anything about the fire, only that it had burned up her livelihood. She had lost not only six cows but a horse and wagon and two tons of coal and two tons of hay. "I had everything that I wanted in for the winter. I could not save five cents' worth of anything out of the barn . . . and upon my word I worked so hard for them."[49]

The commissioners believed her. But the press could not resist a good story. The embers were hardly cool when the now famous song began to circulate:

> *One dark night, when people were in bed,*
> *Old Mrs. O'Leary lit a lantern in her shed,*
> *The cow kicked it over, and winked his eye,*
> *And said,*
> *"There'll be a hot time in the old town tonight."*

Playing on stereotypes about slovenly Irish immigrants, one paper claimed that O'Leary had filed false claims for relief and that when rejected, "The old hag vowed she would be revenged on a city that would deny her a bit of wood or a pound of bacon." Another included a photograph that supposedly pictured her with the miscreant cow. Unfortunately, the photographer couldn't tell a milk cow from a Texas longhorn. Through it all, O'Leary resolutely refused to talk to the press.[50] She didn't ask to be remembered on earth, but she has been.

In contrast, her contemporaries Julia and Abby Smith of Glastonbury, Connecticut, courted public attention by making a spectacle of their town's attempt to confiscate their cows. It all began when, after attending a women's rights meeting in Hartford, they decided to try to register to vote. Abby was then in her late seventies; Julia was eighty-one. When officials refused their request, they stopped paying taxes on their farm, whereupon the town sent the tax collector to confiscate seven of their eight cows.[51] These weren't ordinary cows. They were Alderneys, animals that could trace their pedigree to an island in the English Channel, a breed beloved of aristocrats and agricultural improvers, cows that produced cream so thick and yellow that it stood on its own. Cows of this breed populated the pages of English novels. The most famous Alderney in the 1870s was the one in Elizabeth Gaskell's *Cranford*, a gentle satire of an English village dominated by property-owning spinsters and widows whom she playfully dubbed "Amazons."[52]

Julia and Abby could have inhabited a novel. When the tax collector arrived, they begged him to leave them at least two of their cows, because a single one would be lonely. They insisted that these were special cows, really more like pets than property. They all had names—Jessie, Daisy, Proxy, Minnie, Bessie, Whitey, and Lily—and although the sisters employed a tenant to do the milking, the cows all came when Julia called. When the collector herded the animals into a neighbor's tobacco barn next door, they began to bellow. They would not let the neighbor milk them, and when the town called in the Smiths' tenant to do the work, his wife refused to care for the milk, saying it had been stolen. The sisters had stirred up a mini-feminist revolt in the town.[53]

The town, however, was determined to auction off the cows. At the end of a week, the tax collector marched down Main Street with the best cow. Following behind with the remaining six cows were four men with a dog and a drum. Julia, Abby, their tenant, and his wife rode in a wagon at the end of this strange parade. By the time the auctioneer banged his gavel, reporters from as far away as Boston had arrived to see the fun. In the end, the tenant managed to buy back the cows on the sisters' behalf, but not before the two old ladies had created a national spectacle.[54] With humor—and a bit of help from the Alderneys—they had made their point. A sympathetic writer in *Harper's Illustrated Weekly* asked, "Does taxation without representation cease to be tyranny, and become justice, when the property-owner is a woman? This is a question to which a good-natured laugh at Miss Anthony does not seem to be an entirely satisfactory answer."[55]

Enlivened by the fuss she had created, Julia milked the controversy for all it was worth. In January 1876, she told an audience at a National Woman's Suffrage Association meeting in Washington that "There are but two of our cows left at present, Taxey and Votey. It is something a little peculiar that Taxey is very obtrusive; why, I can scarcely step out of doors without being confronted by her, while Votey is quiet and shy, but she is growing more docile and domesticated every day, and it is my opinion that in a very short time, wherever you find Taxey there Votey will be also."[56] The Smith sisters did not live to see women get the vote, but for a moment, they made history.

By the twentieth century, commercially operated dairies dominated milk production, permanently severing the practical link between women and their cows. But the red heifer has not gone away. In 1996, a Pentecostal minister and cattle-breeder from Mississippi and a group of Orthodox Jews in Israel began collaborating to produce a perfect red heifer whose ashes might be used to purify the Temple Mount in preparation for the reconstruction of Israel's ancient Temple. The first heifer they produced—named Melody— became a disappointment when she sprouted a few white hairs, but the project continues as part of an unusual alliance between fundamentalist Christians who believe the Temple must be rebuilt before the Second Coming of Jesus Christ and fundamentalist Jews who believe that the instructions in ancient writings for the restoration of the Temple should be taken literally.[57]

In contrast to orthodox positions in either faith, a feminist rabbi from New York City named Jill Hammer links the red heifer to the "Divine Feminine," a primordial goddess signifying fertility and the ever-changing cycles of nature. She quotes Starhawk, a self-proclaimed witch who has inspired thousands of women to reclaim goddess worship. "The "Divine Feminine," Starhawk writes, "changes everything she touches, and everything she touches changes."[58]

The same might be said for history.

Artists of the Possible

In *A Room of One's Own,* Virginia Woolf lamented the difficulty of measuring women's achievements.

> One could not go to the map and say Columbus discovered America and Columbus was a woman; or take an apple and remark, Newton discovered the laws of gravitation and Newton was a woman; or look into the sky and say aeroplanes are flying overhead and aeroplanes were invented by women. There is no mark on the wall to measure the precise height of women. There are no yard measures, neatly divided into the fractions of an inch, that one can lay against the qualities of a good mother or the devotion of a daughter, or the fidelity of a sister, or the capacity of a housekeeper.

She concluded that to comprehend women's creativity, a writer would have her work cut out for her "simply as an observer."[59]

The American novelist Alice Walker built on Woolf's insight in her essay "In Search of Our Mother's Gardens," published in *Ms.* magazine in 1974. She said that in looking for female artists, feminists "have constantly looked high, when we should have looked high—and low." Her examples included an appliquéd quilt made by an ex-slave, and the painted houses, woven mats, songs, and stories of Africa. But mostly she thought of the flower gardens her own mother built around every run-down sharecropper's cabin she was forced to inhabit. "I notice that it is only when my mother is working in her flowers that she is radiant, almost to the point of being invisible—except as Creator: hand and eye. She is involved in work her Soul must have."[60]

In the years since Walker wrote, scholars have rediscovered hundreds of such women. In 1987, Elinah Grant and her husband,

Boepetse Busang's *lelapa* wall, 1990

Sandy, began studying the painted houses of her native Botswana, a landlocked country in southern Africa. In Botswana, as in many African countries, women have been builders as well as decorators of houses. The common form here is a round earthen house called a *rondavel*, set in a well-swept courtyard enclosed with a knee-high wall called a *lelapa*. Molded window frames and the sinuous swirls of the *lelapa* give many of these houses the look of sculpture. Local clays, when mixed with cattle dung, produce remarkably durable pigments ranging in hue from pink ochre to light green. Some artists paint their houses with bold diamonds or zigzags; others prefer stylized flowers, animals, or deep curves. For the most ambitious artists, decoration extends to the hand-packed dirt floor of the courtyard. A woman begins by polishing a new layer of earth with a smooth hand-held stone, called a *thitelo*. When the surface is dry, she dampens it again, then adds a layer of cow dung which she finger-paints into complex wheels and lines. The fat in the dung

Mmashadi Sepotlo decorating a *lelapa* entrance, 1992

subtly changes the color of the underlying clay. When the excess dries, the artist sweeps it off, leaving a richly patterned floor.[61]

People sometimes think of "folk art" as static and unchanging, but the women and men who create it are often dealing with a heavy load of history. They demonstrate their creativity in part by adapting traditional forms to changing circumstances. Today in Botswana some women mix clay with commercial paints. Others build one or two small thatched *rondavels* in a walled compound whose main building is a cinder-block house. In neighboring South

Africa, Basotho women use similar techniques to transform rectangular houses like those built by white Afrikaner settlers into stunning works of art. During the struggle against apartheid, they expressed their political beliefs by painting their bold geometric designs in the outlawed colors of Nelson Mandela's party. It was a clever ruse. One could get arrested for displaying a flag or wearing a T-shirt with an African National Congress slogan, but police could hardly condemn a woman for adding fresh paint to her house.[62]

Like other indigenous Americans, the Pomo Indians of northern California were decimated by disease and war in the nineteenth century; in the years following, their children were forced into government schools where they were beaten if they spoke their native language. Yet despite these circumstances, some families managed to perpetuate cherished skills. From her mother and grandmother, Annie Burke learned to gather and process wild plants to make twined and coiled baskets. When attitudes toward Indians improved and a California museum asked Burke to present a program on Pomo traditions, she realized she had no baskets to show. She had sold or given hers away. Nor did she have any made by her beloved grandmother. Like other well-behaved Pomo women, the older woman had insisted that all that remained when she died be buried with her. Burke didn't want the beautiful work of her people to disappear. So she started a collection. Her daughter Elsie Allen picked up where she left off, going door to door to ask other members of her tribe for contributions. Some slammed those doors in her face. Others accused her of violating time-honored tradition by sharing her skills with non–family members, and especially with non-Indians.[63]

Elsie Allen said that a turning point was going out to dinner at a Chinese restaurant with her own daughter. "I was amazed to see other races eating there and saw also how proud the Chinese were of their heritage. Since I felt that the Pomos were one of the great-

Annie Burke and her niece weave a basket

est basket weavers in the world, I resolved in my heart that this wonderful art should not be lost and that I would learn it well and teach others." One of her students was Susan Billy, a Pomo woman whose family had left California years before but who returned in the 1970s to rediscover her heritage. "The baskets began to call me," Billy said. They called others as well. The 1983 poster for National Women's History Week featured Allen's friend Laura Somersal turning a basket.[64]

During these same years, others began to explore quilting as an expression of women's culture. In 1981, Shelly Zegart launched an innovative public project to document Kentucky's historic quilts.

Laura Somersal Twining a Basket, National
Women's History Week Poster, 1983

Establishing "Quilt Days" in a number of sites, she and others
invited people to bring in family heirlooms for documentation. In
succeeding years, groups in all fifty states, Canada, Great Britain,
New Zealand, and Australia catalogued more than 200,000 quilts
made from the late eighteenth to the mid-twentieth century. Meanwhile, contemporary activists revived two seemingly different
nineteenth-century traditions, using quilts to memorialize loved
ones and to express political commitments. The most visible example was the massive AIDS quilt, which was first displayed on the
Mall in Washington, D.C., in October 1987. Larger than a football

Annie Young and her great-granddaughter Shaquetta
Young, Alabama, October, 1993

field, it then had 1,920 panels created by family members and
friends of AIDS victims. Today there are more than 40,000.[65]

Traditional geometric quilts had already attracted the attention
of major museums, though they were usually displayed without
reference to the lives of their creators or to the historical contexts in
which they were made. In 1998, inspired by a photograph in Roland
Freeman's book on African American quilters, folk-art collector
William Arnett began researching "everyday" quilts made by
African American women in Gee's Bend, Alabama. The result was
not only a blockbuster exhibit and two substantial catalogs produced in collaboration with the Museum of Fine Arts in Houston,
Texas, but a richly detailed and moving oral history. The exhibit—
and sometimes a representative group of the quilters—traveled to
major art museums across the United States between 2002 and
2006, transforming the previously anonymous women of Gee's
Bend into an international sensation.[66]

Bars and String-Pieced Columns, 1950s, by Jessie T. Pettway (b. 1929)

Commentators on the quilts made the same three points over and over—that Gee's Bend was an isolated African American community; that quilts made there exemplify improvisation and disdain for fixed patterns; and that their makers are untaught geniuses, artists of the ordinary. It is hard to argue with any of these assumptions. Gee's Bend *is* an out-of-the-way place tucked into an unbridged bend in the Alabama River. The quilts made there *are* wildly original. Their aesthetic appeal comes not only from dazzling shapes and colors but from the materials of which they are made—old feed bags, random bits of calico and wool, and strips of denim cut from used workclothes, the seemingly random designs exposing patches of blue from under ripped-off pockets and a subtle patina created by knees rubbing against earth. To create such beauty out of discarded clothing does require genius.

But there are other elements of the Gee's Bend story. If the community is geographically isolated, it is also one of the best-documented in Alabama, beginning with studies produced by the Federal Farm Security Administration in the 1930s. Though its inhabitants were poor, many owned land, thanks in part to the intervention of the New Deal. Nor did the unsung genius of the Gee's Bend quilters prevent them from participating in the civil rights movement of the 1960s or doing piecework for Sears Roebuck and Bloomingdale's. It is not the separateness of their lives that intrigues but the intersections between their seeming isolation and major forces in twentieth-century U.S. history. Over the last century, this cultural backwater has helped sustain New Deal bureaucracy, sixties activism, eighties mass marketing, and New York chic.[67]

A surviving photograph, taken in 1937 by the Farm Security Administration, shows a woman working at a treadle sewing machine in a room papered with pages from old magazines. Beside her are two children holding a quilt made in the conventional "Dresden plate" pattern popular in that era. Did the New Deal photographer choose that quilt because it demonstrated that, though poor, Gee's Benders could produce work that "looked right"? Or did the quilter herself choose it? Did she distinguish between works she considered worthy of display and those "lazy gal" quilts she made just to keep her children warm?

During the 1960s, China Grove Myles, a single woman who farmed her own land, became famous for her "Pine Burr quilt," later designated the state quilt of Alabama. Notoriously precise, it too differs from the quilts exhibited today. Myles was a fiercely

Jennie Pettway and Another Girl with the Quilter Jorena Pettway, 1937,
by Arthur Rothstein

independent woman who during a civil rights demonstration in
Camden, Alabama, in 1971 banged on the door of a school bus taking demonstrators to jail, yelling, "Take me, too. I want to go to
jail. I need to be with my children." Although she had no biological
children, she had helped to raise her sister's, and she taught many
others to make complex patterns like the "Double Wedding Ring"
or "Monkey's Wrench." She used to go into Camden and buy forty
or fifty yards of cheap cloth at the five-and-dime store and sell it,
piece by piece, to her neighbors. In the months before her death she
and her helpers produced as many as seven Pine Burr quilts to fill
orders generated by a brief mention of her work in a 1975 *National
Geographic* article.[68]

Meanwhile, other women, less visible, more harried, continued
to piece together old clothes to keep their families warm. Anthro-

pologist Nancy Scheper-Hughes fell in love with a pile of old quilts like that when she was working as a civil rights volunteer near Gee's Bend in 1967. Later, living in Cambridge, Massachusetts, she tried to market similar quilts sent by the newly organized Freedom Quilting Bee. A public-spirited gallery pondered displaying "just one," but never did. In Vermont, antique and craft dealers looked askance. People said things like: "*They don't look right.*" "Their method is poor—look at the stitches, they're large, uneven, not even straight." "The colors are garish; they startle rather than soothe. Who would want to sleep under something like this."[69] Today, scattered through the Yankee heartland, there must be dealers kicking themselves for having passed up the opportunity to collect a Gee's Bend masterpiece when it still cost $15.

What is the source of the art in a Gee's Bend quilt? It resides in part in the stories that surround it—appealing and dangerous stories that locate the genius of rural women in simplicity and lack of aspiration. It lies as well in the perceptions of those who have the power to define works of genius, and of course those definitions shift over time. Where does the value lie for the quilters themselves? The oral histories collected as part of the recent Gee's Bend revival provide part of the answer. This was art that grew out of a heartbreaking tension between the probable and the possible. Gee's Bend quilters read the words on magazines pasted to the walls of their houses; then, burdened with too much to do, they "did it their way," patching pieces by eye instead of by pattern, working into bedclothes the passion of their singing, the fervor of their religious faith, and the extravagant generosity of their cooking.[70] Moultree Kennedy told an interviewer that her mother "was the singingest and cookingest person on this earth. Did everything out of her head: singing, cooking, and making quilts." For Kennedy's mother, the joy was clearly in the doing.

A lot of women's art is like that. When Judith Moyer began editing oral histories she and others had gathered in Warner, New

Hampshire, in the 1980s, she found that the words often fell naturally into blank verse. So in planning a public reading of some of
these stories, she let that happen, cutting and pruning a bit to produce small soliloquies that described the poetry of multitasking, the
contrapuntal rhythm of women's work in a rural setting where no
one could be much of an expert on any one thing but where an
ambitious woman might display her talents in unexpected ways.
For one woman, the chance came when a single man in her neighborhood brought her a chicken.

It was old Joe Frenchman that brought the hen.
If I would cook it up, he said, he'd come
to dinner. So I went right to work.
I used to use a lot of chicken fat.
I took that out and put it in a dish
and set it on the back of the stove to melt.
To "try it out," that's what we'd say, to "try it out."
You have to watch it close because
it would burn awful quick.
It wants to be just coming out nice.
I strained it through a little strainer to get
every bit of the stuff that's just oil,
pure oil. I found an egg, an egg inside
that had the shell on it.
I thought I'd see how far I could go on
using that thing, so I made a cake
of the egg and oil, and while he was gone
I got the cake baked. In between all those things,
I put the chicken in the pressure cooker
and cooked it, that's what I did, picked it off
the bones and then mixed up the biscuit dough
and made a chicken pie. This was to show off,

to be kind of smarty. By the time he got back
—it must have been five—I could tell him
I had made all that. When he sat down to eat it
he said, "Most as good as store bought!"[71]

The man's uncomprehending compliment illustrates the problem Virginia Woolf identified so many years ago: "There is no mark on the wall to measure the precise height of women." Little matter. The woman didn't do "all that" to please old Joe Frenchman, but for the pleasure of turning an everyday task into an art.

In some circumstances, however, art was not enough.

Defenders

The picture in Fox's *Book of Days* for February 25–29 shows four energetic women defending a castle. One shoots with a crossbow from the pinnacle of the tower. Below her, another archer pulls back the string of a conventional bow, while two companions fling projectiles from a parapet. These are defiant women, confident and brave, yet there is something strangely wrong with their weapons. The archers have bows but no arrows. Can those be flowers about to sail through the air? Yes, the woman leaning over the edge of the parapet clutches a sprig of posies in each hand. As any medieval reader would recognize, these women are not engaged in a conventional war. They are defending the castle of love. The illustration appears in a sober treatise on kingship presented to Edward III of England sometime between 1325 and 1327. Apparently alluding to the young king's engagement to be married, it promotes the comforting notion that a woman's only weapon is love, an idea that Edward himself might have disputed since he rose to the throne when he did because his mother, Isabella of France, conspired with her lover to have his father deposed and then murdered.[72]

Women defending castle with bow and crossbow, from Walter de Milemete.
De nobilitatibus, sapientiis, et prudentiis regum

The treachery of women like Isabella inspired the attacks on female morals that so distressed Christine de Pizan. She could hardly deny that some women had not behaved well, and she struggled to keep those examples from blackening the names of her sex. Deep into the *Book of the City of Ladies,* she asks Lady Rectitude whether it is true that female misbehavior is the cause of men's unhappiness with marriage. Lady Rectitude is horrified that Christine could even for a moment entertain such an idea. Doesn't she know that women are the true sufferers in marriage? "My God! How many harsh beatings—without cause and without reason—how many injuries, how many cruelties, insults, humiliations, and outrages have so many upright women suffered, none of whom cried out for help? And consider all the women who die of hunger and grief with a home full of children, while their husbands carouse dissolutely or go on binges in every tavern all over town." Lady Rectitude then launches into a string of stories about true and faithful wives.[73]

These women not only nursed sick soldiers; they fought alongside their husbands in battle, roused their men's spirits when they lacked courage, and risked humiliation and physical danger to retrieve men's bodies when they died far from home. Unlike Amazons, they did not compete with men. They enlarged female strengths—and weaknesses. Facing threats to their homes, churches, and communities, they pushed good behavior over the edge into defiance, outdoing men in audacity and sometimes in violence.

Although Lady Rectitude's stories are sometimes fanciful, her themes are echoed in scholarly accounts of female behavior in times of famine, war, religious conflict, or revolution. During the English Peasants' Revolt of 1381, for example, an otherwise anonymous woman named Julia Pouchere goaded rebels from Canterbury and Essex into tearing down a jail. During the same conflict Katherine Gamen untied a boat in which a royal official was trying to escape, allowing a mob to overtake and behead him.[74] Sometimes women acted alone, sometimes as proxies for an entire community. In 1677, during a terrifying war in New England between English colonists and local Indians, a crowd of women in Marblehead, Massachusetts, surrounded two Abenaki prisoners brought into the port. Demanding to know why the prisoners were still alive, they pounded them with stones and clubs until they had separated their heads from their bodies. Then, boasting that they could kill "forty of the best Indians in the country," they faded back into the crowd where no man rose to testify against them.[75]

In tax revolts and bread riots, as in war, crowds of women represented a "world turned upside down." Since women were not supposed to meddle in public affairs, their presence symbolized the depth of a grievance. But since women were also presumed to be weak-minded and given to hysteria, they were less responsible for their actions. If the protest failed, men could save their own necks by claiming that women acted without their permission.[76]

This was not only a Western phenomenon. In so-called rice riots that took place in Japan between 1600 and 1848, women sometimes initiated the action, their pleas for food dramatizing the grievance in a way that appeals from men alone would not do. In one case, 2,500 rioters, mostly women and children, climbed the hill to a castle, sobbing and shouting to attract attention. After one such encounter, an official complained that "this disturbance was due entirely to foolish women." Dismissing the women as "foolish" allowed him to ignore them. It may also have prevented the women from being punished in the way that supposedly more responsible males would have been.[77]

In the Soviet Union, officials called such demonstrations *bab'i bunty*, or "women's riots." A *bab'i* was both more and less than a woman. She was a hag, a noisy, uneducated peasant, an irrational person given to random and uncontrolled protest. Officials nevertheless feared her. When a man named Dobychin called a meeting of peasant women in March 1930 to explain the process of creating a collective farm, they screamed at him and dragged him off the stage. Before he could leave town, the wife of the church watchman rang the bell, summoning the rest of the women in the village. To end the protest, he had to call out the militia.[78]

The French Revolution, with its shifting alliances, offered many models for female action, from the Parisian market women who marched twelve miles to Versailles to demand bread to the Society of Revolutionary Republican Women who demanded the vote and the right to bear arms.[79] A crowd redefined the terms of good behavior, as it did in a number of French villages in 1794 as women, outraged at the Revolutionary government's attacks on religion, banded together to seize the keys or occupy the bell-towers of churches. "It is always the women who are the first to disobey," one official exclaimed. In one protest, a core group walked through their village inviting women to leave their housework or sewing to join them. "Do you want to be with us? Do you want the keys in the church?" they asked. When officials looked for evidence that an outside agitator had led the women, they said again and again, "We incited each other." A woman named Hélène Dujon bragged that she "would have been quite angry to have missed it."[80]

In different times and places, the demonstrative power of such protests derived from the participants' reputations as otherwise well-behaved women. In Wyandotte, Kansas, in 1869, a gaggle of women brought their knitting into a newly opened saloon. The temperance movement was then in full flower, and they weren't about to see their peaceful town contaminated, as they imagined, by drunken husbands and sodden songs. They sat quietly in the saloon, knitting socks or sweaters or whatever it was they had in their bags. At night, they welcomed reinforcements. At the end of the second day, the dismayed saloon-keeper packed up and left town. As long as the ladies sat there, he said, no man would dare to enter.[81] Two decades later in a Midwestern mining town, Mary

Harris Jones, known to her followers as "Mother Jones," led a parade of miners' wives out of the hills carrying brooms and mops for weapons and tin pans for cymbals and drums. Surprising the militia sent to stop male organizers, they marched over a mountain pass into the next town and won the majority of workers to their cause.[82] In demonstrations like this, women parodied their own "best" behavior.

In eastern Nigeria in 1929, women demonstrators went further, inviting officials to recognize the primal power of their reproductive bodies. Outraged at a proposed increase in taxes at a time when prices for palm oil were falling, fifteen thousand Igbo-Ibibio women stripped off their clothes. Wearing only girdles and headdresses of green leaves and armed with nothing but cooking utensils, they converged on British imperial posts, looting stores and humiliating government officials with bawdy songs. When a contingent of soldiers threatened, they lifted their skimpy skirts and said in defiance, "Shoot your mothers." The men did shoot. Fifty women died.[83] But they left an indelible mark on Nigerian history. In July 2002, female protesters from six communities occupied a Chevron-Texaco oil facility, holding British, American, Canadian, and Nigerian workers hostage while they negotiated for community development projects and scholarships for their children. As the *Toronto Star* reported, "The women kept their hold on the terminal by threatening to take off their clothes—a powerful traditional shaming gesture—in a last-ditch gesture to humiliate the company." Soon women from other villages followed, seizing auxiliary flow stations and pipelines. As Dorcas Dakari, one of the leaders explained, "For a long time Chevron has neglected us; they treat us as if we do not exist."[84]

In Argentina in the 1970s, a riot would have been impossible. The ruling junta celebrated nothing so much as order, and after decades of political upheaval, some people welcomed their firmness. Promising to restore respect for God, Country, and Family,

they quietly removed thousands of dissidents, while numbed opponents looked the other way. Many of the "disappeared" were students or young couples with children. In autumn 1977, middle-aged
women wearing white kerchiefs began to appear every Thursday in
the Plaza de Mayo, the central square of Buenos Aires. They
walked quietly, carrying placards that said things like "Where is my
son?" At first, the government tried to dismiss them as *locas*—
"crazy women." Then it tried terror. The women continued to
walk. What began as a simple demonstration became an international movement that eventually attracted the attention of human
rights organizations around the world.[85]

There are hundreds of examples from all over the world of supposedly "traditional" women banding together to make history. In
2004, Wangari Muta Maathai was awarded the Nobel Peace Prize
for her decades of work with rural women in Africa. Born near the
provincial capital of Nyeri, Kenya, in 1940, she grew up in a world
of "abundant rains, rivers, streams, clean drinking water" where
mothers and daughters worked together to cultivate sweet pota-
toes, beans, maize, and wheat, and where storytelling was a female
art. Educated in Catholic mission schools in Kenya, and in the
United States and Germany, she became the first woman in East
and Central Africa to receive a Ph.D. Married in Kenya to an aspiring politician, she became the mother of three children and a university professor. But she did not forget her rural heritage.[86]

In the 1970s, a group of women at the university in Nairobi
where she taught began to meet with rural women "to listen to each
other's problems." She knew that firewood was running out and
that women had to go long distances to get water, but she hadn't
realized that children were also suffering from malnutrition as their
overworked mothers increasingly relied on processed white bread,
rice, margarine, and sweetened tea. A vision of the past animated
her hopes for the future. "Why don't we plant trees?" she said
to her friends in the university. "Why don't you do it?" they

responded. So she did. "I would not have thought of going to organize men," she recalled. "First of all, I don't think they would have
listened to me anyway." But in any case, it was the women who
worked the land. Although some men warned their wives against
Maathai, because she was an educated woman and divorced, both
men and women eventually recognized the value of what she was
doing. As the trees came back, so did water, firewood, and fruit.
Working together, village women discovered that there was no
magic to reforestation, that "a person who cannot read or write can
plant trees that grow with the same dignity as those planted by persons who have a diploma."[87]

As the movement spread, Kenya's repressive one-party state hit
back. "When you start working with the environment seriously, the
whole arena comes: human rights, women's rights, environmental
rights, children's rights—everybody's rights," Maathai explains.
She lost her job, then her home. She and her followers were beaten
and jailed. But the movement grew. "The wind swept me," she told
an interviewer. "That seems to be my way of life. I stand somewhere and the wind sweeps me. But whenever I'm swept, I try to
germinate."[88] Maathai hasn't left her own history to chance. The
author of several books, she makes her speeches and essays available on a sophisticated website devoted to raising money and public
support for her cause.[89] Like Stanton, she knows that a movement is
more likely to survive if its participants take responsibility for pre-
serving its history.

Then and Now

Elizabeth Cady Stanton believed in progress. Vacationing in the
south of France in 1892, she observed rural laborers in the shadows
of cathedrals and fortresses and felt grateful for having been born
in a nation unburdened with the shadows of history. "How everything differed from America, and even from the plain below!" she

wrote. The peasants spoke a strange patois, and they clung to it "with astonishing pertinacity. Their agricultural implements are not less quaint than their speech. The plow is a long beam with a most primitive share in the middle, a cow at one end, and a boy at the other. The grain is cut with a sickle and threshed with a flail on the barn floor, as in Scripture times." She gave thanks for all the progress the world had made in her lifetime.[90]

If she could observe the lives of middle-class women in the United States today, would she conclude that her dream had been worth it?

On April 8, 2005, fifty of the world's leading female photographers filmed American women doing whatever it was they normally did in a day. This would not be a Book of Days but a book built from a single day, a glimpse of dozens of women simultaneously enacting their lives.

At first glance, nothing could be less like the stylized illuminations in medieval manuscripts. These women have names. Many face full-front to the camera, proudly announcing their identities. Some are famous, most obscure. They range from a twenty-nine-year-old former model and aspiring race car driver named Leilani Monter to an institutionalized victim of Alzheimer's disease. The book includes opera diva Denyce Graves, "Queen of Bluegrass" Rhonda Vincent, and a twenty-eight-year-old Muslim hiphop artist named Haero Dizaye. The most astonishing picture may be the one of Pat Derby, a California animal trainer, and the nine-thousand-pound elephant she lives with. "She is like our daughter, our little princess," Derby says. "If she were a human child, she'd probably be at Stanford or Yale by now." There are also pictures of a suburban housewife folding laundry, a cancer patient surrounded by her family, and the plump proprietor of a day-care center sprawled on the floor with her napping charges.[91]

Media celebrities, exotic hobbies, automatic washing machines, and institutional care for infants and the aged—all these things add up to a fast-paced, wealthy, and technologically sophisticated world radically different, one would suppose, from anything Christine de Pizan could have imagined. Yet the overall theme of this work could have come straight out of *The Book of the City of Ladies.* As the preface explains, *A Day in the Life of the American Woman* was created as "a testimony to the energy, ingenuity, determination, bravery, and tenderness" of its subjects. "What a great thing, to celebrate women!" one contributor exclaimed. Leave out Christine's homage to the Virgin Mary, and her argument could have been theirs. Yes, the moral is different. In 2005, the issue is not what will please God, but what a woman might do to create a life "that is personally fulfilling." For most, that means work, family, and friendship.[92]

Given the increased visibility of women in public life over the past thirty years, the emphasis on personal fulfillment is telling. There is very little if anything in this book about commitment to some larger community or cause. A self-professed "girly-girl" now serving as an army medic in Baghdad talks about the challenge of proving herself as a soldier but not about the war itself. The biographical sketch of a double-amputee wounded in Iraq notes that she ended up in the military because "she found that friends whose values she shared all seemed to be in the National Guard," but it says nothing about what those values might be. Nor do the sketches of a pregnant prosecutor in Philadelphia or a Hmong state senator in Minnesota say anything at all about politics.[93]

The closest anyone in this collection comes to a political statement is Cherilyn Holter, pictured outside her home in Hydaburg, Alaska, where she works to record and preserve stories told in her native Haida. She was herself a fluent speaker until her parents enrolled her in a Head Start program. Her grandparents warned her "that from now on it had to be English only. In their day, when the missionaries came to civilize us, it was brutal. If the children spoke Haida, they were beaten." Now she is trying to recover what has been lost.[94] This is, of course, a feel-good book. Too many allusions to controversial topics would surely have gotten in the way of the celebration.

Yet the stance of the book is surprising, especially given the backgrounds of the contributors. Among the fifty-six photographers and journalists were women who had covered an Armenian earthquake, the Three Mile Island nuclear disaster, the impact of Agent Orange in Vietnam, the Palestinian intifada, the release of Nelson Mandela from prison, and events in Iraq before as well as after the 2003 American invasion. On previous assignments, they had photographed Mexican volcanoes, Australian aborigines, and victims of domestic violence, as well as American celebrities. They have been based in New Delhi, Hong Kong, Budapest, and Hanoi, as well as in Austin, Texas; Portland, Oregon; Fort Lauderdale, Florida; and Park City, Utah. One has covered ten Olympic competitions. Another has worked as an official photographer for Vice President Cheney. Eleven have received the Pulitzer Prize. This assignment seemed different. One photographer said, "I felt a complete connection in a way I'd never experienced before." An editor summed up the feeling of the group when she said, "It was truly a rewarding time and the process was so supportive. Women work well together and I made some great friends."[95]

Was stepping aside from public issues a kind of furlough? Or would politics have intruded on the harmony they hoped to find among American women?

Anne Day's two-page spread on the Salisbury, Connecticut, chapter of the Red Hat Society captures the spirit of celebration that pervades the book. Devoted to women over fifty, the Red Hat Society has only one objective—having fun. Founded in California in 1998, it now has a million members. The official Red Hat website reports that the standard answer to the question "What do you do?" is "Nothing." The Salisbury group meets once a month to attend movies, Broadway shows, or just for cocktails. "We're not interested in saving the world," one woman explained, "just having a good time." In Day's photographs, they are surely doing that. Dressed in bright red hats, they are gathered around a park bench blowing bubbles with the abandon of a group of toddlers. As the official website explains, "We see this group as an opportunity for those who have shouldered various responsibilities at home and in the community their whole lives, to say goodbye to burdensome responsibilities and obligations for a little while."[96]

Still, some members of the society express an interest in being noticed, if not remembered. A Red Hat website features a bright purple T-shirt with the motto "Well-behaved women seldom make history."[97] These women have decided to make history by resisting the impulse to solve other people's problems, at home and at work, and by concentrating on their own friendships and pleasure. What will be the long-term impact of that behavior, only history will tell.

Chapter Six

ॐ

WAVES

$\mathcal{W}$here did they come from, those brash young women sprawled in living rooms talking through the night, or crowded into borrowed offices mimeographing manifestos? In the 1960s as Vietnam war protests disrupted college campuses and Black Power erupted in urban ghettoes, a surprising number of women in the United States began to misbehave. They disturbed public meetings, defaced subway posters, and shouted their irreverent slogans in the streets. In January 1968, some of them carried a papier-mâché coffin to an antiwar parade in Washington, D.C., and declared that traditional womanhood was dead.

In March of 1968, in a long article in the *New York Times Magazine*, Martha Lear acknowledged the emergence of a new movement. "Proponents call it the Second Feminist Wave," she wrote, "the first having ebbed after the glorious victory of suffrage and disappeared, finally, into the great sandbar of Togetherness."[1] Her label stuck. "Second-wave feminism" became the catchall label for a resurgent women's movement.[2]

First wave/second wave. The image was inherently historical, but also confusing. In the 1960s, few Americans knew anything any longer about the campaign that had culminated in the passage of the Women's Suffrage Amendment in 1920. The illustrations in the

Times article reinforced that ignorance. One was an oversized cartoon of a 1910 suffragist holding a limp pennant proclaiming "Votes for Women." In her plumed hat, the banner-waving suffragist looked like a bespectacled version of Mrs. Banks, the ditzy mother who neglects her children while parading for women's rights in the 1964 Disney movie *Mary Poppins*. Lear admitted that her own initial response to the new militancy was amusement; she could not help associating it with the old-fashioned suffragists who, to career women like herself, were almost comic in their intensity. But as she researched her story, she realized that something new and important was happening, not only among the professional women who had organized the National Organization for Women (NOW) in 1966 but among young radicals. Lear's article is now forgotten, but her notion that the new movement represented a "second wave" persists.

In fact, some aspects of second-wave feminism do have an uncanny resemblance to the nineteenth-century women's movement—which helps to explain why Elizabeth Cady Stanton's memoir, *Eighty Years and More*, was so appealing when it reappeared in the 1970s. Stanton's book described the silencing of women at the World Anti-Slavery Convention in 1842, her domestic discontent after she and Henry moved to Seneca Falls a few years later, and the seemingly accidental gathering that led to the landmark women's rights convention. She recounted her own forays onto the speaker's circuit, the disruptive behavior of demonstrators at Independence Hall in 1876, and the outrage following the publication of *The Woman's Bible* in 1895. All this seemed familiar. Sixties feminism had its own harried housewives, silenced activists, happenstance gatherings, provocative demonstrations, and outraged public. Like Stanton's movement, second-wave feminism developed out of the ferment of racial conflict and the frustrations of educated women denied full participation in public life. As in the nineteenth century, the movement of the 1960s spread into unexpected corners, transforming fundamental aspects of American life. And, like its predecessor, it aroused female as well as male opposition.

Just as scholars have reassessed the history of the nineteenth-century movement, they are now beginning to reinterpret the "second wave." The broad distinction between student radicals and the professional women who founded NOW persists, but recent research has identified a much broader movement, one shaped by the activities of women of color and by religious organizations like the YWCA. The new feminism penetrated divinity schools and small-town PTAs as well as universities and communes. The new scholarship also broadens the chronological scope of the story, showing how the supposedly quiet fifties actually prepared the way for the explosions that followed. Because so many activists have now written memoirs, their stories provide a fascinating counterpoint to the quite different memoir Stanton wrote a century earlier.

The Emergence of Second-Wave Feminism

The harried housewife is by now a classic figure in the history of the 1960s. In 1963, so the story goes, Betty Friedan diagnosed "the problem that has no name," the mysterious angst of suburban women who seemingly had it all, yet felt empty and unfulfilled. Women were depressed, Friedan argued, because they sought fulfillment in the empty rituals of housework, sex, and consumption. Middle-class housewives didn't need therapy, they needed more to do. Grateful readers turned *The Feminine Mystique* into a best seller and its title into a household word. "My secret scream as I stir the oatmeal, iron the blue jeans, and sell pop at the Little League baseball games is 'Stop the World, I want to get on before it's too late!'" a thirty-seven-year-old Wyoming mother wrote.[3]

The Feminine Mystique reassured readers who had already begun to make changes in their lives. In Thunder Bay, Ontario, Canada, Lois Miriam Wilson, ministerial candidate and mother of four,

devoured the book. Her oldest daughter, who was thirteen at the
time, remembers that as her mother read, she would periodically
cry out, "That's right!" But, contrary to popular assumption, its
appeal was not confined to housewives. Susan Brownmiller, single
and a free-lance writer living in Manhattan, found herself on every
page. "*The Feminine Mystique* changed my life," she recalls.[4]

It also helped to motivate women in the U.S. government who
were already engaged in expanding opportunities for women. They
found their moment in 1964, when a conservative Southern congressman, hoping to defeat a comprehensive civil rights act, introduced an amendment barring discrimination in employment on the
basis of sex as well as race. He assumed his addition was so ridiculous it would induce Northern congressmen to vote no on the
whole bill. But Martha Griffiths, a Republican congresswoman
from Michigan, had long wanted just such a law. With the support
of aging suffragists and the blessing of the first lady, "Lady Bird"
Johnson, Griffiths forged a coalition who lobbied for the bill. Her
speech on the floor of the House warned that a "vote against this
amendment today by a white man is a vote against his wife, or his
widow, or his daughter, or his sister." The *Wall Street Journal* was
aghast. If the government actually tried to enforce this ridiculous
law, employers needing typists might be forced to advertise for
"people with small nimble fingers," then hire the "first male midget
with unusual dexterity" who showed up.[5]

They needn't have worried. Although the bill passed, the new
Equal Employment Opportunity Commission showed no inclination to challenge sex discrimination. On June 20, 1966, Congresswoman Griffiths denounced the EEOC in Congress. "I would
remind them," she said, "that they took an oath to uphold the law,
not just the part of it that they are interested in." Ten days later, at a
conference of state commissions on the status of women, she and a
dozen other women met in Betty Friedan's hotel room to talk about
forming a national women's lobby. The next day, as they sat around

two lunch tables plotting strategy, Friedan took a napkin and wrote down a name: the National Organization for Women. Then she added a line defining its mission—to "bring women into the mainstream of American society, *now*."[6]

The formal "Statement of Purpose" passed at NOW's first convention that fall expressed the same urgency. Although nearly half of women in the United States now worked outside the home, they were clustered in low-paying service and clerical occupations. Only 1 percent of federal judges were female, fewer than 4 percent of the nation's lawyers, and merely 7 percent of its doctors. Despite studies and reports produced since President John F. Kennedy appointed the first Commission on the Status of Women in 1961, things were actually getting worse. Women earned on average 60 percent of the wages paid to men. The NOW manifesto insisted that "*the time has come* for a new movement," "*the time has come* to move beyond . . . abstract argument, discussion and symposia," and "*the time has come* to confront, with concrete action, the conditions that now prevent women from enjoying the equality of opportunity and freedom which is their right."[7]

Most of the signatories had indeed waited a long time. Pauli Murray was an experienced civil rights lawyer. A graduate of Howard University, she had the distinction of having been rejected by the University of North Carolina on the basis of her race and for advanced study at Harvard University Law School on the basis of her sex. She had been working hard on the problem of racial discrimination and was ready as well to do something about sex discrimination. She was not alone. Women who had worked in government agencies or in labor unions were stepping forward. As Murray recalled, "unconsciously we had been trained in everybody else's business and when we finally turned to ourselves we had all of this conditioning and training." Although the *New York Times* reported NOW's first convention on the women's pages beneath recipes for turkey and stuffing, experienced activists were poised to take on the turkeys. In the words of Ruth Gage-Colby, a veteran of many causes, the new movement had made feminism "a living thing."[8]

During these same years, as the standard histories have long told us, a different, more radical, version of feminism was taking shape in the heat and danger of the segregated South. In 1964, two young civil rights workers, Casey Hayden and Mary King, circulated an anonymous position paper to staff members of the Student Non-Violent Coordinating Committee in Mississippi. The simplified version of their story says they were upset at being handed typing and other routine tasks while male activists dominated leadership positions. The story is actually more complex than that. Hayden and King were both themselves in the inner circle. They came to feminism through a combination of reading, experience, and shared discussion. In college, King's philosophy professor had introduced her to the works of the French feminist Simone de Beauvoir, whose 1953 book *The Second Sex* had condemned marriage as a form of slavery and challenged women to make their own history. While living in poverty as organizers for SNCC, King and Hayden worked through King's copy of *The Second Sex* until it "was underlined, creased, marked up, and finally coverless." They applied De Beauvoir's insight that human beings are responsible for their own destiny both to their work as organizers and their situation as women.[9]

When King sat down to draft the now famous position paper, she was "shaken with doubt," fearing that others would ridicule the ideas she and Hayden had so fervently discussed. "Assumptions of male superiority are as widespread and deep-rooted and every much as crippling to the woman as the assumptions of white supremacy are to the Negro," she wrote. Why else would SNCC leaders routinely refer to adult women as "girls"? Why did they automatically assign them clerical work and cooking "and the assistant kind of administrative work but rarely the 'executive' kind"?

Her heart was palpitating as she typed, but she persisted, hoping that her beloved SNCC was different from other groups, that it "had the potential to see itself both as the oppressed and the oppressor." She was wrong about that.[10]

One night, SNCC staff went to a cool spot to relax and drink wine. (Some people remember marijuana as well.) Stokely Carmichael, handsome and witty, began joking around, making fun of himself and everybody else. As King recalls, "He began to gesticulate dramatically, slapping his thighs and spinning around, thrusting his arm, silhouetted against the moon like a Javanese shadow puppet." Finally he came to the paper on women. Looking straight at King, he asked, "What is the position of women in SNCC?" Collapsing in hilarity, he answered his own question: "The position of women in SNCC is prone!" She laughed too, believing he was "poking fun at his own attitudes."[11] But nothing changed.

A year later, King and Hayden sent out forty copies of a revised version of the paper to other women in the peace and freedom movements. Sex, like race, created a "common-law caste system," it began. "Many people who are very hip to the implications of the racial caste system, even people in the movement, don't seem to be able to see the sexual-caste system and if the question is raised they respond with: 'That's the way it's supposed to be. There are biological differences.' "[12] Within SNCC itself, this was not the best time to make such an argument; the organization was then wracked by internal dissension and would soon invite white volunteers to leave.[13] Outside SNCC, however, the response was electric.

In December 1965, two women took copies of the "memo" to the national convention, at the University of Illinois, of Students for a Democratic Society, a radical antiwar group. "When the SNCC letter from Mary and Casey was read aloud," Marilyn Webb recalls, "it precipitated a three-day marathon discussion about women in SDS. We'd been dealing with civil rights, with the Vietnam War, we'd been urging resistance to the draft with slogans like

'Women Say Yes to Men Who Say No'—that had been our mentality. This was one of the first conversations where we talked about what was happening with *us*." The following spring a pacifist periodical called *Liberation* reprinted the memo, further spreading the flames.[14]

The personal encounters and small-group discussions that fueled women's liberation had begun. The new consciousness grew person to person, as converts exchanged books, manifestos, and their own stories. When Stokely Carmichael repeated his joke about the women in SNCC, women who had experienced sexual harassment or rape in student movements were outraged, and said so.[15] Visits from friends turned into all-night sessions of consciousness-raising. Activists carried mimeographed position papers in their backpacks as they entered graduate school or took new jobs. As historian Ruth Rosen has wryly observed, "A good epidemiologist could have traced the rapid transmission of the infectious enthusiasm."[16]

Enthusiasm led to action. In New York, radicals released white mice at a commercial bridal fair in Madison Square Garden. In Seattle, a frightened young student spontaneously stood against *Playboy* and its bunnies by staging a protest at a student event. At Yale Divinity School, female graduate students occupied the only toilet in the library until the school agreed to remove the sign that said "Men."[17]

The most famous demonstration occurred in Atlantic City in September 1968. A hundred women, some of whom had come from as far away as Florida, carried posters and paraded a live sheep on the boardwalk outside the Miss America Pageant. The *New York Post* reported that they planned to burn their bras. But since city regulations forbade fires on the boardwalk, they threw bras, girdles, eyelash curlers, home permanents, and copies of *Good Housekeeping* and *Playboy* into a "Freedom Trash Can." "Down with these shoes," said a sixty-eight-year-old woman as she dumped her high heels. "And down with bound feet!" yelled another. "Had the media called us 'girdle-burners,' nearly every woman in the country would have rushed to join us," Carol Hanisch recalls. As it was, the organizers were deluged with mail. "I've been waiting all my life for something like this to come along," one woman wrote.[18]

Poet Robin Morgan probably started the rumor about bra-burning as a device to get press attention. A recent convert to feminism, she had polished her skills as a political prankster among the Yippies, a countercultural antiwar group led by Abbie Hoffman and Jerry Rubin. When Yippie leaders asked her to help with a demonstration at the Democratic National Convention in Chicago, she said she was too busy organizing the action in Atlantic City. "You've got to be kidding," they said, "the revolution is going to start in Chicago." "No, the revolution is going to start in Atlantic City," she responded. The violence that erupted in Chicago framed the women's demonstration a week later. "We don't want to incite or provoke," Morgan told the *New York Times*. "We don't want another Chicago." In Atlantic City, there was neither tear gas nor tears. Although angry onlookers taunted, "Go back to Russia!" "Man-haters!" "Lesbians!," the demonstrators were jubilant. "We had broken some chains," Carol Hanisch recalls. "We had dared to expose and defy this idol of femininity and replace it with the hope of feminism."[19]

Feminism Spreads, Explodes, and Splinters

In February of 1970, Robin Morgan and her friends took over an underground newspaper called *Rat* and produced an all-woman issue. In her own essay, Morgan issued a defiant challenge to the men of the radical student movements:

> We are rising, powerful in our unclean bodies; bright glow-
> ing, mad in our inferior brains; wild hair flying, wild eyes

staring, wild voice keening. . . . We are rising with a fury
older and potentially greater than any force in history, and
this time we will be free or no one will survive. *Power to all
the people or to none.*[20]

When her anthology *Sisterhood Is Powerful* was published later that
year, its red-and-white cover featured a logo designed by Morgan
and her husband, Kenneth Pitchford. Over the symbol for
"female," they superimposed the radicals' clenched fist.[21]

Classic histories of the movement distinguish "liberal feminists"
like the founders of NOW from "radical feminists" like Morgan.
Liberals, so the story goes, worked within the political system,
drafting legislation, lobbying legislators, and supporting candidates for office. Radicals thrived on street theater and contentious,
small-group discussions devoted to consciousness-raising. There is
truth in these distinctions. NOW had a president and board of
directors; radicals disdained top-down leadership. Attempting to
operate by consensus, they splintered into dozens of short-lived
cadres with provocative names, like WITCH, which stood for
"Women's International Terrorist Conspiracy from Hell." (Or was
it "Women Inspired to Tell Their Collective History"? Or
"Women Interested in Toppling Consumer Holidays"? Radicals
liked to keep people guessing.) For some women, the greatest liberation was in embracing the very stereotypes critics used against
them. "WITCH may not have known much about the real history
of witches," writer Robin Morgan recalled, "but WITCH had joie
de vivre."[22]

Up close, however, such distinctions break down. Some members of NOW plotted sit-ins and demonstrations. Some radicals
morphed into savvy businesswomen. More important, neither
NOW nor the most visible of the radical organizations encom-
passed the full range of feminist energy. In the late sixties and early
seventies, there were multiple feminisms, sometimes acting in con-

Radcliffe graduates, from the Radcliffe Archives. Their placards employ a
symbol used on Robin Morgan's 1970 book, *Sisterhood Is Powerful*.

cert, more frequently bubbling up in separate places and taking
their own direction.[23] Midwestern housewives, Manhattan activists,
California college students, Catholic nuns, nursing mothers, teachers, secretaries, and even a few eighth-graders were finding new
ways of making a difference in the world. By the early seventies,
brushfires of feminism were erupting all over the United States.

Bev Mitchell was spending a weekend in Chicago when she
stumbled onto a women's liberation rally in Grant Park. "It was
just about the most exciting thing I had ever been to," she recalls.
Back home in Cedar Rapids, Iowa, she helped to establish a
women's liberation group that lobbied for changes in the state's
civil rights code. She jokes that her group included "scary, hippie
women . . . dripping with beads," as well as the wife of a major

industrialist. The men on the civil rights commission "were scared to death that between their wives, who were capable of incredible fury, and these hippies, God knows what would happen. So protection for women was put in the code." Her group celebrated at a summer encampment for women and children. Every morning they "raised a bra on an improvised flagpole while a member . . . played 'God Bless America' on her kazoo."[24]

In New York in the summer of 1973, Jane Galvan-Lewis and other black activists began meeting in the backroom of a beauty parlor. That August, they held a press conference announcing their intention to form a National Black Feminist Organization and inviting those interested to call. "We thought we were going to have about twenty-five phone calls," Galvan-Lewis recalls. Instead, the "phones rang for about a week. Solid. . . . We didn't know what to do with ourselves." To their surprise, they discovered that black women as far away as Los Angeles were already meeting in small consciousness-raising groups. In November, four hundred women showed up for an Eastern Regional Conference held at the Cathedral of St. John the Divine on New York's Upper West Side. The testimonies of the women "filled the crowded room like vapor," wrote a reporter for *Essence*. "The talk was of being on welfare, of not having day care facilities and black men; of color discrimination within the race, salary and job discrimination, of being a lesbian, of being treated as a sex object, of learning to love oneself and black men." When a Chicago woman read a report of the conference, she was ecstatic. "I thought I was the only black woman on the planet Earth who felt the way I felt."[25]

At Long Beach State University in California in 1969, Ana Nieto-Gómez and her friends named their consciousness-raising group Las Hijas de Cuauhtémoc after an early women's organization that had operated on both sides of the Mexico–United States border in the early twentieth century. They were also inspired by the feistiness of older women they knew. "In my mind, I was acting like my mom, like my aunts, like the Chicanas from San Bernardino," Nieto-Gómez remembers. Male leaders of the Chicano student group at Long Beach felt threatened. When she won the group's election for president, some of them hung her in effigy, then staged a mock mass and burial. She responded to all this intimidation by "learning to cuss." The room was silent the first time she used a four-letter word, but "all of a sudden I had everybody's attention." Swearing, especially in Spanish, was "the only way to stop the dudes, the only way to get them to listen to you."[26]

When Nancy Hawley heard a radical feminist dismiss pregnancy as "barbaric," she decided the women's movement needed her voice. In the spring of 1969, shortly after giving birth to her second child, she offered a workshop on women's bodies at a New England gathering of women's liberation groups. By December 1970, she and her friends had borrowed $1,500 and published a 136-page self-help booklet that interspersed personal stories with factual information. Its title, *Women and Their Bodies,* was straightforward but unimaginative. When it came time to print a second edition, somebody shouted, "Hey, it isn't women and *their* bodies—it's us and our bodies." By 1980, the Simon and Schuster edition of *Our Bodies, Ourselves* had earned over half a million dollars in royalties for their nonprofit foundation.[27]

Ada Maria Isasi-Diaz, a Cuban refugee who had been a Catholic missionary in Peru, was working in a Sears store in Rochester, New York, when a friend invited her to attend a conference on women's priestly ordination. When a speaker invited those who felt called to ordination to stand, she turned to a Dominican friend next to her and said, "Mary, I do not want to stand. I am tired of battles." But she was soon on her feet, sustained by the "cloud of witnesses" around her. When she sat down, she thought, "I have been born, baptized, and confirmed in this new life all at once!"[28]

Cheri Register and Gerri Heseltine met in a picket line outside a men-only grill in Minneapolis in the late summer of 1970.

Frustrated with the slow pace of change, they founded the Emma Willard Task Force to address sexism in the public schools. Working without compensation, they were soon regular speakers at training programs run by the Minnesota Department of Education. Although they had to put their own education and career objectives on hold, they began to see results. One of their curriculum packets included a paper by Connie Dvorkin, an eighth-grader in a New York suburb who had heard about women's liberation on the radio and had sent away for information. "Ironically the very night I was reading it I was baby-sitting and watching TV," Dvorkin wrote. Five months before, she would have laughed at the antics of two women on *I Love Lucy* who tried unsuccessfully to "be equal to the men for one night." Instead she was horrified at the unconscious sexism she had learned from the media and in school.[29]

As word spread, previously invisible women began their own revolutions. In a Chicago law firm, one morning in 1977, a legal secretary named Iris Rivera decided not to make coffee. "I don't drink coffee," she said. "It's not listed as one of my job duties, and ordering the secretaries to fix the coffee is carrying the role of homemaker too far." When her firm fired her, a feminist group called Women Employed took up the cause. As network cameras hummed, they dragged a coffee-maker and a bag of used grounds into the office and staged a demonstration for lawyers on how to make coffee. Rivera got her job back.[30]

Stories like these make it all sound easy. In fact, there was intense, often wounding, opposition. Women in minority groups were pilloried as traitors to their people. Feminists everywhere were stigmatized as "man-haters" or "crazies." After Irene Blea organized a conference on Chicana feminism at the University of Colorado in 1977, name-calling escalated into vandalism. "There's nothing worse in a Colorado winter than having somebody egg your car and then 't.p.' it and then have it freeze," she remembers.[31]

When the Equal Rights Amendment slid through Congress in

1971 with little discussion and virtually no opposition, a lawyer and political writer named Phyllis Schlafley spun into action. Her flagship organization, Stop ERA, forged a powerful alliance of women, clergy, and conservative politicians. The response from the mainstream media was more subtle. In an editorial titled "Henpecked Congress," the *New York Times* scolded the nation's lawmakers for paying more attention to the "ladies' gallery" than to sober lawyers who predicted chaos should the amendment pass.[32]

By then, the FBI was investigating the new feminism. Some in the Bureau thought the women's movement might have a "positive" effect in fragmenting radical groups, but they weren't sure whether the women themselves posed a danger. They simply didn't know what to make of groups that called themselves things like BITCH, Uppity Women, or Keep on Truckin', or how to deal with reports from the field that said things like "This group has no leaders, dues, or organization." A Washington, D.C., group ended up on the FBI's armed and dangerous list, even though its only identifiable weapon was a newspaper called *off our backs*. As historian Ruth Rosen has suggested, the fragmented politics of the movement "flummoxed even the most experienced agents."[33]

That didn't stop them from recruiting informants. One of these unnamed observers was entranced by "the extreme fuzzy appearance" of some feminists' hair. She believed they achieved this effect by braiding their hair while wet. From the looks of it, she reported, "they apparently really didn't bother to try and comb it out afterward." This kind of material makes entertaining reading today, but it also suggests the confusion the new feminism provoked. Who were these women? And what did they want? The person who infiltrated a consciousness-raising group in Baltimore in 1968 was similarly puzzled. Most of the members were young women who appeared to be "either lonely or confined to the home with small children." Their main purpose seemed to be to get together to talk about their problems, but they also wanted "to go out and work in what kind of jobs they wanted," and they thought their husbands ought "to share in the housework and in raising their children." The FBI didn't see any immediate danger, though, being men, they might have worried a bit about the housework.[34]

The most wrenching conflicts were within the movement. Black feminists accused predominantly white groups of racism. Socialists disdained the constant rounds of consciousness-raising as bourgeois self-indulgence. Groups committed to "leaderless" organizing condemned "stars" who they thought hogged media attention. While Schlafley condemned the new *Ms.* magazine, launched in 1971, as "a series of sharptongued, high-pitched, whining complaints by unmarried women," aggrieved feminists launched more creative attacks on its editor, Gloria Steinem, claiming she had covered up a "ten-year association with the CIA stretching from 1959 to 1969." According to the radical New York group Redstockings, *Ms.* magazine was actually "hurting the women's liberation movement." When the *Ms.* foundation helped to fund a women's conference in Vermont, angry radicals walked out. "You can't take that money," they insisted. "That money is tainted, that money is suspect."[35]

Meanwhile, NOW was dealing with a more difficult issue. After the riot at the Stonewall Inn in June 1969 launched the modern gay rights movement, lesbian feminists began to assert their own identity. When Rita Mae Brown, a younger staffer at NOW, casually referred to herself as the "token lesbian in the room," Betty Friedan was incensed. Fearing that public discussions of sexuality would derail progress toward economic and political reforms, she began muttering about "the lavender menace." When Susan Brownmiller, in an article in the *New York Times,* lightly dismissed Friedan's charge as a "lavender herring," lesbians among New York radicals thought she was dismissing *them.* On May 1, 1970, they got their revenge on the entire movement. As four hundred women listened to the opening speeches at a purported Second Congress to Unite Women, the lights went out, then came up on seventeen women dressed in custom-made lavender T-shirts and carrying posters that said things like "TAKE A LESBIAN TO LUNCH" or "LESBIANISM *IS* A WOMEN'S LIBERATION PLOT." For two hours the demonstrators controlled the mikes, announcing to all the world that they would not be silenced by fellow feminists. "What is a lesbian?" they asked. "A lesbian is the rage of all women condensed to the point of explosion."[36]

The rifts were predictable. The new feminism was not one thing but many. It was a *movement*—a tremor in the earth, a lift in the wind, a swelling tide. Although there were many groups, there was no unified platform, no single set of texts. Instead there was an exhilarating sense of discovery, a utopian hope that sometimes collapsed into factionalism. Self-appointed vanguards fought sexism, racism, capitalism, compulsory heterosexuality, and each other. The one common commitment was that women be heard.

Rosalyn Baxandall has written: "What I'd like to convey—what I think has been neglected in the books and articles about the women's liberation movement—is the joy we felt. We were, we believed, poised on the trembling edge of a transformation. All the walls and boundaries inside and outside us might be knocked down. There was a yeastiness in the air that made us cocky and strong. Sure, there were splits and backbiting among us, but . . . also fun and great times. For me, the women's liberation movement was love at first sight."[37]

Sara Evans puts it this way: "As it dawned on us that a new movement was coming into being, we had a thrilling sense that we could, in fact, make history."[38]

Making History

When the National Black Feminist Organization convened in New York in 1973, the young Alice Walker was there. In the report she sent to *Ms.*, she said that if this meeting had happened in the

nineteenth century, Frederick Douglass, the legendary black abolitionist who attended the women's rights convention at Seneca Falls
in 1848, would have approved. Douglass's "newspaper would have
been pleased to cover our conference. . . . Women who wanted
their rights did not frighten him, politically or socially, because he
knew his own rights were not diminished by theirs." So why
weren't there any representatives of black magazines and newspapers at this meeting? "Are not black women black news?" she
asked. When she went home and stood in front of a picture of
Douglass that hung on her wall, she asked herself another question:
Why wasn't there a picture of Harriet Tubman on her wall, or a
drawing of Sojourner Truth? "And I thought that if black women
would only start asking questions like that, they'd soon—all of
them—have to begin reclaiming their mothers and grandmothers—and what an enrichment that would be!"[39]

Walker's experience captures an essential quality of the new
feminism. Second-wave feminists rediscovered the past in the act of
making their own history. The Minneapolis educators who rediscovered Emma Willard, or the Chicana activists who named themselves after a revolutionary Mexican group, were not alone. As Ana
Nieto-Gómez explained, history let people know that oppression
"was a result of policy, of policy that could be changed."[40] History
could also offer comfort in a storm. During the turmoil in SNCC, a
volunteer in Tupelo, Mississippi, handed Mary King a typed quotation from Frederick Douglass: "When I ran away from slavery, it
was for myself; when I advocated emancipation, it was for my people; but when I stood up for the rights of women, self was out of the
question, and I found a little nobility in the act." This affirmation
from the past helped King know she was not alone.[41]

Women's stories were virtually absent from formal history as it
was taught in the United States in the 1960s. Female historians were
largely absent as well. The few who wrote about women were outside the academy; those who had managed to land positions in col-

leges or universities knew better than to write about anything that
appeared feminine. Jo Freeman, who entered Berkeley in 1961 as a
precocious fifteen-year-old, looks back in astonishment at the male-
centered education she received. "During my four years in one of
the largest institutions of higher education in the world—and one
with a progressive reputation—I not only never had a woman professor, I never even saw one. Worse yet, I didn't notice."[42]

Ignorance of women's issues was not confined to the fifties or to
state universities. Even in the sixties few undergraduates imagined
the contradictions that would face them on graduation. When
Estelle Freedman was a student at Barnard College, her adviser
suggested she take the one women's history course offered. She
responded that she would rather study "real" history. "Two years
later, my values shaken by the antiwar and student movements, I
was questioning all of my old priorities," she recalls.[43] Sara Evans
remembers only one class at Duke "in which women were
acknowledged to have some historical agency." The professor was
Anne Firor Scott, who "drew on her research on southern white
women to tell us about the importance of women in Progressive
Era politics." But Evans, then preoccupied with other issues, was
unprepared to listen. Again, time away from school and a brief
encounter with a women's liberation group in Chicago in 1968
changed her mind. When she entered graduate school at the University of North Carolina in 1969, she was hungry for more. Since
there were no courses in women's history at UNC, she and other
women students had to teach themselves. "Little did we know that
we were part of a cohort of several thousand across the country,
collectively inventing women's history as a major field of historical
inquiry and women's studies as a discipline."[44]

Fortunately, young women were welcomed into the field by a
few stalwart pioneers, including Evans's undergraduate teacher
Anne Firor Scott. Born into an old Southern family in 1921, Scott
had majored in history at the University of Georgia, then com-

pleted an M.A. at Northwestern before taking a job with the League of Women Voters in 1946. Field trips through New England and the Middle West introduced her to strong-minded women, but the real surprise came in Kentucky and Tennessee. Her astonishment comes through in her journal: "Certainly it is not true, as is sometimes alleged, that Southern women are no good outside the home. The only difference is they don't make such a fuss about it." Scott began graduate work at Harvard in 1947, at the same time as her husband, political scientist Andrew Scott. Six years later, he left with a Ph.D., she with a box full of notes and a toddler. Through two moves and another pregnancy, she continued to work on her dissertation, finally receiving her degree in 1958, when she was thirty-seven years old. By then she was doing a little part-time teaching at the University of North Carolina, where her husband was a faculty member. "An invitation to teach at Duke 'until we can find somebody' launched what would become a thirty-year career." When *The Southern Lady* was published in 1970, former students like Evans were ready to receive it.[45]

Scott's career belies the notion that women were universally in thrall to "the feminine mystique" in the 1950s. Her feminism was nurtured by the women she interviewed in her study of progressive politics but also by the intrepid Southern ladies on her own family tree. "We sometimes say, only half in jest, that historians write their autobiographies into scholarship," she wrote in an afterword to the twenty-fifth-anniversary edition of *The Southern Lady*. Her own work, she admitted, "might give some credence to that notion."[46]

Scott's family were storytellers. She grew up with stories about a "widowed great-great-grandmother left in charge of a plantation in Orange County, Virginia, who was said to have slept in a chair, fully dressed, through the whole Civil War (only of course it was called the War Between the States) so she would not be taken unawares by Yankee soldiers. She had, we were told, with feigned reluctance allowed Ben Butler's men to requisition a barrel of lime which she assured them was the finest flour." There were also stories about "the patriarchal sins" of her Georgia great-grandfather, who was so opposed to women working outside the home he built a schoolhouse in the backyard so his spinster sister could teach without violating his notions of propriety. "Not content with commanding his own children, he forbade an intellectually ambitious daughter-in-law to sign her name when she wrote, as she often did, for the newspaper." That daughter-in-law, Anne's grandmother, was a clubwoman and suffragist, an active member of the League of Women Voters, and "a respected leader in the Baptist church though all her husband's family were staunch Methodists."[47]

Long before the new feminists began their parades, Scott knew that women's history mattered. She was unusual. Gerda Lerner believes that in 1970 there were only five specialists in U.S. history who identified themselves primarily as historians of women. Lerner was one of them. Born in Austria in 1920, she came to the United States in 1939 as a Jewish refugee from Nazism. A passionate student, she was forced to put her dreams of a college education on hold as she labored in a series of unskilled jobs, eventually working herself up to medical technician. After she and her husband, film-writer Carl Lerner, moved to Hollywood, she worked in hospitals, cared for their children, and volunteered for various left-wing groups. In Vienna, the Communist Party had been her one refuge from Hitlerism. In the United States, she was impressed with its commitment to racial justice and equality for women. When she and Carl moved back to New York in 1950, they chose to live in a mixed-race neighborhood, where she worked with local activists to protest blockbusting, and helped to strengthen the public schools. In 1958, almost twenty years after graduating at the head of her class in her lyceum in Austria, she enrolled at the New School in New York, completing a B.A. in four years of part-time study. By 1966, she had a Ph.D. in history from Columbia. To the amusement of her male mentors, she insisted on specializing in women's history. She explains how she came to that decision. "I had long worked with women in their community organizations and I knew in my bones that women build communities. But as I entered academic life as a student, I encountered a world of 'significant knowledge,' in which women seemed not to exist. I never could accept that patriarchal mental construct and resisted it all through my training. My commitment to women's history came out of my life, not out of my head." In 1967, she published *The Grimké Sisters of South Carolina*, a scholarly biography of the two Southern women whose work in the antislavery movement led them to become advocates for women's rights.[48]

Lerner became an engine of change. In 1972, she founded an M.A. program in women's studies at Sarah Lawrence College. When she wrote to the faculty inviting them to assist in developing courses, Joan Kelly congratulated her on the new program but said that because her own field was Renaissance history she wouldn't be able to help. Lerner invited her to lunch. Four hours later, Kelly was still not convinced she had anything to contribute, but she promised to go home and think about it. "That turned out to be the most exciting intellectual adventure I can recall," Kelly later wrote. All she did was ask herself a new question: How would the European Renaissance, "reputed for its liberation from old and confining forms," look if studied from the vantage point of women? "The change I went through was kaleidoscopic. I had not read a new book. I did not stumble upon a new archive. No fresh piece of information was added to anything I knew. But I knew now that the entire picture I had held of the Renaissance was partial, distorted, limited, and deeply flawed by those limitations." In a series of pathbreaking articles, she challenged the familiar time line in Western history. In an essay first published in 1977, she declared flatly that "there was no renaissance for women—at least, not during the Renaissance."[49]

Together, older scholars like Lerner and Scott and new converts like Evans and Kelly began to transform the historical profession in the United States. In the late sixties, the American Historical Association remained, in the words of Berenice Carroll, a "gentlemen's protection society." Although it had admitted women from its founding in 1884, in its first hundred years it had only one female president. Eileen Boris remembers her first attempt to attend an AHA convention. "A jean-clad graduate student, I walked into the Sheraton Boston but turned away at the first sight of men in suits, before even inquiring about the program." Things were little different in the Organization of American Historians, a society for those specializing in U.S. history. When Lerner attended her first OAH convention in 1963, there seemed no way to break into the tightly knit clusters of male professors and their devoted followers. Lerner decided to create her own network. "I just walked up to one or more of the nuns present and asked if I could have lunch or dinner with them. The nuns were always friendly and cheerful and I made some splendid contacts and lifelong friendships."[50]

Similar circumstances had led to the founding in the 1930s of the Berkshire Conference of Women Historians. Excluded from the "smokers" and other informal gatherings through which men built professional connections, a group of about twenty women teaching in women's colleges in the Northeast met for breakfast at the annual AHA convention and later for annual spring retreats somewhere in the Berkshires. The Berkshire group was still meeting in the 1960s, but few younger historians knew anything about it.[51]

Change began in 1969, when two dozen women met at the annual AHA convention in Washington, D.C., and organized a Coordinating Committee on Women in the Historical Profession, which remains today a kind of umbrella organization linked to the AHA and the OAH, and acts as a network for women's issues in other historical organizations.[52] Hilda Smith, then a graduate student at the University of Chicago, helped to produce its newsletter in borrowed quarters at the national office of NOW. "One of my fonder memories is of my elder son as a baby sleeping on mailbags in the NOW headquarters while we were producing the newsletter. It was a cooperative effort on the part of NOW officials (who knew how to operate the printer), my husband, and a number of U of C graduate students, both male and female."[53]

Meeting to meeting, person to person, the new ideas spread. Renate Bridenthal discovered women's history in a free seminar Lerner gave at the Graduate Center of the City University of New York. "Like so many others at the time, I suddenly wondered: Where have all the women been in history? Where have they been in German history, my field of specialization? I had written a Master's thesis on a nineteenth-century male utopian socialist and a Ph.D. dissertation on a nineteenth-century male German historian. Now my mother's stories came to the forefront of my mind. Where was she in German history?"[54] In 1972, Bridenthal and two other historians of Europe gave one of the first women's history panels at an AHA convention. They then delivered the same papers at the spring retreat of the Berkshire conference. "We noticed an age gap between ourselves, then in our thirties, and members of the audience, in their seventies," Bridenthal recalls. "The missing generation was an absent presence, making a statement about the historical profession! Out of this mini-Berks emerged a whole conference in women's history, which was held at Douglas College . . . with about 700 people attending."[55]

The official Berkshire Conference website says there were three hundred people at the Douglas conference, but no matter. There were many times the number the organizers had planned. The Second Berkshire Conference on Women's History, held at Radcliffe College in 1974, drew well over a thousand participants, prompting a long story in the *New York Times*. The male reporter noted that there were cheers in Sanders Theater when Carol Smith-Rosenberg of the University of Pennsylvania challenged the assumption that "women have not been trendsetters, activists or protagonists in the drama of great events." Alice Kessler-Harris of Sarah Lawrence pursued a similar theme, arguing "that women trade unionists were generally tougher bargainers than men, more selfless on the picket line and less willing to compromise in strikes." A Berkeley professor exulted, "Twenty years ago the thought of holding such a conference would never have occurred to me in all my wildest feminist fantasies." Although it was too soon to evaluate the impact of the new enthusiasm, the *Times* reporter predicted that "serious and readable books will be published in profusion."[56] "The Berks" became one of the best-attended history conferences in the United States, in some years rivaling the conventions of much older organizations.

In 1970, Florence Howe, then an assistant professor at Goucher College, approached publishers about reprinting lost works by nineteenth- and early-twentieth-century American women writers. The response was blunt: "There is no money in it." So with the help of fellow activists, she founded the Feminist Press, a nonprofit collective that became a pioneering force in women's history. The first volume off the press was *Life in the Iron Mills*, an 1861 novel by Rebecca Harding Davis, soon followed by Charlotte Perkins Gilman's *The Yellow Wallpaper*, which shortly became a standard text in women's studies courses. By 1979, they had reintroduced readers to the Harlem Renaissance writer Zora Neale Hurston. Other presses began to fill a similar market for historic texts. In 1971, Schocken Books brought out Elizabeth Cady Stanton's 1898 memoir, *Eighty Years and More*. In 1974, Arno Press did a reprint of Stanton's controversial commentary on selected passages in the Bible, calling it *The Original Feminist Attack on the Bible*. In 1978, the University of Illinois Press published Mary Jo and Paul Buhle's one-volume abridgment of the massive *History of Women's Suffrage* produced by Stanton and her associates.

As scholars began to push further and further back into time, they discovered wave after wave of what Gerda Lerner called "feminist consciousness." Long before there was an organized women's rights movement, there were women who questioned the time-honored arrangements between the sexes, and argued for the advancement of women.

Charity Willard came across Christine de Pizan in the 1930s, when she was studying for an M.A. in French at Smith College. For her Ph.D. at Harvard, she prepared an edition of Pizan's unpublished *Livre de la paix* (*Book of Peace*), transcribing it in Paris during the frightening summer of 1939. But the disruptions of war and the lack of a general interest in women's lives ensured that Willard's work, like Pizan's, would remain obscure. Willard defended her thesis on May 28, 1940, "the day Belgium fell to the German invader," and accepted her doctoral diploma during "the week in June that marked the fall of France." During the war, she considered herself "an intellectual refugee" without access to sources. After the war ended, she still found little reinforcement for her interest. When she sought out a renowned medieval scholar at his rural retreat in Ontario, she found him more interested in his stamp collection than in Pizan's manuscripts. In the fall of 1951, Willard was finally able to return to Paris, where, at the Bibliothèque Nationale, she met Suzanne Solente, who was working on a scholarly edition of another of Pizan's manuscripts. But Solente's work, like Willard's, was addressed to specialists.[57]

Natalie Davis, then a graduate student at Harvard, ran across Pizan's *Book of the City of Ladies* that same year. "It was a stunning revelation. I had not known a woman of such literary accomplishment existed in the late medieval period; she had never been mentioned in any of my undergraduate courses. All the more remarkable were her consciousness of women's predicament and the arguments she marshaled in defense of her sex." Although Davis wrote a seminar paper titled "Christine de Pizan as the Prototype of the Professional Literary Woman," she soon turned to other topics, writing her Ph.D. dissertation at Michigan on French artisans. Twenty years later, however, inspired by the women's movement, she pulled out her old paper and began to assign extracts from *City of Ladies* to students in her courses. She did her own translations from the French, or made do with extracts from an English edition printed in London in 1521. As publishers discovered the growing demand for historical works by women, all this changed. In 1982, Davis wrote the preface to a new paperback edition of *City of Ladies,* translated by Earl Jeffrey Richards. Two years later, the same publisher brought out Willard's biography of Pizan.[58]

At the same time, scholars were reassessing the significance of well-known women writers, like Jane Austen, Harriet Beecher Stowe, and Virginia Woolf. "It may seem amazing that so many women of my generation are reading Virginia Woolf for the first time," historian Blanche Cook wrote in an essay in *Signs* in 1979. "But of course it is not at all amazing. She understood that the freedom—personal, economic, and political—to which we aspire connects our work with passion to all our human relations. We were told, on the other hand, that she was a mad, virginal Victorian spinster-wife, precious and elitist. And so we were denied access to the most eloquent creator of a woman-loving socialist feminist vision of the early twentieth century."[59]

Woolf inspired partisans on both sides of the debate over the inclusion of works by women on the list of "great books" taught in colleges and universities. Conservatives seized on those passages in *A Room of One's Own* that disdained feminist advocacy. Reformers responded with counterarguments that unpacked Woolf's subtle distinctions between advocacy and silence. In May 1986, the debate over the canon hit the pages of the *New York Times* when a Columbia University student was arrested for unfurling across the front of Butler Library a 140-foot banner adding the names of women writers to the pantheon enshrined there. The list included Christine de Pizan at one end and Virginia Woolf at the other.[60]

Meanwhile, historians were discovering new/old work in every field. As a student activist, Beverly Guy-Sheftall had read plenty of black literature, but she was unprepared for the discovery she made in the Emory University library one day when she stumbled on Anna Julia Cooper's *A Voice from the South by a Black Woman of the South.* "I was literally awestruck when I read Cooper's insightful and original pronouncement, which she wrote in 1892 long before there was any mention of Black feminism: 'The colored woman of to-day occupies, one may say, a unique position in this country. . . . She is confronted by both a woman question and a race problem, and is as yet an unknown or an unacknowledged factor in both.'" For Guy-Sheftall, that passage shifted the earth in a new direction.[61]

For Susan Kohler the earth shifted in much the same way when, browsing in the stacks of Harvard's Widener Library, she stumbled on bound volumes of a prosuffrage, pro–women's rights periodical published in Utah from 1872 to 1914. To her astonishment, she realized that its creators were the same ostensibly well-behaved Mormon women she had revered as foremothers. She lugged the *Woman's Exponent* home from the library, one heavy volume at a time, sharing her discovery with other LDS feminists in the Boston area. In 1974, they launched *Exponent II*, christening it "The Spiritual Descendant of the *Woman's Exponent*." The homemade cover, printed on cheap newsprint, borrowed a motto from nineteenth-century abolitionism, exploiting the double meanings of feminist and religious kinship to ask: "Am I Not a Woman and a Sister?"[62] For these women, as for many others, the past became a guide to the future.

The new field of women's history was built through books, conferences, and small epiphanies. Some scholars had their epiphanies on picket lines. Renate Bridenthal writes that her anthology on women in European history "was born on the sidewalk in front of

Cover of *Exponent II*

the Honeywell Corporation, where I was part of a group of antiwar faculty protesting the manufacture of antipersonnel bombs." Because the "police left us sitting there for hours," she got to talking with another historian and cooked up the idea for her influential anthology, *Becoming Visible.*[63]

Activism didn't provide answers, but it provoked new questions, and it offered irrefutable evidence that history mattered. Estelle

Freedman says that during the years she was writing her dissertation "at a university that remained unwelcoming to women," she was sustained by local gatherings of feminists. When she moved to San Francisco in the mid-seventies, she recalls, "local study groups on sexuality and on socialist feminism, the grassroots Lesbian and Gay History Project, and the creative and political writing by diverse women of color, all transformed my own feminism from its middle-class, East Coast origins to a broader and more diverse political entity." She went on to write important books on prison reform and the history of sexuality.[64]

One of the most remarkable effects of the new feminism was its impact on the cataloging of historical materials. Linda Kerber admits that until the early seventies, she didn't have the courage "to intrude into a manuscript library to ask what women's collections they had without feeling like a fool. In 1968 it was a dumb question, revealing that the asker was on a fishing expedition and need not be taken seriously."[65] Others learned how to ferret out women's materials from conventional catalogs, but the process was time-consuming and difficult. In 1971, Gerda Lerner, with support from the Rockefeller Foundation, helped to organize a conference on women's history sources. The result was Andrea Hinding's marvelous *Women's History Sources: A Guide to Archives and Manuscript Collections in the United States,* published in 1979.[66] (Through Hinding's entry on the Maine State Library, I found the manuscript diary of Martha Moore Ballard two years later.)

If a renaissance involves a rediscovery of lost knowledge, then without question there was a renaissance for women in the 1970s.

Tides and Waves

Sara Evans called her survey of the new feminism *Tidal Wave,* suggesting that the feminist wave of the 1970s was different—bigger, faster-moving, and more powerful than anything that came before.[67] *The Oxford English Dictionary* says the term *tidal wave* originally meant the "high water wave caused by the movement of the tide." But by the 1870s, it connoted something out of the ordinary, a wave generated by an unseen cataclysm, often far out at sea, like an earthquake. The destruction caused by such waves can be immense.[68]

So if seventies feminism was that sort of tidal wave, what did it destroy? The achievements Evans lists do not appear cataclysmic. "It is startling to realize," she writes, "that in the early 1960s married women could not borrow money in their own names, professional and graduate schools regularly imposed quotas of 5–10 percent or even less on the numbers of women they would admit, union contracts frequently had separate seniority lists for women and men, and sexual harassment did not exist as a legal concept. It was perfectly legal to pay women and men differently for exactly the same job and to advertise jobs separately: 'Help Wanted—Men' and 'Help Wanted—Women.' "[69] The new feminism turned some households upside down, but, despite conservative fears, it didn't topple capitalism, the Bible, or the United States Constitution, nor did it end male dominance in *The New York Review of Books* or the use of women's bodies to sell beer.

But without question it transformed many aspects of American life. Some people are happy to give feminists credit for things they fear—like abortion rights, contraception for teenagers, or gay liberation—but less willing to acknowledge that feminist activism brought about things they support, like better treatment for breast cancer or the opportunity for young girls to play soccer as well as lead cheers. As Rosalyn Baxandall and Linda Gordon observe, "Although the word 'feminist' has become a pejorative term to some American women, most women (and most men as well) support a feminist program: equal education, equal pay, child care, freedom from harassment and violence," and so on. Because of the feminist movement, airline flight attendants, many of whom are now male, no longer have to retire at thirty-two. In Washington, there are female senators in both parties, and in the House of Representatives, a woman has at last become Speaker. Meanwhile, on playgrounds, in supermarkets, and at children's classroom conferences, fathers as well as mothers appear.[70]

These changes are so entrenched in American life that it is hard to remember a time when they seemed radical. That's what worries some historians. Waves are inherently cyclical. They move in. They move out. They pound the shore then disappear, often leaving changes too subtle to be observed. If earlier waves of female consciousness disappeared, surely the same thing can happen again. A new generation might forget where their freedoms came from, drifting back once again into the sandbar of silence. Sara Evans thinks that concern helps explain why so many second-wave feminists became scholars. "Certainly I am not the only historian," she writes, "who wishes to spare the next generation the rage we experienced about having been cut off from our own history in all its complexity."[71]

Afterword

꒳

MAKING HISTORY

*T*here are many ways of making history. Some people enter contests. Others fill family scrapbooks with snapshots, greeting cards, and locks of hair. A few people devote their lives to bringing about change.

Jill Portugal is one of these. For her, making history is all about the future. In 1996, she pulled together $100 to start a small business putting feminist slogans on T-shirts. She was twenty-three years old then, single, and working for a temp agency in Portland, Oregon. Today she is a school guidance counselor, wife, and mother, living in New England. But she still does business as "one angry girl." She worries a lot about the impact of popular culture on the young people she works with, which is why her website offers a scathing but witty denunciation of pornography and a list of companies that deserve "girlcotts." Alongside that famous T-shirt with the slogan about women and history, she sells shirts that say things like "Anti-porn star" and "Ignore celebrities." Portugal wants to make a difference. She knows the odds are against her. The profits in T-shirts are small, and the cash flow in porn is in the billions. But with determination and a wry sense of humor, she remains true to her motto: "Taking over the world one shirt at a time."[1]

Scholars have other ways of making history. At the University of Edinburgh specialists are working with the British Library to produce an online edition of the collected works of Christine de Pizan, using the manuscript that she herself prepared in 1413–14.[2] At Rutgers University in New Jersey, historians have been busy since 1982 collecting and editing the complete works of Elizabeth Cady Stanton and Susan B. Anthony. So far, the Stanton-Anthony project has produced a microfilm edition of fourteen thousand documents gathered from 202 libraries and government offices, and published four of a projected six-volume print edition. Stanton's memoir, *Eighty Years and More,* is among the works now online.[3]

There are now dozens of similar ventures. In the past fifteen years, the Women Writers Project at Brown University has rescued hundreds of Shakespeare's female contemporaries from oblivion.[4] In Canada, the Harriet Tubman Resource Centre on the African Diaspora at York University has begun documenting the twenty thousand slave refugees who arrived in Ontario in the 1840s and 1850s.[5] At Michigan State University, textile scholars have launched an ambitious "Quilt Index" that when complete will provide digital images and supporting information for thousands of quilts documented in state and regional projects.[6] At Pace University in New York, researchers are beginning work on a scholarly edition of the papers of Harriet Jacobs.[7] Even the venerable *Dictionary of National Biography,* the project that Virginia Woolf's father, Leslie Stephen, helped to create, has found a more substantial place for women. A new online edition has added 3,869 entries on women, a 200 percent increase over the older version.[8]

The accumulation of resources is overpowering. Where once only a handful of "notable women" sat in printed volumes, there are now crowds of uppity, outrageous, inspiring, or dutiful women—inventors, union activists, combat pilots, government photographers, Salvation Army commanders, physicians, spiritualists, letter-writers, diarists, assembly-line workers, rural housewives, servants, and slaves whose lives are documented in print and on the web. Harvard University's "Open Collections" program, for example, has recently released, free and open to the public, an online edition of half a million pages documenting women's work in the United States between 1800 and 1930.[9] If Virginia Woolf were to go to the British Library today and search for "Women and Poverty" in the online catalog, she would find hundreds of books addressing her topic. They would deal with women in São Paulo and Cairo as well as London.[10] Woolf's "supplement to history" has grown up. In the libraries of once all-male universities, there are now sober volumes on female mountain climbers, pottery workers, radio broadcasters, philanthropists, archaeologists, and cross-dressers.[11] At Harvard there are almost three hundred books dealing with Amazons, a third of them published since 1990, with cross-references to "Women Soldiers" in Canada, China, Colombia, Egypt, England, Eritrea, Ethiopia, France, and so on through the alphabet to Uganda, Ukraine, and Zimbabwe.[12]

Some archives have also discovered the importance of artifacts. Tucked away among suffrage banners and campaign buttons at Harvard's Schlesinger Library for the History of Women are three dozen T-shirts dating from 1968 to 2004. Some are printed with the pictures of famous women, others with slogans like the one from 1990 that reads, "Dare to Use the F-word . . . Feminism."[13]

Christine de Pizan would delight in the variety. Elizabeth Cady Stanton would look beneath the clutter to find a common thread of narrative that might explain where women have made progress and where they have lost ground. Virginia Woolf would complicate the task by asking whether fitting women into existing notions of history enlarges or reduces their lives. She might argue that doubling the proportion of women in the *Dictionary of National Biography* from 5 to 10 percent does little in itself to change the assumptions that exclude them.

Still, the expansion of women's history over the past thirty years is impressive. If Gerda Lerner is right in claiming that the core of women's oppression has been an inability to access their own history, then this explosion of resources may presage more lasting change.[14] It is too soon to tell. Without question, however, history continues to animate contemporary politics, sometimes in surprising ways.

Recently, a group calling themselves "Feminists for Life" paid for full-size billboards near Stanton's home at Seneca Falls proclaiming that the legendary suffragist opposed abortion. Declaring that pro-life activists are the true heirs to nineteenth-century feminism, they have appropriated the humor and feistiness usually associated with pro-choice groups. This took Ann Gordon, editor of the Stanton-Anthony papers, by surprise. Deluged by phone calls, she prepared a package for the press pointing out that the terms of debate in the nineteenth century were radically different and that the quotations attributed to Stanton were taken out of context. Little matter. Today the "Feminists for Life" website sells a commemorative mug displaying a picture of a bonneted Elizabeth Cady Stanton with a baby on her lap and the caption "Another humorless old biddy for life." The explanatory legend urges supporters to invite their "feminist foremothers over for coffee this morning and start a *Revolution* by tea time!"[15]

As we have seen over and over again in this book, historical icons can be appropriated for contradictory causes. On one side of an argument, a biblical figure like Esther may ratify political action, on another justify silence. To one writer Penthesilea represents chastity, to another unbridled lust. In less than a decade, Mary Wollstonecraft was transformed from sage to harpy. Confronting these shifting meanings, some people wonder whether history has any value at all. At any given moment it is hard to know whom to believe or what to trust. That's why details matter. Details provide the contexts in which Wollstonecraft, Stanton, and Friedan mounted their arguments. Details help us understand the precise circumstances that allowed Artemisia Gentileschi to become an artist, or Harriet Jacobs a writer. Details keep us from falling into the twin snares of "victim history" and "hero history." Details let us out of boxes created by slogans.

Serious history reminds us that women have been on both sides of most revolutions. There is no universal sisterhood, no single history of women. Women were among the accusers as well as the victims in European witch hunts. They supported as well as worked against slavery. As Virginia Woolf understood so well, women have figured in history not only as actors but as mirrors for competing dreams and fears. In Brazilian folktales, female water sprites mutate into witches, dangerous creatures whose songs entice women to barbecue their husbands. Anxiety over female power shows up as well in intimate letters written with quill pens, as in John Adams's playful but no less revealing allusion to the "despotism of the petticoat." In times of trouble, images of ignorant, disorderly, or slovenly women have been useful scapegoats. In Chicago in the 1870s, nobody noticed Mrs. O'Leary's milk route until a fire broke out.

If history is to enlarge our understanding of human experience, it must include stories that dismay as well as inspire. It must also include the lives of those whose presumed good behavior prevents us from taking them seriously. If well-behaved women seldom make history, it is not only because gender norms have constrained the range of female activity but because history hasn't been very good at capturing the lives of those whose contributions have been local and domestic. For centuries, women have sustained local communities, raising food, caring for the sick, and picking up the

Christine de Pisan at Her Computer, by Mary Yaeger

pieces after wars. Today, because more women are educated and communication is easier, more of these projects get noticed, but the work has just begun. It isn't easy to give Anon. a history.

A few years ago, a fifteenth-century image of Christine de Pizan at her desk inspired textile artist Mary Yaeger to create an unusual work of art. She calls it an emblem. First she painted a picture of the medieval writer at a computer. Then she photographically transferred the image to a small piece of satin, highlighting the border and details with hand-stitched embroidery. Yaeger's witty art links contemporary feminism with historical feminism just as Christine linked her own age with stories from antiquity. In the original image, Christine had a dog at her side. In Yaeger's embroidery, she is joined instead by a bright-green dragon, whom she studiously ignores. A woman who writes her own stories has no fear of demons, Yaeger's emblem seems to say. That is an idea worth contemplating.[16]

Well-behaved women make history when they do the unexpected, when they create and preserve records, and when later generations care.

ACKNOWLEDGMENTS

Thanks to Kay Mills for elevating my sentence to an epigram and Jill Portugal for printing it on a T-shirt. A bundle of thanks to all those who have e-mailed to ask about the slogan, to request permission to use it in your own projects, or to report seeing it in unusual places. I owe the beginning of this book to your collective enthusiasm. Thanks also to the women of *Exponent II*, who gave me the first opportunity to explore the implications of the slogan, in a talk and then in an essay.

The actual contents of the book have a more complex origin. When I came to Harvard University in 1995, my first assignment was to teach an introductory course in women's history. All of it! That daunting course, co-taught for several years with Maura Henry, led me way beyond my own areas of expertise. Eventually I developed a Harvard Core Course, Historical Studies A-10, "Women, Feminism, and History," that focused on the uses of history in the long history of feminism in the West. I thank the undergraduate students who took that course and the fabulous graduate students who served as my teaching assistants for continually pushing me in new directions. As I drafted this book, I kept hearing their voices asking, "But what about . . . ?" Fortunately, Mark Hanna, Eliza Clark, Kirsten Sword, Erica Evasdottar, and others who served as teaching fellows in that course are now answering those questions with their own books and courses.

I tried out parts of this book in talks at Utah Valley State College, the University of Nebraska–Omaha, the University of Pennsylvania, Keene State College (NH), Fitchburg State College (MA), Snow College (Utah), Loyola University (New Orleans), Holy Cross University (Worcester), Notre Dame University, Yale University, Randolph-Macon Women's College, Hofstra University, Miami University of Ohio, and annual meetings of the Australian American Studies Association, the American Historical Association, and the Mormon History

Association. Many of these lectures were given under the auspices of the Organization of American Historians. I thank Annette Windhorn for her skillful handling of those assignments.

Participants in workshops at the Massachusetts Historical Society, the Newberry Library, and the Harvard University History Department gave helpful comments on particular chapters, as did Mark Kishlansky, Suzanne Blier, Kirsten Sword, Sarah Pearsall, Susan Gong, Amy Ulrich, Julie Livingston, and Janet Polasky. I also thank Nancy Cott, James Hankins, Katherine Park, John Thornton, Jeffrey Hamburger, Jane Mangan, and Ann Blair for answering my strange queries, and Adam Morris for helping me with Italian sources. Jill Lepore read an almost-finished draft and helped me see what else needed to be done. Michelle Morris gave the entire manuscript the benefit of her careful reading and judicious editorial hand, and in addition jumped in to help with unresolved research questions. Gael Ulrich proved that an engineer can be an astute, if picky, reader. Most of the time I took his advice.

Thanks, too, to Donald Lamm, who thought that a slogan was a good title for a book and never once complained when he found himself answering more queries about T-shirts than chapters. Once again, I have had the privilege of working with Jane Garrett at Knopf. I appreciate her encouragement and wisdom. I also appreciate the production team at Knopf and especially Mel Rosenthal for thoughtful as well as meticulous copyediting.

Finally, let me thank the many scholars who together have built the field of women's history by founding and editing journals, establishing archives, organizing conferences, sharing syllabi, raising money for prizes, compiling encyclopedias, dictionaries, and anthologies, creating fellowships, and writing essays, articles, and books. This book is an inadequate effort to pay tribute to your work.

L.T.U.

NOTES

The Slogan

1. *The Oxford English Dictionary* says that *seldom* was present in Old English by the ninth century C.E. *Rarely* came along five or six hundred years later as a borrowing from French or Latin.
2. See her website at http://www.oneangrygirl.net/.
3. Lori Pearson to Laurel Ulrich, January 23, 2004, copy of e-mail in my possession, used by permission.
4. "Inciteful insight: Wisdom of a simple phrase, challenges, inspires women," *Cleveland Plain Dealer*, May 1, 2003, Section F, pp. 1, 5; Chris Sheper, "Plain Dealer's Connie Schultz wins Pulitzer," ibid., April 5, 2005, Section A, p. 1.
5. Jeanne Coverdale to Laurel Ulrich, October 2, 2003, copy of e-mail in my possession, used by permission.
6. Kacey Jones and Jill Conner Browne, "Well-Behaved Women Rarely Make History," on *The Sweet Potato Queens Big Ass Box of Music* (Igo Records, 2003).
7. Kacey Jones to Laurel Ulrich, January 19, 2004, copy of e-mail in my possession, used by permission.
8. "Mayor Cargo's baggage riles foes," *Denver Post*, September 22, 2002, Section A, pp. 1, 18.
9. Suzanne Bruno, *The Misbehaving Women Quilt Companion Booklet* (Raymond, Me., 2002). On Bates, see Judith Schwarz, " 'Yellow Clover': Katharine Lee Bates and Katharine Coman," *Frontiers: A Journal of Women Studies* 4 (1979): 59–67; and a brief biography on the Wellesley College website, http://www.wellesley.edu/Anniversary/bates.html.
10. *Cool Women* was written by Dawn Chipman, Mari Florence, and Naomi Wax, and edited by Pam Nelson (Chicago: Girl Press, 1998).
11. Nor have Curie's scientific contributions gone unquestioned. When she was nominated to the French Academy in 1911, opponents argued that she was a mere assistant, though a good one, to her husband. *Le Journal des Débats*, in its issue of January 20, 1911, found it a "very delicate problem to determine with certainty . . . what part was really played by Mme Curie." See J. L. Davis, "The Research School of Marie Curie in the Paris Faculty, 1907–14," *Annals of Science* 52 (1995): 348. For a fascinating account of the tabloid accusations and their significance, see Susan Quinn, *Marie Curie: A Life* (New York: Simon & Schuster, 1994), Chapter 14. As Quinn points out, Curie's fame made her an easy target.
12. Marina Warner, *Joan of Arc: The Image of Female Heroism* (New York: Alfred A. Knopf, 1981), is the essential study. Also see Deborah Fraioli, "The Literary

Image of Joan of Arc: Prior Influences," *Speculum* 56 (1981): 811–83; Eric Jennings, " 'Reinventing Jeanne': The Iconology of Joan of Arc in Vichy Schoolbooks, 1940–44," *Journal of Contemporary History* 29 (1994): 711–34; Lisa Tickner, *The Spectacle of Women: Imagery of the Suffrage Campaign 1907–1914* (London: Chatto & Windus, 1987), pp. 208–11, 234.

13. John Ogilby, *Africa . . . collected and translated from the most authentick authors* (London: T. Johnson, 1970), quoted in Antonia Fraser, *The Warrior Queens* (New York: Alfred A. Knopf, 1989), pp. 241–42.

14. Fraser, *Warrior Queens*, pp. 242–43; Heinrich Loth, *Woman in Ancient Africa*, trans. Sheila Marnie (Westport, Conn.: Lawrence Hill, 1987), p. 58; Joseph C. Miller, "Nzinga of Matamba in a New Perspective," *Journal of African History* (1975): 201–16. Africanists Linda Heywood and Catherine Skidmore-Hess are now engaged in full-length studies of Njinga. I thank them both for telling me about their projects.

15. Daniel Donoghue, *Lady Godiva: A Literary History of the Legend* (Malden, Mass., and Oxford: Blackwell, 2003), pp. 1–25, 45, 81, 104–5.

16. Jill Watts, *Mae West: An Icon in Black and White* (New York: Oxford University Press, 2001), pp. 21, 56, 156.

17. Marybeth Hamilton, *When I'm Bad, I'm Better: Mae West, Sex, and American Entertainment* (New York: HarperCollins, 1995), pp. 2, 236–37, 248–50, 254; Watts, *Mae West*, pp. 70–92; Emily Wortis Leider, *Becoming Mae West* (New York: Farrar, Straus & Giroux, 1997), p. 351. Watts suggests that one of West's grandfathers may have been black. On this point, see Heather O'Donnell, "Signifying Sex," *American Quarterly* 54 (2002): 499–505.

18. Shana Pearson to Laurel Ulrich, August 4, 2003, copy of e-mail in my possession, used by permission.

19. Robert Hughes Wright, *The Birth of the Montgomery Bus Boycott* (Southfield, Mich.: Charro Press, 1991), p. 27; Rita Dove, "Rosa Parks: Her simple act of protest galvanized America's civil rights revolution," http://www.time.com/time/time100/heroes/profile/parks01.html.

20. C. Alvin Hughes, "A New Agenda for the South: The Role and Influence of the Highlander Folk School, 1953–1961," *Phylon* 46 (1985): 242–50.

21. David J. Garrow, ed., *The Walking City: The Montgomery Bus Boycott, 1955–1956* (Brooklyn, N.Y.: Carlson, 1989), p. 546.

22. Steven M. Millner, "The Montgomery Bus Boycott: A Case Study in the Emergence and Career of a Social Movement," in Garrow, *Walking City*, p. 443.

23. Ellen Goodman, "The mythology of Rosa Parks," *Boston Globe*, October 28, 2005, p. E10.

24. Awele Makeba's powerful one-woman show, "Rage Is Not a 1-Day Thing," dramatizes the lives of sixteen little-known participants, male and female, black and white. For details see her website, http://www.awele.com/programs.htm. For a list of resources prepared for the fiftieth anniversary of the boycott in 2005, see http://www.teachingforchange.org/busboycott/busboycott

.htm. Additional document can be found in Stewart Burns, ed., *Daybreak of Freedom: The Montgomery Bus Boycott* (Chapel Hill and London: University of North Carolina Press, 1997). Herbert Kohl, *She Would Not Be Moved: How We Tell the Story of Rosa Parks and the Montgomery Bus Boycott* (New York and London: The New Press, 2005), urges teachers to move from the theme "Rosa Was Tired" to the more historically accurate concept "Rosa Was Ready."

25. *American Quarterly* 28 (1976): 20–40.

26. Denis de Rougemont, *Love in the Western World*, trans. Montgomery Belgion (New York: Pantheon, rev. ed., 1956), p. 15.

27. Earlier I had made a systematic search of Andrea Hinding's then newly published *Women's History Sources: A Guide to Archives and Manuscript Collections in the United States* (New York: R. R. Bowker, 1979). If I hadn't already noted the existence of two eighteenth-century diaries at the Maine State Library, housed in the same building as the archives, I might not have discovered the Ballard diary. The Maine State Library is generally off the beaten track for scholars.

28. Gerda Lerner, *Why History Matters* (New York: Oxford University Press, 1997), p. 199.

Chapter One: Three Writers

1. Christine de Pizan, *The Book of the City of Ladies*, ed. Earl Jeffrey Richards (New York: Persea Books, rev. ed., 1998), pp. 3–5.

2. Ibid., pp. 6, 12–14.

3. Elizabeth Cady Stanton, *Eighty Years and More: Reminiscences 1815–1897* (New York: Schocken Books, 1971, orig. pub. T. Fisher Unwin, 1898), pp. 30–32.

4. Ibid., p. 32.

5. Virginia Woolf, *A Room of One's Own* (San Diego, New York, London: Harcourt Brace Jovanovich, 1981, orig. 1929), pp. 8, 25, 26.

6. Ibid., pp. 28, 31–32.

7. Ibid., pp. 32, 33–34.

8. Ibid., pp. 37, 39.

9. Ibid., p. 26; R. Q. Peddie, *The British Museum Reading Room: A Handbook for Students* (London: Grafton, 1912), pp. 2, 3.

10. Richards, Introduction to Pizan, *Ladies*, p. xlviii.

11. *Room of One's Own*, p. 37. When the British House of Lords passed the women's suffrage bill in 1918, Woolf told her diary, "I don't feel much more important—perhaps slightly less so." *The Diary of Virginia Woolf*, eds. Anne Olivier Bell and Andrew McNeillie, vol. 1 (London: Hogarth Press, 1977), p. 104, quoted in Hermione Lee, *Virginia Woolf* (New York: Vintage, 1999), p. 339.

12. Charity Cannon Willard, *Christine de Pizan: Her Life and Works* (New York: Persea Books, 1984), pp. 15–32. For a brief survey, with illustrations of art

production during her lifetime, see "Patronage at the Early Valois Courts, 1328–1469 A.D.," on a Timeline of Art History, Metropolitan Museum of Art, New York, http://www.metmuseum.org/toah/hd/valo_2/hd_valo_2.htm. On manuscript production, see Jonathan J. G. Alexander, *Medieval Illuminators and Their Methods of Work* (New Haven and London: Yale University Press, 1992), pp. 35–51, and on Paris in particular, Brigitte Buettner, *Boccaccio's Des cleres et nobles femmes: Systems of Signification in an Illuminated Manuscript* (Seattle and London: University of Washington Press, 1996), pp. 4–24.

13. Willard, *Christine de Pizan*, 38–40; Enid McLeod, *The Order of the Rose: The Life and Ideas of Christine de Pizan* (London: Chatto & Windus, 1976), pp. 1–33.

14. Lesley Smith, "*Scriba, Femina:* Medieval Depictions of Women Writing," in Lesley Smith and Jane H. M. Taylor, *Women and the Book: Assessing the Visual Evidence* (British Library and University of Toronto Press, 1996), pp. 26–27; Willard, *Christine de Pizan*, p. 47; Pizan, *Ladies*, 1.41.4, p. 85.

15. Willard, *Christine de Pizan*, pp. 47, 51, 73, 84.

16. Christine de Pizan, *The Book of Fortune's Transformation*, 1.12, in *The Selected Writings of Christine de Pizan*, ed. Renate Blumenfeld-Kosinski (New York: Norton, 1997), pp. 104–5. On Christine's "transformation," see Jacqueline Cerquiglini, "The Stranger," in Blumenfeld-Kosinski, ed., pp. 269–70.

17. Pizan, *Ladies*, p. 155.

18. Ibid., p. 120.

19. Ibid., pp. 75, 94–95.

20. Katherine Usher Henderson and Barbara F. McManus, *Half Humankind: Contexts and Texts of the Controversy About Women in England, 1540–1640* (Urbana and Chicago: University of Illinois Press, 1985), p. 8; Pizan, *Ladies*, pp. 130–31.

21. Pizan, *Ladies*, pp. 44–45, 7, 82, 153, 155.

22. Ibid., p. 6.

23. Virginia Brown, Introduction to Giovanni Boccaccio, *Famous Women* (Cambridge, Mass., and London, England: Harvard University Press, 2003), pp. xi–xii.

24. Richards, Introduction to Pizan, *Ladies*, pp. xxxviii–xlii.

25. Pizan, *Ladies*, 143–50, 155–58.

26. Pizan, *Ladies*, pp. 82–83; Eleni Stecopoulos with Karl D. Uitti, "Christine de Pizan's *Livre de la Cité des Dames:* The Reconstruction of Myth," in Earl Jeffrey Richards, ed., *Reinterpreting Christine de Pizan* (Athens and London: University of Georgia Press, 1992), pp. 52–56.

27. Pizan, *Ladies*, pp. xx–xxi, xxxix–xlv, 51.

28. Giovanni Boccaccio, *Concerning Famous Women*, trans. Guido A. Guarino (New Brunswick, N.J.: Rutgers University Press, 1963), pp. 101–3.

29. Pizan, *Ladies*, pp. 160–62.

30. Sheila Delany, "History, Politics, and Christine Studies: A Polemical Reply," in Margaret Brabant, ed., *Politics, Gender, and Genre: The Political Thought of Christine de Pizan* (Boulder, San Francisco, Oxford: Westview Press, 1992), p.

195. Also see Eric Hicks, "The Political Significance of Christine de Pizan," and Christine M. Reno, "Christine de Pizan: 'At Best a Contradictory Figure'?," in the same volume.

31. Beatrice Gottlieb, "The Problem of Feminism in the Fifteenth Century," in *Selected Writings of Pizan*, ed. Blumenfeld-Kosinski, pp. 282, 284, 295; Earl Jeffrey Richards, "Somewhere Between Destructive Glosses and Chaos: Christine de Pizan and Medieval Theology," and Rosalind Brown-Grant, "Christine de Pizan as a Defender of Women," in Barbara K. Altmann and Deborah L. McGrady, eds., *Christine de Pizan: A Casebook* (New York and London: Routledge, 2003), pp. 47–48, 91. Also see Roberta L. Krueger, "Christine's Treasure: Women's Honor and Household Economies in the *Livre des trois vertus*," in the same volume, pp. 101–14.

32. Pizan, *Ladies*, pp. 234–40. On the complexity of the image of the disembodied tongue in French history, see Lori J. Walters, "Christine de Pizan as Translator and Voice of the Body Politic," in Altmann and McGrady, eds., *Pizan: Casebook*, pp. 34–35.

33. *Selected Writings of Pizan*, ed. Blumenfeld-Kosinski, pp. xiv–xv, 252–62; *The Writings of Christine de Pizan*, ed. Charity Cannon Willard (New York: Persea Books, 1993), pp. 348–63.

34. "The Poem of Joan of Arc," trans. Thelma S. Feinster, in *Writings of Pizan*, ed. Willard, pp. 352, 356, 358.

35. *Writings of Pizan*, ed. Willard, p. 207.

36. Elisabeth Griffith, *In Her Own Right: The Life of Elizabeth Cady Stanton* (New York: Oxford, 1984), pp. 191, 207–8, 211–13; Lois W. Banner, *Elizabeth Cady Stanton: A Radical for Women's Rights* (Boston: Little, Brown, 1980), pp. 161–65.

37. Stanton, *Eighty Years*, pp. 20–21.

38. Ibid., pp. 23, 33–34.

39. Ibid., pp. 3–4, 10.

40. Ibid., p. 17.

41. Ibid., pp. 51, 63.

42. Ibid., p. 44.

43. Ibid., p. 49.

44. Ibid., pp. 58–60, 71–72.

45. Ibid., pp. 72, 80–83.

46. Ibid., pp. 113–20.

47. Ibid., pp. 136, 133–34.

48. Ibid., pp. 147, 148.

49. Ibid., pp. 148–49; Banner, *Stanton*, pp. 40–42; Griffith, *In Her Own Right*, pp. 54–55.

50. "Declaration of Sentiments," in Mari Jo and Paul Buhle, eds., *The Concise History of Woman Suffrage* (Urbana: University of Illinois Press, 1978), pp. 94–97.

51. Stanton, *Eighty Years*, pp. 152–53, 192.

52. Ibid., p. 166; Banner, *Stanton*, pp. 58–61.

53. Stanton, *Eighty Years,* pp. 186–88.

54. Griffith, *In Her Own Right,* pp. 30, 80–84.

55. Stanton, *Eighty Years,* pp. 200–4.

56. Ibid., p. 308.

57. Ibid., p. 317.

58. Lee, *Virginia Woolf,* pp. 98–99; Trev Lynn Broughton, *Men of Letters, Writing Lives* (London and New York: Routledge, 1999), pp. 33–36.

59. Lee, *Virginia Woolf,* pp. 146–47.

60. Ibid., pp. 122–24, 151–55.

61. Ibid., pp. 238–41, 258–59.

62. Ibid., p. 550; Herbert Marder, *The Measure of Life: Virginia Woolf's Last Years* (Ithaca and London: Cornell University Press, 2000), p. 22.

63. Virginia Woolf, *Orlando* (San Diego, New York, and London: Harcourt, 1956, orig. pub. 1928), pp. 138, 153, 168.

64. Ibid., pp. 160–61, 251. As Woolf's biographers have noted, Orlando is both a celebration and a parody of Sackville-West, whose lesbian affairs were notorious. Lee, *Virginia Woolf,* pp. 480–83, 515–18; Mitchell Leaska, *Granite and Rainbow: The Hidden Life of Virginia Woolf* (New York: Farrar, Straus & Giroux, 1998), pp. 272–76.

65. Woolf, *Room of One's Own,* pp. 98–99, 104.

66. Virginia Woolf, *Jacob's Room* (London: Vintage, 2000), pp. 99, 100–101.

67. Some readers of Woolf's book took offense at the disparaging description of the prunes and custard served at "Fernham," or argued that the sumptuous luncheon she served up at "Oxbridge" was a product of her imagination. S. P. Rosenbaum, Introduction to Virginia Woolf, *Women & Fiction* (Oxford: Blackwell, 1992), pp. xv–xviii.

68. Quentin Bell, *Virginia Woolf: A Biography,* vol. 2 (London: Hogarth Press, 1990), p. 144.

69. Woolf, *Room of One's Own,* pp. 6, 7–8, 25.

70. Ibid., pp. 22, 50–51, 65, 68, 69.

71. Ibid., pp. 46–49, 113–14.

72. Ibid., pp. 87–88.

73. Ibid., pp. 49, 85.

74. Ibid., p. 45.

75. Ibid., pp. 88–89.

Chapter Two: Amazons

1. Josine Blok, *The Early Amazons: Modern and Ancient Perspectives on a Persistent Myth* (Leiden, New York, Koln: E. J. Brill, 1995), 1–3, 146–73.

2. Christine de Pizan, *The Book of the City of Ladies,* trans. Earl Jeffrey Richards (New York: Persea, 1982), pp. 40–51.

3. Louis Montrose, "The Work of Gender in the Discourse of Discovery," *Representations* 33 (1991), pp. 27–28. For other uses of the Amazon motif in early modern Europe, see Annette Dixon, ed., *Women Who Ruled: Queens, Goddesses, Amazons in Renaissance and Baroque Art* (London: Merrell, in association with University of Michigan Museum of Art, 2002); Kathryn Schwarz, *Tough Love: Amazon Encounters in the English Renaissance* (Durham and London: Duke University Press, 2000), pp. 16, 11, 109–33, and passim; Ben Jonson, *The Masque of Queenes*, The Holloway Pages, www.hollowaypages.com/jonson1692fame.htm, p. 352; Kirstin Belkin, *Rubens* (London: Phaidon, 1998), pp. 157–61.

4. Alfred F. Young, *Masquerade: The Life and Times of Deborah Sampson, Continental Soldier* (New York: Knopf, 2004), pp. 9, 195; Laurel Thatcher Ulrich, *The Age of Homespun: Objects and Stories in the Creation of an American Myth* (New York: Knopf, 2001), p. 243.

5. Gay Gullickson, *Unruly Women of Paris: Images of the Commune* (Ithaca and London: Cornell University Press, 1996), pp. 9, 102–4.

6. Abby Wettan Kleinbaum, *The War Against the Amazons* (New York: McGraw-Hill, 1983), pp. 6–7, 36, 8, 79, 101–34; Jorge Magasich-Airola and Jean-Marc de Beer, *America Magica: When Renaissance Europe Thought It Had Conquered Paradise*, trans. Monica Sandor (London: Anthem Press, 2006), pp. 103–10; Edna G. Bay, *Wives of the Leopard: Gender, Politics, and Culture in the Kingdom of Dahomey* (Charlottesville and London: University of Virginia Press, 1998), pp. 278–79 (photographs).

7. On the lawsuit, see Patty Mariscano, "Amazon Women Flex Their Muscles," *The Minnesota Women's Press*, April 28, 1999, online at http://www.womens press.com/newspaper/1999/15-03%20articles/15-3amazon.html, and Katharine Mieszkowski, "Battle of the Amazons," Salon.com, http://www.salon .com/tech/log/1999/10/28//amazon/; and Kristen A. Hogan, "Defining Our Own Context," *thirdspace*, March 2003, http://www.thirdspace.ca/articles/pr_hog.htm. After a public relations debacle, Amazon.com paid damages. The Minneapolis store continues in business under the name "Amazon Bookstore Cooperative." Their website is at http://www.amazonFEMBKS .com/.

8. Jeannine Davis-Kimball, with Mona Behan, *Warrior Women: An Archaeologist's Search for History's Hidden Heroines* (New York: Warner, 2002), pp. xii–xiii, 1–2, 12, 30–31; Jeannine Davis-Kimball, telephone interview and follow-up e-mail to Laurel Thatcher Ulrich, March 17, 2004; Jeannine Davis-Kimball, "Warrior Women of the Eurasian Steppes," *Archaeology*, January/February 1997, 44–48; NPR website, http://www.npr.org/rundowns/segment.php ?wfId=1030134.

9. Davis-Kimball, "Warrior Women," 48.

10. Essays collected in Bettina Arnold and Nancy L. Wicker, eds., *Gender and the*

Archaeology of Death (Walnut Creek, Calif.: Altamira Press, 2002), exemplify the change and at the same time emphasize the complexity of the evidence and vast differences among societies and across time.

11. Davis-Kimball, "Warrior Women," 45–49.

12. Pennington, *From Amazons to Fighter Pilots*, vol. 1: 58–60, 68–69, 113–15, 214–15, 267–68; vol. 2: 407–08, 437–39. For the reference to Maria the drummer, see Young, *Masquerade*, p. 8; DeAnne Blanton and Lauren M. Book, *They Fought Like Demons: Women Soldiers in the American Civil War* (Baton Rouge: Louisiana State University Press, 2002), pp. 6–7, 128–29, 147, 204; Elizabeth D. Leonard, *All the Daring of the Soldier: Women of the Civil War Armies* (New York and London: W. W. Norton, 1999), pp. 209, 218–19, 220; the statement from the general appears on p. 219.

13. Pizan, *Ladies*, pp. 37–38.

14. Mady Wechsler Segal, "Women's Military Roles Cross-Nationally: Past, Present, and Future," *Gender and Society* 9 (1995): 757–75.

15. Donald Reynolds Dudley and Graham Webster, *Rebellion of Boudicca* (London: Routledge and Kegan Paul, 1962), pp. 54, 99–112, and pictures between pp. 66 and 67; Paul R. Sealey, *The Boudican Revolt Against Rome* (Buckinghamshire: Shire Publications, 1997), pp. 22–37.

16. Jerome R. Adams, *Notable Latin American Women: Twenty-nine Leaders, Rebels, Poets, Battlers and Spies, 1500–1900* (Jefferson, N.C., and London: McFarland, 1995), pp. 67–74.

17. Pennington, *Amazons to Fighter Pilots*, vol. II, pp. 355–57.

18. Sarah Womack, "The Remakings of a Legend: Women and Patriotism in the Hagiography of the Trung Sisters," *Crossroads: An Interdisciplinary Journal of Southeast Asian Studies* 9 (1996): 31–50; Hue-Tam Ho Tai, "Face of Remembrance and Forgetting," in *The Country of Memory: Remaking the Past in Late Socialist Vietnam* (Berkeley: University of California Press, 2001), p. 174.

19. Merry Wiesner-Hanks, "Women's Authority in the State and Household in Early Modern Europe," in Dixon, ed., *Women Who Ruled*, p. 38.

20. Hue-Tam Ho Tai, "Face of Remembrance and Forgetting," p. 174. On festivals honoring Lady Trieu, see http://www.thanhhoa.gov.vn/english/vanhoa-dulich/lehoi.html.

21. Fraser Easton, "Gender's Two Bodies: Women Warriors, Female Husbands and Plebeian Life," *Past and Present* 180 (2003): 137.

22. Young, *Masquerade*, pp. 9, 195.

23. The most detailed account of her story and later reputation is Sherry Velasco, *The Lieutenant Nun: Transgenderism, Lesbian Desire & Catalina de Erauso* (Austin: University of Texas Press, 2000). Kathleen Ann Myers, *Neither Saints nor Sinners: Writing the Lives of Women in Spanish America* (New York: Oxford University Press, 2003), includes a brief excerpt from her autobiography.

24. Sandra E. Holliman, "Warfare and Gender in the Northern Plains: Osteologi-

cal Evidence of Trauma Reconsidered," in Arnold and Wicker, eds., *Gender and the Archaeology of Death*, p. 182.

25. Claude E. Schaeffer, "Kutenai Female Berfdache: Courier, Guide, Prophetess, and Warrior," *Ethnohistory* 12 (1965): 193–236, quote on page 216.

26. John K. Thornton, *The Kongolese Saint Anthony: Dona Beatriz Kimpa Vita and the Antonian Movement, 1684–1706* (Cambridge: Cambridge University Press, 1998), pp. 184, 26–27.

27. Ibid., pp. 112–18, 159–63, 168, 183–84, 210–14.

28. Geraldine Brooks, *Nine Parts of Desire: The Hidden World of Islamic Women* (New York: Doubleday, 1995), pp. 107–18; Adrienne A. R. Brooks, "Women in the Emirati Military: Spearhead of Change," *Military Review* (March–April 2002), online edition http://www.cgsc.army.mil/milrev/english/MarApr02/insight.asp. On their English-language website, the United Arab Emirates uses their success in training women for the military as a mark of their nation's modernity, http://www.uaefootball.org.ae/uae-e.htm.

29. Robert C. Edgerton, *Warrior Women: The Amazons of Dahomey and the Nature of War* (Boulder, Colo.: Westview Press, 2000), 154–55.

30. Bay, *Wives of the Leopard*, pp. 8–9, 18–19, 46, 72, 144–45, 312, 313, 317, 320–21, 199.

31. Ibid., pp. 145, 205–8.

32. *New York Times*, September 2, 1876, p. 4.

33. Stanley B. Alpern, *Amazons of Black Sparta: The Women Warriors of Dahomey* (London: Hurst, 1998), pp. 11–12, 202.

34. Bay, *Wives of the Leopard*, pp. 209, 278–79.

35. Suzanne Preston Blier, "The Wild Women of Africa: Dahomey Amazon Performances in the West (1890–1925)," unpublished paper. Prof. Blier kindly shared an advance copy of her paper. She analyzes artistic representations of the *ahosi* both in Dahomey and in the West; "Les Amazones a la rencontre de l'Occident," in *Memoire Colonal: Zoos Humaines* (*Paris:* Editions la Decouverte, 2002) and book in progress, *Imaging African Amazons: The Art of Dahomey Women Warriors*.

36. Blier, "The Wild Women of Africa."

37. Louise Edwards, "Women Warriors and Amazons of the Mid Qing Texts, Jinghua Yuan and Honglou Meng," *Modern Asian Studies* 29 (1995): 227.

38. Maxine Hong Kingston, *The Woman Warrior: Memoirs of a Girlhood Among Ghosts* (New York: Alfred A. Knopf, 1976), pp. 24, 54, 62–63, 243.

39. Beth Hannan Rimmels, "Disney's Latest Heroine Saves Its Reputation," *Long Island Voice*, June 18–24, 1998, at http://www.comicsutra.com/cs/comics/reprints/liv/mulan.htm.

40. Kleinbaum, *War Against the Amazons*, p. 1.

41. Virginia Woolf, *A Room of One's Own* (San Diego, New York, London: Harcourt Brace Jovanovich, 1981, orig. 1929), p. 35.

42. For an overview of scholarship, see Lorna Hardwick, "Ancient Amazons: Heroes, Outsiders, or Women?," in Ian McAuslan and Peter Walcot, eds., *Women in Antiquity* (Oxford: Oxford University Press, 1996), pp. 158–76.

43. Blok, *Early Amazons*, p. 174.

44. Ibid., pp. 146–73. The phrase appears twice in Homer's *Iliad*, though the references are casual, almost incidental. In both cases the speaker is remembering a distant battle. Blok explains that the word *Amazones*, though given an appropriate Greek grammatical form, is not Greek. By itself it could connote an ethnic group composed of men alone or perhaps of men, women, and children. But tradition and the other half of the phrase introduce a paradox. The prefix *anti* in this period meant *equivalent to* rather than *against*. When linked with *anier* (*male* or *masculine*) and completed with the feminine ending *ai*, it turns back on the word *Amazones* to create a puzzle—a nation of women who are equivalent to men.

45. Blok, *Early Amazons*, pp. 199, 218, 410–19, 434–35, 437, 441–42; Kleinbaum, *War Against the Amazons*, pp. 23–26.

46. Kleinbaum, *War Against the Amazons*, pp. 49, 50–60.

47. Giovanni Boccaccio, *Famous Women*, trans. Virginia Brown (Cambridge, Mass.: Harvard University Press, 2003), pp. 64–65.

48. Pizan, *Ladies,* pp. 48–51. Christine's patron, Charles VI, owned a set of tapestries telling Penthesilea's story. What these looked like and whether they were commissioned before or after *The City of Ladies,* we do not know.

49. Marina Warner, *Joan of Arc: The Image of Female Heroism* (New York: Alfred A. Knopf, 1981), pp. 205–6.

50. Montrose, p. 27; Schwarz, *Tough Love,* pp. 16, 11, 109–33; Ben Jonson, *The Masque of Queenes,* The Holloway Pages, www.hollowaypages.com/jonson1692fame.htm, p. 352.

51. Heinrich von Kleist, *Penthesilea: A Tragic Drama,* trans. Joel Agee (New York: HarperCollins, 1998), p. 52.

52. Kleist, *Penthesilea,* pp. 95–96, 127–28, 145. Not surprisingly, Kleist's play was a dismal failure at the time it was written, though many years later Sigmund Freud found it interesting. See William Reeve, *Kleist on Stage, 1804–1987* (Montreal and Kingston: McGill-Queen's University Press, 1993), pp. 78–111; Kleinbaum, *War Against the Amazons*, pp. 174–78, 219.

53. William Reeve, *Kleist on Stage, 1804–1987* (Montreal and Kingston: McGill-Queen's University Press, 1993), pp. 78–111; Joel Agee, Introduction to Kleist, *Penthesilea,* pp. xi–xxix; Kleinbaum, *War Against the Amazons*, pp. 170–80; Kate Rigby, "The Return of the Repressed, or, the Strange Case of Kleistian Feminism," *Southern Review* (Australia) 25 (1992): 320–32; Jost Hermand, "Kleist's Penthesilea: Battleground of Gendered Discourses," in Bernd Fischer, ed., *A Companion to the Works of Heinrich von Kleist* (Rochester, N.Y.: Camden House, 2003), pp. 43–60; Robert Sayre and Michael Lowy, "Romanti-

cism as a Feminist Vision: The Quest of Christa Wolf," *New German Critique* 64 (Winter 1995): 105–34.

54. Agee, Introduction, pp. xxvi–xxix; Hélène Cixous, *Readings: The Poetics of Blanchot, Joyce, Kafka, Kleist, Lispector, and Tsvetayeva*, ed. and trans. Verena Andermatt Conley (Minneapolis: University of Minnesota Press, 1991), pp. 71, 64.

55. Mary Daly, *Gyn/ecology: The Metaethics of Radical Feminism* (Boston: Beacon Press, 1978), pp. 44–49, 39, 111, 368–69.

56. Les Daniels, *Wonder Woman: The Complete History* (San Francisco: Chronicle Books, 2000), pp. 19–22.

57. Pizan, *Ladies*, pp. 44–47.

58. Lillian S. Robinson, *Wonder Women: Feminism and Superheroes* (New York and London: Routledge, 2004), pp. 27–28.

59. Ibid., pp. 40–41; Daniels, *Wonder Woman*, pp. 28–30.

60. Robinson, *Wonder Women*, pp. 82–83, Daniels, *Wonder Woman*, pp. 131–32.

61. Daniels, *Wonder Woman*, pp. 103–55; Robinson, *Wonder Women*, pp. 132–35.

62. On the lawsuit, see Patty Mariscano, "Amazon Women Flex Their Muscles," *Minnesota Women's Press*, April 28, 1999; Katharine Mieszkowski, "Battle of the Amazons," Salon.com, http://www.salon.com/tech/log/1999/10/28/amazon/; and Kristen A. Hogan, "Defining Our Own Context," *thirdspace*, March 2003, http://www.thirdspace.ca/articles/pr_hog.htm. After a public relations debacle, Amazon.com paid damages. The Minneapolis store, as mentioned earlier, remains in business, calling itself "Amazon Bookstore Cooperative."

63. *The Discovery of the Amazon*, ed. José Toribio Medina, trans. Bertram T. Lee (New York: Dover reprint, 1988, orig. pub. 1935), pp. 219–22.

64. Sir Walter Raleigh, *The Discoverie of the Large, Rich, and Bewtiful Empyre of Guiana*, ed. Neil L. Whitehead (Manchester: Manchester University Press, 1997), p. 146.

65. Ibid., p. 196.

66. Schwarz, *Tough Love*, pp. 53–56.

67. Batya Weinbaum, *Islands of Women and Amazons: Representations and Realities* (Austin: University of Texas Press, 1999).

68. Neil L. Whitehead, "The Historical Anthropology of Text: The Interpretation of Raleigh's *Discoverie of Guiana*," *Current Anthropology* 36 (1995): 53–74, and response by Elizabeth Reichel, "Comments," p. 67. Also see Magasich-Airola and de Beer, *America Magica*, pp. 118–27.

69. Alex Shoumatoff, *In Southern Light: Trekking Through Zaire and the Amazon* (New York: Simon and Schuster, 1986), p. 29.

70. Ibid., pp. 32, 34.

71. Ibid., pp. 75, 77–81.

72. Ibid., pp. 105–6.

73. Ibid., pp. 106–8.
74. Ibid., p. 108.
75. Mindlin, *Barbecued Husbands*, pp. 253–54, 1.
76. Ibid., pp. 30–36.
77. Ibid., pp. 264–67.
78. Ibid., pp. 292, 294, 301–3.
79. Ibid., pp. 37–47.
80. Ibid., pp. 292, 294, 297–99. The six native groups who live in the Rio Branco and Guapore' Indigenous Areas have a combined population of about 750 people.
81. Ibid., pp. 292, 294, 301–3.
82. Neil L. Whitehead, Introduction to Raleigh, *Guiana*, pp. 94–99.
83. Goldstein has published the most comprehensive examination of the biological and social factors which contribute to male dominance in war. He believes that in the creation of war, culture works overtime. "Contrary to the idea that war thrills men, expresses innate masculinity, or gives men a fulfilling occupation, all evidence indicates that war is something that societies impose on men, who most often need to be dragged kicking and screaming into it, constantly brainwashed and disciplined once there, and rewarded and honored afterwards." Like many feminist theorists, Goldstein argues that the relationship between war and gender is circular. Men fight because it is manly to do so, and in fighting they reinforce the connection between manhood and war. Joshua S. Goldstein, *War and Gender: How Gender Shapes the War System and Vice Versa* (Cambridge: Cambridge University Press, 2001), pp. 162–63, 283, 253, 408, 411.
84. Scheherezade Faramarszi, "Iraqi says U.S. guards stripped him naked," *Boston Globe*, May 3, 2004, p. A9.
85. Douglas Herman, "Let Us Now Thank Lynddie England," www.strike-the-root.com/4/herman/herman22.html, and Cathy Hong, "How Could Women Do That?," www.salon.com/mwt/feature/2004/05/07/abuse_gender/.
86. Rick Bragg, *I Am a Soldier, Too: The Jessica Lynch Story* (New York: Alfred A. Knopf, 2003), pp. 7–12, 30–35, 76–81, 102–04, 129–30, 5; David D. Kirkpatrick, "Jessica Lynch Criticizes U.S. Accounts of Her Ordeal," *New York Times*, November 7, 2003, p. A25; Frank Rich, "Jessica Lynch Isn't Rambo Anymore," *New York Times*, November 9, 2003, Section 2, p. 1. A made-for-television drama focusing on the rescue was based in part on interviews with an Iraqi lawyer who tipped off marines to her whereabouts. He later published his own account: Mohammed Odeh Al-Rehaief, with Jeff Coplon, *Because Each Life Is Precious: Why an Iraqi Man Risked Everything for Private Jessica Lynch* (New York: HarperCollins, 2003).
87. Thomas Curley, "Chasing Eyeballs and Remembering Jessica Lynch," in Kristina Borjesson, ed., *Feet to the Fire: The Media After 9/11* (New York: Prometheus Books, 2005), p. 70; Bragg, *I Am a Soldier, Too*, pp. 129–30, 5.

88. James Bennett, "Arab woman's path to unlikely 'martyrdom,' " *New York Times,* January 30, p. A1; "Arab press glorifies bomber as heroine," *New York Times,* February 11, 2002, p. A8.

89. Bennett, "Arab woman's path."

90. Lisa Tickner, *The Spectacle of Women: Imagery of the Suffrage Campaign, 1907–14* (London: Chatto & Windus, 1987), pp. 209–13; Warner, *Joan of Arc,* see colored illustrations opposite p. 101.

91. Obrad Kesić, "Women and Gender Imagery in Bosnia: Amazons, Sluts, Victims, Witches, and Wombs," in Sabrina P. Ramet, ed., *Gender Politics in the Western Balkans* (University Park: Pennsylvania State University Press, 1999), pp. 188–90.

Chapter Three: Shakespeare's Daughters

1. Virginia Woolf, *A Room of One's Own* (San Diego, New York, London: Harcourt Brace Jovanovich, 1981, orig. pub. 1929), pp. 28, 41–43, 45–46.

2. Ibid., pp. 46–49.

3. Barry Weller and Margaret W. Ferguson, Introduction to *The Tragedy of Mariam: The Faire Queene of Jewry with the Lady Falkland: Her Life* (Berkeley, Los Angeles, and London: University of California Press, 1994), p. 1; Susanne Woods, *Lanyer: A Renaissance Woman Poet* (New York and Oxford: Oxford University Press, 1999), p. vii; Nandini Das, "Biography," on a Mary Wroth website managed by the Faculty of English, University of Cambridge, http://www.english.cam.ac.uk/wroth/biography.htm; Barbara Keifer Lewalski, Introduction to *The Polemics and Poems of Rachel Speght* (New York and Oxford: Oxford University Press, 1996), p. xi.

4. Elizabeth H. Hageman and Sara Jayne Steen, "Teaching Judith Shakespeare," *Shakespeare Quarterly* 47 (1996): v–viii, and other articles in the same issue. For a vigorous critique of the influence of Woolf's fable on twentieth-century literary history, see Margaret J. M. Ezell, *Writing Women's Literary History* (Baltimore and London: Johns Hopkins University Press, 1993).

5. David Cressy, "Literacy in Seventeenth-Century England: More Evidence," *Journal of Interdisciplinary History* 8 (1977): 141–50.

6. Susan Groag Bell, *The Lost Tapestries of the City of Ladies: Christine de Pizan's Renaissance Legacy* (Berkeley, Los Angeles, London: University of California Press, 2004), pp. 2, 33–40.

7. For brief overviews of social history concerning women in early modern Europe, see Olwen Hufton, "Women, Work, and Family," in Natalie Zemon Davis and Arlette Farge, eds., *A History of Women in the West: Renaissance and Enlightenment Paradoxes* (Cambridge, Mass., and London: Harvard University Press, 1993), pp. 15–45; and Maryanne Kowaleski, "Singlewomen in Medieval and Early Modern Europe," in Judith M. Bennett and Amy M. Froide, eds., *Singlewomen in the European Past, 1250–1800* (Philadelphia: University of

Pennsylvania Press, 1999), pp. 38–81. Also see Olwen Hufton's comprehensive survey, *The Prospect Before Her: The History of Women in Western Europe* (New York: Alfred A. Knopf, 1996), which offers comparative insights and discusses changes over time. For an overview of English population history, see John Hatcher, "Understanding the Population History of England," *Past and Present* 180 (2003): 83–130.

8. Laura Gowing, *Domestic Dangers: Women, Words, and Sex in Early Modern London* (Oxford: Clarendon Press, 1996), pp. 12–17, 146.

9. For a comprehensive description, see David Cressy, *Birth, Marriage, and Death: Ritual, Religion, and the Life-Cycle in Tudor and Stuart England* (Oxford and New York: Oxford University Press, 1997).

10. E. R. C. Brinkworth, *Shakespeare and the Bawdy Court of Stratford* (London and Chichester: Phillimore, 1972), pp. 78–84.

11. On the distribution of Judith's story on material objects, see Margarita Stocker, *Judith: Sexual Warrior* (New Haven and London: Yale University Press, 1998), pp. 50–52.

12. Quotations are from the modern edition of Christine de Pizan, *The Book of The City of Ladies*, II.37.1, pp. 155–56.

13. Ibid., II.31.1., pp. 143–45.

14. Scott Smith-Bannister, *Names and Naming Patterns in England, 1538–1700* (Oxford: Clarendon Press, 1997), pp. 196–201.

15. Woolf, *Room of One's Own*, p. 49.

16. The couple did have to answer in court for rushing into the marriage too soon after posting their intentions. Stephen Greenblatt, *Will in the World: How Shakespeare Became Shakespeare* (New York and London: W. W. Norton, 2004), pp. 118–25.

17. Cressy, *Birth, Marriage, and Death*, pp. 73–75; Martin Ingram, *Church Courts, Sex and Marriage in England, 1570–1640* (Cambridge: Cambridge University Press, 1987), pp. 219–37, 259–68.

18. Brinkworth, *Shakespeare and the Bawdy Court*, pp. 78–84; Greenblatt, *Will in the World*, 385–86.

19. Brinkworth, *Shakespeare and the Bawdy Court*, pp. 76–77, 151, 156–57.

20. Gowing, *Domestic Dangers*, pp. 30–38; Ingram, *Church Courts*, p. 240; Bernard Capp, "The Double Standard Revisited: Plebeian Women and Male Sexual Reputation in Early Modern England," *Past and Present* 162 (1999): 70–100; Garthine Walker, "Rereading Rape and Sexual Violence in Early Modern England," *Gender & History* 10 (1998): 1–25.

21. Walker, "Rereading Rape," p. 11.

22. Ibid., p. 7. I have modernized the spelling in Walker's transcriptions from the court records.

23. Ibid., p. 17.

24. Capp, "The Double Standard," p. 91.

25. Ibid., pp. 85–89.

26. Bernard Capp, "The Poet and the Bawdy Court: Michael Drayton and the Lodging-House World in Early Stuart London," *Seventeenth Century* X (1995).

27. Bernard Capp, *When Gossips Meet: Women, Family, and Neighbourhood in Early Modern England* (New York and Oxford: Oxford University Press, 2003), pp. 127, 144–45.

28. Capp, "The Double Standard," pp. 80–81.

29. Gowing, *Domestic Dangers*, pp. 60, 1.

30. Ibid., pp. 100–05.

31. Ibid., pp. 84–85. I have modernized the spelling in Gowing's transcriptions from the court records.

32. David Cressy, *Travesties and Transgressions in Tudor and Stuart England: Tales of Discord and Dissension* (Oxford: Oxford University Press, 2000), pp. 9–28, quotation on p. 14.

33. Ibid., pp. 18, 13.

34. Ibid., pp. 35–37.

35. Ibid., pp. 17–18.

36. Steve Hindle, "The Shaming of Margaret Knowsley: Gossip, Gender and the Experience of Authority in Early Modern England," *Continuity and Change* 9 (1994): 391–419.

37. Ibid., p. 400.

38. Ibid., pp. 403–4.

39. Ibid., pp. 405–6, 408–9. For an illuminating commentary on twentieth-century implications of Knowsley's story, see Lynda Boose, "The Priest, the Slanderer, the Historian and the Feminist," in *English Literary Renaissance* 25 (1995): 320–40.

40. Susanne Woods, *Aemilia Lanyer: A Renaissance Woman Poet* (New York and Oxford: Oxford University Press, 1999), pp. 4–7; Barbara Kiefer Lewalski, *Writing Women in Jacobean England* (Cambridge, Mass., and London: Harvard University Press, 1993), p. 221. Some scholars have speculated that Lanyer's father was a Jew. If so, he had abandoned that identity even before leaving Italy.

41. Susanne Woods, Introduction to *The Poems of Aemilia Lanyer*, pp. xv–xxx.

42. Since Carey was the patron of Shakespeare's theater company, the discovery of Forman's case notes led one writer to claim, without any evidence at all, that Lanyer was the mysterious "dark lady" of Shakespeare's sonnets. Sexual intrigue was a staple of the court in the 1590s, but there was nothing dark or particularly mysterious about Lanyer. Woods, *Aemilia Lanyer*, pp. 16–18; on sexual intrigue, see Paul E. J. Hammer, "Sex and the Virgin Queen: Aristocratic Concupiscence and the Court of Elizabeth I," *Sixteenth-Century Journal* 31 (2000): 77–97.

43. Woods, Introduction to *The Poems of Aemilia Lanyer*, pp. xv–xxi; Woods, *Aemilia Lanyer*, pp. 25–27; Lewalski, *Writing Women*, pp. 214–16.

44. Compare "To the Queenes most Excellent Majestie," lines 19–24, *The Poems of*

Aemilia Lanyer, p. 4, with Ben Jonson, *The Masque of Queenes* (London: King's Printers, 1930), pp. 37–38.

45. Woods, *Aemilia Lanyer*, pp. 28–30.

46. "To the Ladie Margaret, Countesse Dowager of Cumberland," lines 1–14, "To the Vertuous Reader," lines 30–40, *Salve Deus Rex Judaeorum*, lines 193–96, 1481–1504, 1529–53, in *The Poems of Aemilia Lanyer*, pp. 34, 48, 49, 59, 114–17.

47. *Salve Deus Rex Judaeorum*, lines 193–208, pp. 59–60.

48. "To the Queenes most Excellent Majestie," lines 77–78, p. 6.

49. "To the Vertuous Reader," p. 48.

50. Woods, *Aemilia Lanyer*, pp. 9–14, x; *Salve Deus Rex Judaeorum*, lines 797–98, 778–80, 831–32, pp. 86, 85, 87.

51. "The Lady Falkland," in Weller and Ferguson, *Tragedy of Mariam*, p. 186.

52. Quoted in Bernard H. Newdigate, *Michael Drayton and His Circle* (Oxford: Basil Blackwell, 1961), p. 77.

53. "The Lady Falkland," in Weller and Ferguson, *Tragedy of Mariam*, p. 188.

54. Introduction, and "The Lady Falkland," in Weller and Ferguson, *Tragedy of Mariam*, pp. 5–6, 179, 188.

55. *The Tragedy of Mariam*, p. 136, lines 587–92; Weller and Ferguson, Introduction to *Tragedy of Mariam*, pp. 17–20; Dympna Callaghan, "Rereading Elizabeth Cary's *The Tragedie of Mariam, Faire Queene of Jewry*," in Margo Hendricks and Patricia Parker, eds., *Women, Race, and Writing in the Early Modern Period* (London and New York: Routledge, 1994), pp. 163–77.

56. "The Lady Falkland," p. 202.

57. Weller and Ferguson, Introduction to *Tragedy of Mariam*, pp. 8–10.

58. Dolan, *Whores of Babylon*, pp. 143–47; Lewalski, *Writing Women*, pp. 189–90.

59. Weller and Ferguson, Introduction to *Tragedy of Mariam*, p. 11.

60. Frances E. Dolan, *Whores of Babylon: Catholicism, Gender, and Seventeenth-Century Print Culture* (Ithaca and London: Cornell University Press, 1999), p. 126.

61. Elizabeth Cropper, "Life on the Edge: Artemisia Gentileschi, Famous Woman Painter," in Christiansen and Mann, pp. 273–75.

62. Mary D. Garrard, *Artemisia Gentileschi: The Image of the Female Hero in Italian Baroque Art* (Princeton: Princeton University Press, 1989), Appendix, pp. 414–16.

63. Elizabeth S. Cohen, "The Trials of Artemisia Gentileschi: A Rape as History," *Sixteenth-Century Journal* 31 (2000): 47–75.

64. Patrizia Cavazzini, "Documents Relating to the Trial of Agostino Tassi," in Keith Christiansen and Judith W. Mann, eds., *Orazio and Artemisia Gentileschi* (New Haven and London: Yale University Press for the Metropolitan Museum of Art, New York, 2001), pp. 432, 443–44.

65. Mann, "Documented Chronology," pp. xv–xvi.

66. Cropper, "Life on the Edge," pp. 268, 269.

67. Garrard, *Artemisia Gentileschi*, p. 175.
68. Ibid., pp. 183–209; Judith W. Mann, "Documented Chronology," and catalog entries in Christiansen and Mann, eds., *Orazio and Artemisia*, pp. xix, 296–99, 355–58, 424–26.
69. Garrard, *Artemisia Gentileschi*, p. 173.
70. On contemporary treatments of Artemisia's story, including those in fiction and film, see Richard E. Spear, "Artemisia Gentileschi: Ten Years of Fact and Fiction," *Art Bulletin* 82 (2000), 568–79.
71. See images and catalog descriptions in Christiansen and Mann, eds., *Orazio and Artemisia*, pp. 308–11, 330–33, 349–50, 368–70.
72. Woolf, *Room of One's Own*, p. 41.

Chapter Four: Slaves in the Attic

1. Elizabeth Cady Stanton, *Eighty Years and More: Reminiscences 1815–1897* (New York: Schocken Books, 1971, orig. 1898), pp. 62–64.
2. Recent scholarly studies of Tubman, Jacobs, and Stowe include: Jean M. Humez, *Harriet Tubman: The Life and the Life Stories* (Madison: University of Wisconsin Press, 2003); Kate Clifford Larson, *Bound for the Promised Land: Harriet Tubman, Portrait of an American Hero* (New York: Ballantine, 2004); Catherine Clinton, *Harriet Tubman: The Road to Freedom* (New York and Boston: Little, Brown, 2004); Jean Fagan Yellin, *Harriet Jacobs: A Life* (New York: Basic Books, 2004); Joan Hedrick, *Harriet Beecher Stowe: A Life* (New York: Oxford University Press, 1994); Barbara Anne White, *The Beecher Sisters* (New Haven: Yale University Press, 2003). For the stories mentioned here, see below.
3. Stanton, *Eighty Years and More*, pp. 60–61.
4. Ibid., pp. 64, 71.
5. Ibid., p. 83.
6. This is not only an American story. Historian Clare Midgley has identified a "triple discourse" of antislavery in the writing of British feminists in the years 1790 to 1869. Although "overwhelmingly preoccupied with the position of white middle-class women in Britain, they critiqued British women's oppression with reference to three different forms of slavery existing outside Britain: black chattel slavery in Britain's West Indian colonies and North America; the slavish position of women in 'savage' societies; and the enslavement of women in the harem under 'Oriental despotism.' " Clare Midgley, "Anti-slavery and the roots of 'imperial feminism,' " in Clare Midgley, ed., *Gender and Imperialism* (Manchester and New York: Manchester University Press, 1998), p. 166.
7. A carefully edited and annotated copy of this speech appears in *Stanton and Anthony Papers Project Online*, at: http://ecssba.rutgers.edu/docs/ecswoman1 .html. Stanton, like Grimké, took her ethnographic examples from Lydia Maria

Child's two-volume 1835 work, *History of the Condition of Women, in Various Ages and Nations.*

8. "Declaration of Rights and Sentiments," Elizabeth Cady Stanton et al., eds., *History of Women's Suffrage,* vol. 1 (1887), p. 70.

9. Milton C. Sernett, *North Star Country: Upstate New York and the Crusade for African American Freedom* (Syracuse: Syracuse University Press, 2002), pp. 4–10, 53.

10. Ralph Volney Harlow, *Gerrit Smith: Philanthropist and Reformer* (New York: Henry Holt, 1939), pp. 268–69; Sernett, *North Star Country,* pp. 145–46.

11. *The Friend of Man,* October 16, 1839; October 23, 1839. I would like to thank Donna Burdick of the Madison County (N.Y.) Freedom Trail Commission for providing photocopies of these papers.

12. Ibid., October 23, 1839.

13. Ibid., December 25, 1839.

14. Ibid., October 23, November 6, December 25, 1839.

15. Walter Johnson, *Soul by Soul: Life Inside the Antebellum Slave Market* (Cambridge, Mass., and London: Harvard University Press, 1999), pp. 138–61.

16. Ibid., pp. 113–15.

17. *Friend of Man,* November 6, 1839.

18. Ibid., April 1, 1840.

19. Information from Canadian records kindly supplied by Joanne Stanbridge, Kingston Frontenac Public Library, Kingston, Ontario.

20. Joan D. Hedrick, *Harriet Beecher Stowe: A Life* (New York: Oxford University Press, 1994), pp. 133–37.

21. Ibid., pp. 139, 121.

22. Harriet Beecher Stowe, "Trials of a Housekeeper," *The Lady's Book* 18 (New York: Jan. 1839): 4.

23. Hedrick, *Harriet Beecher Stowe,* pp. 102–9; Lois W. Banner, *Elizabeth Cady Stanton: A Radical for Woman's Rights* (Boston: Little, Brown, 1980), p. 18; Elisabeth Griffith, *In Her Own Right: The Life of Elizabeth Cady Stanton* (New York: Oxford University Press, 1994), pp. 26–27.

24. Hedrick, *Harriet Beecher Stowe,* pp. 106–8.

25. Ibid., pp. 190–91.

26. Ibid., pp. 206–7, 223–25.

27. Ibid., pp. 222, 223, 232–33.

28. Harriet Beecher Stowe, *A Key to Uncle Tom's Cabin* (Port Washington, N.Y., Kennikat Press, 1968, orig. pub. 1853), pp. 21–23.

29. Harriet Beecher Stowe, *Uncle Tom's Cabin; or, Life Among the Lowly* (Boston: John P. Jewett, 1852), pp. 265, 286, 288.

30. Harriet Jacobs, *Incidents in the Life of a Slave Girl,* ed. Jean Fagan Yellin (Cambridge and London, England: Harvard Press, 1987), pp. 5, 269 n. 4; and Yellin, *Harriet Jacobs,* pp. 3–4, 20–21.

31. Yellin, *Harriet Jacobs,* pp. 23–27.

32. The advertisement is reproduced in Yellin, *Harriet Jacobs*, between pp. 264 and 265.

33. Jacobs, *Incidents*, pp. 95–117, and Yellin, *Harriet Jacobs*, pp. 30–62.

34. Yellin, *Harriet Jacobs*, pp. 57–58, 72–73; Jacobs, *Incidents*, pp. 148–55, 224.

35. Yellin, *Harriet Jacobs*, p. 110.

36. Ibid., pp. 118–20.

37. Ibid., p. 121; Harriet Jacobs to Amy Post, April 4, 1853, and October 9, 1853, in Jacobs, *Incidents*, pp. 234–37.

38. Jacobs, *Incidents*, p. 1.

39. Ibid., pp. 54–55.

40. Clinton, *Harriet Tubman*, pp. 17–20; Humez, *Harriet Tubman*, pp. 11–15, 178; Larson, *Bound for the Promised Land*, pp. 41–44, 62–63.

41. Humez, *Harriet Tubman*, p. 178.

42. *Friend of Man*, Vol. 1, No. 4 (November 6, 1839); Child, Introduction to *Incidents*, p. 4; Humez, *Harriet Tubman*, pp. 37, 38.

43. Sarah H. Bradford, *Scenes in the Life of Harriet Tubman* (Auburn: W. J. Moses, 1869), pp. 1–3; *Harriet: The Moses of Her People* (New York: Geo. R. Lockwood and Son, 1886), pp. 4–6. Bradford explained that she used the name *Moses* because it was the name the public had long given her.

44. Clinton, *Harriet Tubman*, p. 20; Humez, *Harriet Tubman*, pp. 20–23, 349–52.

45. Humez, *Harriet Tubman*, pp. 133–38.

46. Larson, *Bound for the Promised Land*, pp. 156–63, 177; Humez, *Harriet Tubman*, pp. 38–40; Clinton, *Harriet Tubman*, 124–39.

47. Clinton, *Harriet Tubman*, pp. 168–72.

48. Ibid., Larson, *Bound for the Promised Land*, pp. 213–14.

49. Humez, *Harriet Tubman*, pp. 58–61.

50. Bradford, *Incidents*, pp. 24–25; Humez, p. 188; Larson, *Bound for the Promised Land*, p. 254.

51. Humez, *Harriet Tubman*, pp. 188–89, 216; Kimberly Wulfert, "The Underground and Uses of Quilts as Messengers for Fleeing Slaves," http://www.antiquequiltdating.com/ugrr.html.

52. Yellin, *Jacobs*, pp. 175–76.

53. Ibid., pp. 176–78.

54. See Chronology in Jacobs, *Incidents*, pp. 224–25.

55. Larson, *Bound for the Promised Land*, pp. 213–14.

56. Ibid., pp. 230, 252–53.

57. Thomas Paine, *The American Crisis*, No. 1, Dec. 23, 1776, in *The Complete Writings of Thomas Paine*, ed. Philip Foner (New York, 1945), 1:50. On the broader point, see Eric Foner, "The Meaning of Freedom in the Age of Emancipation," *Journal of American History* 81 (1994): 438–42.

58. David Herlihy, "Family," *American Historical Review* 96 (1991): 1–3.

59. Jean Bodin, *Six Books of the Common-Weale*. Trans. Richard Knolles (London: 1606) 9.

60. Abigail Adams to John Adams, March 31, 1776. Digital images and a transcription can be found on the Massachusetts Historical Society "Digital Adams" website at: http://www.masshist.org/digitaladams/aea/cfm/doc.cfm?id= L17760331aa.
61. John Adams to Abigail Adams, April 14, 1776, available on "Digital Adams."
62. Abigail Adams to John Adams, May 7, 1776.
63. There is a vast literature on this topic. I have taken the quotations in this paragraph from Michèle Crampe-Casnabet, "A Sampling of Eighteenth-Century Philosophy," in Natalie Zemon Davis and Arlette Farge, eds., *A History of Women in the West*, vol. 3: *Renaissance and Enlightenment Paradoxes* (Cambridge, Mass., and London: Harvard University Press, 1993), p. 318.
64. "Sentiments of an American Woman," Library of Congress, American Memory website, http://memory.loc.gov/cgi-bin/query/r?ammem/rbpebib:@ field(NUMBER+@band(rbpe+14600300)).
65. Gary Nash, *The Forgotten Fifth: African Americans in the Age of Revolution* (Cambridge, Mass., and London: Harvard University Press, 2006), pp. 1, 17–18, and Chapter One passim.
66. Wheatley's letter was published in the *Connecticut Journal*, April 1, 1774. For Wheatley's response to the Revolution, see Frank Shuffleton, "On Her Own Footing: Phillis Wheatley in Freedom," in Vincent Carretta and Philip Gould, eds., *Genius in Bondage: Literature of the Early Black Atlantic* (Lexington: University Press of Kentucky, 2001), pp. 175–89.
67. Gary Nash, *Forgotten Fifth*, pp. 1, 10–13, 25–27, 33–34, 39.
68. Evelyn Gerson, "Ona Judge Staines: Escape from Washington," based on the author's M.L.A. thesis at Harvard Extension School and online at http:// seacoastnh.com/blackhistory/ona.html. The attempt to retrieve Ona is well documented in three letters: Joseph Whipple to Oliver Wolcott, Jr., September 10 and October 4, 1796, and Joseph Whipple to George Washington, December 22, 1796, "George Washington Papers in the Library of Congress, 1741–1799," American Memory website, http://1cweb2.loc.gov/ammem/ gwhtml/.
69. Quoted in Charlotte Sussman, *Consuming Anxieties: Consumer Protest, Gender, and British Slavery, 1713–1833* (Stanford, Calif.: Stanford University Press, 2000), pp. 117, 116.
70. Sussman, *Consuming Anxieties*, pp. 110–29; Charlotte Sussman, "Women and the Politics of Sugar, 1792," *Representations* 48 (Autumn 1994): 48–69.
71. Clare Midgley, *Women Against Slavery: The British Campaigns, 1780–1870* (London and New York: Routledge, 1992), p. 27.
72. Joan Wallach Scott, *Only Paradoxes to Offer: French Feminists and the Rights of Man* (Cambridge, Mass., and London: Harvard University Press, 1996), pp. 19–23, 30–33, 39, 42–47. For a succinct examination of ideas about women and slavery, see Nancy Cott, *Public Vows: A History of Marriage and the Nation* (Cambridge, Mass., and London: Harvard University Press, 2000), Chapter 3.

73. Robert C. Smith, "Liberty Displaying the Arts and Sciences: A Philadelphia Allegory by Samuel Jennings," *Winterthur Portfolio* 2 (1965): 84–89, 94; and "A Philadelphia Allegory," *The Art Bulletin* 31 (1949): 323–26. Also see the Library Company's website at: http://www.librarycompany.org/instance.htm.

74. Yvonne Korshak, "The Liberty Cap as a Revolutionary Symbol in America and France," *Smithsonian Studies in American Art* I (1987): 52–69; J. David Harden, "Liberty Caps and Liberty Trees," *Past and Present* 146 (1995): 66–102; David Hackett Fischer, *Liberty and Freedom* (New York: Oxford University Press, 2005), pp. 40–41, 188, 198, 200, 201, 205, 211; Laurel Thatcher Ulrich, *The Age of Homespun* (New York: Alfred A. Knopf, 2001), pp. 166–71. Liberty as a white goddess appeared in the earliest designs for the Great Seal of the United States. In the years immediately following the war, she appeared on newspaper mastheads, in political cartoons, and even on printed fabric.

75. Phillip Lapsansky, "Graphic Discord: Abolitionist and Antiabolitionist Images," in Jean Fagan Yellin and John C. Van Horen, eds., *The Abolitionist Sisterhood: Women's Political Culture in Antebellum America* (Ithaca and London: Cornell University Press, 1994), pp. 201–3.

76. *The Lady's Magazine, or Repository of Entertaining Knowledge* (Philadelphia: 1792), pp. 189–98. The frontispiece is reproduced in *American women: A Library of Congress guide for the study of women's history and culture in the United States*, Sheridan Harvey, ed. (Washington, D.C.: Library of Congress, 2001), p. 105. Susan Branson, *These Fiery Frenchified Dames* (Philadelphia: University of Pennsylvania Press, 2001), p. 39, suggests that the frontispiece was modeled on one in the London periodical that was the model for the Philadelphia magazine. There is indeed a similar frontispiece in *The Lady's Magazine, or Entertaining Companion for the Fair Sex* (London: 1792). In it, a kneeling figure who appears to be male presents a book to a standing image of Britannia accompanied by a figure who may represent Fame. Although the composition is similar, the Philadelphia image explicitly links the revolutionary image of Liberty with the work of Wollstonecraft.

77. Lori Ginzberg, *Women and the Work of Benevolence* (New Haven and London: Yale University Press, 1990), pp. 11–18, 40–58; Julie Roy Jeffrey, "Permeable Boundaries: Abolitionist Women and Separate Spheres," *Journal of the Early Republic* 21 (2001): 79–93. Two landmark works on the relationship between female societies and the development of a women's rights movement are Nancy Cott, *Bonds of Womanhood: Woman's Sphere in New England, 1780–1835* (New Haven: Yale University Press, 1977), and Nancy Hewitt, *Women's Activism and Social Change: Rochester, New York, 1822–1872* (Ithaca: Cornell University Press, 1988).

78. Mary Hershberger, "Mobilizing Women, Anticipating Abolition: The Struggle Against Indian Removal in the 1830s," *Journal of American History* 86 (1999): 25–26.

79. Ibid., 27–29.

80. Midgley, *Women Against Slavery*, pp. 62–66.

81. Sussman, *Consuming Anxieties*, pp. 130–58; Gillian Whitlock, "Volative Subjects: *The History of Mary Prince*," in Vincent Carretta and Philip Gould, eds., *Genius in Bondage: Literature of the Early Black Atlantic* (Lexington: University of Kentucky Press, 2001), pp. 72–86.

82. Nancy Isenberg, *Sex and Citizenship in Antebellum America* (Chapel Hill and London: University of North Carolina Press, 1998), pp. 64–69; Susan Zaeske, *Signatures of Citizenship: Petitioning, Antislavery, & Women's Political Identity* (Chapel Hill and London: University of North Carolina Press, 2003), pp. 54–59.

83. Jeffrey, "Permeable Boundaries," pp. 83, 87, 89, 91–92.

84. Zaeske, *Signatures of Citizenship*, pp. 114–15.

85. Ibid., p. 117.

86. Catharine E. Beecher, "Essay on Slavery and Abolitionism, with Reference to the Duty of American Females" (Philadelphia: Perkins, 1837), in Sklar, ed. *Women's Rights Emerge*, pp. 108–9.

87. August 2, 1837, reprinted in Angelina E. Grimké, *Letters to Catharine E. Beecher in Reply to an Essay on Slavery and Abolitionism*, in Sklar, ed. *Women's Rights*, pp. 143, 144.

88. Stephanie McCurry, *Masters of Small Worlds: Yeoman Households, Gender Relations, and the Political Culture of the Antebellum South Carolina Low Country* (New York and Oxford: Oxford University Press, 1995), pp. 136–37, 211–23. McCurry also discusses this theme in "The Two Faces of Republicanism: Gender and Proslavery Politics in Antebellum South Carolina," *The Journal of American History* 78 (1992): 1245–64.

89. McCurry, *Masters of Small Worlds*, pp. 215–16.

90. Margaret Hope Bacon, "By Moral Force Alone: The Antislavery Women and Nonresistance," in Jean Fagan Yellin and John C. Van Horne, eds., *The Abolitionist Sisterhood: Women's Political Culture in Antebellum America* (Ithaca and London: Cornell University Press, 1994), pp. 282–86.

91. Bacon, "By Moral Force Alone," pp. 286–88.

92. Sernett, *North Star Country*, pp. 49–52; Judith Wellman, *The Road to Seneca Falls: Elizabeth Cady Stanton and the First Woman's Rights Convention* (Urbana and Chicago: University of Illinois Press, 2004), pp. 36–41; Ralph Volney Harlow, *Gerrit Smith, Philanthropist and Reformer* (New York: Holt, 1939), p. 268.

93. Sernett, *North Star Country*, pp. 24–34, 43–44; Wellman, *Road to Seneca Falls*, pp. 41–46, 53.

94. Elizabeth Cady Stanton, *Eighty Years and More* (New York: Schocken Books, 1971, orig. pub. 1898), pp. 309–24; "Declarations of Sentiments," and "Women's Declaration of Rights," in Anne Firor Scott and Andrew MacKay Scott, eds., *One Half the People* (Urbana and Chicago: University of Illinois Press, 1982), pp. 56–59, 90–95.

95. Mari Jo and Paul Buhle, eds., *The Concise History of Woman Suffrage: Selections*

from the Classic Work of Stanton, Anthony, Gge, and Harper (Urbana, Chicago, London: University of Illinois Press, 1978), pp. 297–303.

96. *Eighty Years and More,* pp. 5–6, 17; "1790 Census of the Town of Caughnawaga," transcribed by Judy Dolanski, http://www.rootsweb.com/~nyherkim/census/caughna1790.html; also see James F. Morrison, ed., "Colonel James Livingston: The Forgotten Livingston Patriot of the War for Independence," http://www.rootsweb.com/~nyfulton/military/livingston.html.

97. Sernett, *North Star Country,* pp. 3–6; Kathi Kern, *Mrs. Stanton's Bible* (Ithaca and London: Cornell University Press, 2001), pp. 22–30.

98. *Eighty Years and More,* pp. 16–17.

99. Sernett, *North Star Country,* pp. 4–11.

100. Stanton, *Eighty Years and More,* pp. 240–41; United States Constitution, Amendment XIV.

101. Zaeske, *Signatures of Citizenship,* pp. 117–18.

102. Humez, *Harriet Tubman,* pp. 153–54, 272–75; Larson, *Bound for the Promised Land,* pp. 290–95.

103. Clinton, *Harriet Tubman,* pp. 217–20; W. K. Kellogg Foundation, "Greater Battle Creek General Grantmaking," http://www.wkkf.org/Programming/Resources.aspx?CID=289; "Library Mural," University of Maryland Eastern Shore, http://www.umes.edu/fdl/SpecCol/mural.htm; Annie Baxter, "Spreading Politics Across the Walls," http://news.minnesota.publicradio.org/features/2004/10/01_baxtera_alewitz/.

104. Yellin, *Harriet Jacobs,* pp. xv–xxi, 262.

Chapter Five: A Book of Days

1. Virginia Woolf, *A Room of One's Own,* pp. 49, 89.

2. "The Story of National Women's History Month," NWHP website, http://www.nwhp.org/whm/themes/history-of.html.

3. Laurel Thatcher Ulrich, interviews with Sally Fox, Cambridge, Mass., April 28 and June 2, 2004.

4. *The Medieval Woman: An Illuminated Book of Days* (Boston, Toronto, and London: Little, Brown and Company, 1985). *An Illuminated Address Book* followed in 1988, then *An Illuminated Book of Postcards* in 1991. In 1992, Fox began producing wall calendars, extending her search for images from manuscripts to full-size paintings and tapestries.

5. "Young Unwed Mothers Learn a Trade," *New York Times,* June 26, 1985, p. C1. Also see John Cavanaugh, "More Women Join Building Trades," *New York Times,* Sunday, July 18, 1982, p. 15 and R. B. Lynch, "Carpentry Class Helps Rebuild Lives," *New York Times,* Aug 19, 1984, p. 55. In a letter to the editor (*New York Times,* September 11, 1985, p. A26), Mary Ellen Boyd, Director, Non-traditional Employment for Women, complained that the Reagan

Administration was dismantling the affirmative action guidelines that made such gains possible. Women, she said, composed barely 2 percent of workers in the construction industry. On the decline of government support, see Sara M. Evans, *Tidal Wave: How Women Changed America at Century's End* (New York: Free Press, 2003), pp. 176–77.

6. Fox, *Book of Days*, July 19–24, from *Collected Works of Christine de Piʒan: Cité des Dames*, MS. Harley 4431.f.190, British Library, London. The Persea edition of the paperback translation by Earl Jeffrey Richards has this image on the cover.

7. For a concise summary of Alice Clark, *Working Life of Women in the Seventeenth Century* (1919), see Sharon Howard, "Alice Clark, Working Women's Historian," *Early Modern Notes* (March 23, 2005), http://www.earlymodernweb.org.uk/emn/index.php/archives/2005/03/alice-clark-working-women/. For the influence of Clark's work on later scholarship, see Amanda Vickery, "Golden Age to Separate Spheres? A Review of the Categories and Chronology of English Women's History," *Historical Journal* 36 (1993): 383–414. For colonial America as a "golden age," see Mary Beth Norton, "The Evolution of White Women's Experience in Early America," *American Historical Review* 89 (1984): 593–619.

8. David Cowling, "Verbal and Visual Metaphors in the Cambridge Manuscript of the *Douʒe Dames de Rhétorique* (1463)," *Journal of the Early Book Society* 3 (2000): 107–8. The illuminations varied among various manuscripts of the poems. The arrangement of the books in the picture of the miner is slightly different in the edition reproduced in George Chastelain, Jean Robertet, and Jean de Montferrant, *Les Douʒe Dames de Rhétorique,* ed. David Cowling (Geneva: Librairie Droz, 2002), cover and Plate 12. For additional commentary on the poems and their illustrations, see Claudine A. Chavannes-Mazel, "The Twelve Ladies of Rhetoric in Cambridge," *Cambridge Bibliographical Society Proceedings* X (1991–1995): 139–55.

9. Christina Vanja, "Mining Women in Early Modern European Society," in Thomas Max Safley and Leonard N. Rosenband, eds., *The Workplace Before the Factory* (Ithaca and London: Cornell University Press, 1993), pp. 100–17; Susan C. Karant-Nunn, "The Women of the Saxon Silver Mines," in Sherrin Marshall, ed., *Women in Reformation and Counter-Reformation Europe* (Bloomington and Indianapolis: Indiana University Press, 1989), pp. 29–46; P. M. P. Goldberg, ed. and trans., *Women in England, c. 1275–1525: Documentary Sources* (Manchester and New York: Manchester University Press), pp. 177, 199; Geraldine Sheridan, "Views of Women at Work by the Royal Academicians: The Collection *Descriptions des arts et métiers (1761–1789),*" *Studies in Eighteenth-Century Culture* 32 (2003): 155, 162–71; "A Coal Miner's Life During the Late Ottoman Empire," in Donald Quataert and Yüksel Duman, eds., *International Labor and Working Class History* 60 (2001): 172–73; John Hannavy, "Amazons Among the Coal Tubs," *History Today* 54 (2004): 27–29.

10. Goldberg, ed. and trans., *Women in England,* 199; Nancy Armstrong and Leonard Tennenhouse, "Gender and the Work of Words," *Cultural Critique* 13 (1989): 229–30; Ellen Jordan, "The Exclusion of Women from Industry in Nineteenth-Century Britain," *Comparative Studies in Society and History* 31 (1989): 290.

11. The *Romance of the Rose* is an allegorical narrative that describes the adventures of a lover in his conquest of a garden-enclosed rose. Scholars have interpreted the long speech by Dame Nature in various ways, but the poem makes clear that her primary work is "forging individual creatures to continue the species": Guilaume de Lorris and Jean de Meun, *The Romance of the Rose,* trans. Charles Dahlberg, 3d edition (Princeton: Princeton University Press, 1995), p. 270. Other medieval texts make the symbolism of the hammer and anvil quite explicit. See E. C. Knowlton, "Nature in Old French," *Modern Philology* 20 (1923): 318–21; Sylvia Huot, *The Romance of the Rose and Its Medieval Readers* (Cambridge: Cambridge University Press, 1993), pp. 31, 32; R. A. Shoaf, *Dante, Chaucer, and the Currency of the Word* (Norman, Okla.: Pilgrim Books, 1983), chapter 12; Elise Boneau, "Obscenity Out of the Margins: Mysterious Imagery Within the Cent nouvelles, MS Hunter 252," *eSharp* 6 (Spring 2006), http://www.sharp.arts.gla.ac.uk/issue6/issue_6_part2/Boneau.pdf.

12. Fox, *Book of Days,* opp. July 7–12, orig. Jean Bondol, *Histoires anciennes jusqu'à César,* France, 1375, Kraus Rare Books and Manuscripts, New York; Renate Blumenfeld-Kosinski, *Not of Woman Born: Representations of Caesarean Birth in Medieval and Renaissance Culture* (Ithaca and London: Cornell University Press, 1990), pp. 38–47, 70–71, 121–22, 125–38, 156; Marcus I. Goldman and Louise M. Ackerman, "Caesarean Section," *American Speech* 38 (1963): 302–03. Also see the entry in the online encyclopedia Wikipedia, at http://en.wikipedia.org/wiki/Cesarian_section; Monica Green, "Women's Medical Practice and Health Care in Medieval Europe," *Signs* 14 (1989): 434–73; Katharine Park, "The Criminal and the Saintly Body: Autopsy and Dissection in Renaissance Italy," *Renaissance Quarterly* 47 (1994): 1–33.

13. Ibn Butlán, *Four Seasons of the House of Cerruti,* trans. Judith Spencer (New York: Facts on File, 1984) p. 106. Silvano Servanti and Françoise Sabban, *Pasta: The Story of a Universal Food,* trans. Anthony Shugaar (New York: Columbia University Press, 2000), pp. 8–10, 57–59.

14. Fox, *Book of Days* (May 19–24). Fox titles it simply "Sculptor." The source is Giovanni Boccaccio, *Le livre des clères et nobles femmes,* MS. Fr. 599, f. 58 French, fifteenth century, Bibliothèque Nationale, Paris. Giovanni Boccaccio, *Famous Women,* trans. Virginia Brown (Cambridge, Mass., and London: Harvard University Press, 2003), pp. 135–37; Pizan, *Book of the City of Ladies,* 1.41.4, p. 85. Catherine King, "Looking a Sight: Sixteenth-Century Portraits of Woman Artists," *Zeitschrift für Kunstgeschichte* 58 Bd., H. 3 (1995): 381–406; Dorothy Miner, *Anastaise and Her Sisters: Women Artists of the Middle Ages*

(Baltimore: Walters Art Gallery, 1974). Cf. Jonathan J. G. Alexander, *Medieval Illuminators and Their Methods of Work* (New Haven and London: Yale University Press, 1992), pp. 16–20; Lorna Campbell and Susa Foister, "Gerard, Lucas and Susanna Horenbout," *The Burlington Magazine* 128 (1986): 717–19.

15. Giorgio Vasari, *The Lives of the Artists*, trans. Julia Conaway Bondanella and Peter Bondanella (New York: Oxford University Press, 1991), pp. 339–42; Katherine McIver, "Vasari's Women," in Anne B. Barriault, Andrew Ladis, Norman E. Land, and Jeryldene M. Wood, eds., *Reading Vasari* (Atlanta: Georgia Museum of Art, 2005), pp. 179–88; Fredrika H. Jacobs, "The construction of a life: Madonna Properzia De'Rossi '*Schultrice*' Bolognese," *Word & Image* 9 (1993): 122–32; "Women Artists of Bologna," in Vera Fortunati Pietrantonio, *Lavinia Fontana of Bologna, 1552–1651* (Washington, D.C.: National Museum of Women in the Arts, and Milan: Electa, 1998), pp. 120–23; Caroline P. Murphy, *Lavinia Fontana: A Painter and Her Patrons in Sixteenth-Century Bologna* (New Haven & London: Yale University Press, 2003), 77–78; Paula Findlen, "Science as a Career in Enlightenment Italy: The Strategies of Laura Bassi," *Isis* 84, no. 3. (September 1993): 441–69, and "Translating the New Science: Women and the Circulation of Knowledge in Enlightenment Italy," *Configurations* 3 (1995): 167–206.

16. Rebecca Messgarger, "Re-membering a Body of Work: Anatomist and Anatomical Designer Anna Morandi Manzolini," *Studies in Eighteenth-Century Culture* 32 (2003): 123–54, and "Waxing Poetic: Anna Morandi Manzolini's Anatomical Sculptures," *Configurations* 9 (2001): 65–97.

17. For a brief history of the Guerilla Girls and images of their posters, see http://www.guerrillagirls.com/.

18. Roger S. Wieck, *Time Sanctified: The Book of Houses in Medieval Art and Life* (New York: George Braziller, 2000).

19. Laurel Thatcher Ulrich, *A Midwife's Tale* (New York: Alfred A. Knopf, 1990), p. 336.

20. Luke 1:381, King James Version.

21. *Emily: The Diary of a Hard-Worked Woman*, ed. Janet Lecompte (Lincoln: University of Nebraska Press, 1987), pp. 90, 14.

22. Judith Moyer and the Warner Women's Oral History Project, "It Had to Be Done So She Did It: Women's Work," in Warner, N.H., 1900–1960, unpublished script, used by permission. Rebecca Courser, Lucy Metting, Dot Bean, Peg Wurtz, Jane Bliss, and Beverly Hill were among the thirty women who developed this project.

23. Jonathan Alexander, "Labour and Paresse: Ideological Representations of Medieval Peasant Labor," *Art Bulletin* 72 (1990): 436–52. This is also a central theme in Camille, *The Luttrell Psalter*.

24. Moyer, "It Had To Be Done."

25. Pizan, *Book of the City of Ladies*, I.43.2, I. 44.1, pp. 88–90.

26. E. Patricia Tsurumi, *Factory Girls: Women in the Thread Mills of Meiji Japan* (Princeton, N.J.: Princeton University Press, 1990), p. 12.

27. *The True Woman; or, Life and Happiness at Home and Abroad* (New York: Carlton and Porter, 1857), p. 243, quoted in Jeanne Boydston, *Home and Work: Housework, Wages, and the Ideology of Labor in the Early Republic* (New York and Oxford: Oxford University Press, 1990), p. 146.

28. *Eighty Years and More*, pp. 145–47, 154.

29. Virginia Woolf, "Professions for Women," in *The Death of the Moth and Other Essays* (New York: Harcourt, Brace, and Company, 1942), pp. 237–38.

30. *Discourses of Brigham Young*, pp. 216–17, quoted in Claudia Lauper Bushman, "Women in Dialogue: An Introduction," *Dialogue: A Journal of Mormon Thought* 6 (1971): 7.

31. "Working Women Are a Great Revolutionary Force," May 8, 1973, Historical Reprints from Revolutionary China, http://www.awtw.org/back_issues/1998-24/womenholduphalfthesky.htm.

32. Sheridan Harvey, "Rosie the Riveter: Real Women Workers in World War II," transcript of Library of Congress video presentation, available online at http://www.loc.gov/rr/program/journey/rosie-transcript.html. The lyrics to the song can be found at http://www.1clark.edu/~ria/rosie.html.

33. "The Pasture," in *North of Boston* (New York: Henry Holt, 1915). For the entire poem, see http://www.bartleby.com/118/1.html.

34. *Bestiary, Being an English Version of the Bodleian Library*, Oxford M.S. Bodley 764, trans. Richard Barber (Woodbridge: Boydell Press, 1993), p. 92.

35. Adelheid Heimann, "The Capital Frieze and Pilasters of the Portail Royal, Chartres," *Journal of the Warburg and Courtauld Institutes* 31 (1968): 73–102.

36. Matthew 11: 28–30, King James Version.

37. Lyndal Roper, *Witch Craze: Terror and Fantasy in Baroque Germany* (New Haven and London: Yale University Press, 2004), pp. 1–3, 158–59.

38. Ibid., pp. 15–43, 117–23; Robin Briggs, *Witches & Neighbours: The Social and Cultural Context of European Witchcraft* (New York: HarperCollins, 1996), pp. 3–13; Anthony Fitzherbert, *The Boke of Husbandry*, and "Ballad of a Tyrannical Husband," in P. M. P. Goldberg, ed. and trans., *Women in England, c. 1275–1525: Documentary Sources* (Manchester and New York: Manchester University Press, 1995), pp. 167, 169.

39. David D. Hall, ed. *Witch-Hunting in Seventeenth-Century New England: A Documentary History, 1638–1692* (Boston: Northeastern University Press, 1991), p. 71.

40. Briggs, *Witches & Neighbours*, pp. 85–86.

41. Ibid., pp. 91, 87.

42. *Twelve Ingenious Characters: Or, Pleasant Descriptions, of the Properties of Sundry Persons & Things* (London: 1650), pp. 38–40; *The Journals of Dorothy Wordsworth*, vol. 1, ed. William Knight (London: Macmillan, 1897), p. 292;

Mary Waldron, *Lactilla, Milkwoman of Clifton: The Life and Writings of Ann Yearsley, 1753–1806* (Athens and London: University of Georgia Press, 1996).

43. Martha Moore Ballard Diary (Maine State Library, Augusta, and online at dohistory.org), November 26, 1795; June 7, 1797, December 23, 1793, August 11, 1805.

44. *Diary of Elizabeth Sandwith Drinker*, ed. Elaine Forman Crane (Boston: Northeastern University Press, 1991), 3: 787.

45. *Boston Evening Post*, December 30, 1751, p. 2; *Pennsylvania Gazette*, August 21, 1755, p. 4; *New York Gazette*, June 22, 1761, p. 4, and October 22, 1764, p. 3.

46. *The Irish Journals of Elizabeth Smith, 1840–1850*, eds. David Thomson and Moira McGusty (Oxford: Clarendon Press, 1980), p. 326.

47. A. T. Lucas, *Cattle in Ancient Ireland* (Kilkenny, Ireland: Boethius Press, 1989), pp. 6–12, 60; Clodaugh Brennan Harvey, "Some Irish Women Storytellers and Reflections on the Role of Women in the Storytelling Tradition," *Western Folklore* 48 (1989): 120–21.

48. Sally McMurry, "Women's Work in Agriculture: Divergent Trends in England and America, 1800 to 1930," *Comparative Studies in Society and History* 34 (1992): 248–70; L. DeAne Lagerquist, *In America the Men Milk the Cows: Factors of Gender, Ethnicity, and Religion in the Americanization of Norwegian-American Women* (Brooklyn, N.Y.: Carlson, 1991), pp. 20, 72–75.

49. The text of O'Leary's testimony and the conclusion of the Board, among other primary sources, are available on a Chicago Historical Society Website, at http://www.chicagohs.org/FIRE/oleary/report.html.

50. Richard F. Bales, *The Great Chicago Fire and the Myth of Mrs. O'Leary's Cow* (Jefferson, N.C.: McFarland, 2002), pp. 51, 165–70; Karen Sawislak, *Chicagoans and The Great Fire, 1871–1874* (Chicago and London: University of Chicago Press, 1995), pp. 43–45.

51. Kathleen L. Housley, *The Letter Kills But the Spirit Gives Life: The Smiths— Abolitionists, Suffragists, Bible Translators* (The Historical Society of Glastonbury, Conn., 1993), pp. 138–40; Linda K. Kerber, *No Constitutional Right to Be Ladies: Women and the Obligations of Citizenship* (New York: Hill & Wang, 1998), pp. 86–89.

52. "The Alderney Cow," The Alderney Society and Museum website, http://www.alderneysociety.org/aldcow.html; Eileen Gillooly, "Humor as Daughterly Defense in Cranford," *ELH* [English Literary History] 59 (1992): 883–910, quotation on p. 893.

53. Housley, *The Letter Kills*, pp. 147–50.

54. Ibid., pp. 150–52; Kerber, *No Constitutional Right*, pp. 90–92.

55. "Sam Adams and Miss Abby H. Smith," *Harper's Illustrated Weekly*, February 7, 1874, p. 23 accessed on online database, *HarpWeek*.

56. Housley, *The Letter Kills*, pp. 167–80.

57. David S. New, *Holy War: The Rise of Militant Christian, Jewish and Islamic Fundamentalism* (Jefferson, N.C., and London: McFarland, 2002), pp. 131–36;

Graeme Carlé, *The Red Heifer's Ashes: Mysteries of Ancient Israel* (Wellington, New Zealand: Emmaus Road Publishing, 2001). Also see a 1998 website sponsored by the Pentecostal-Jewish alliance: http://www.templemount.org/heifer.html.

58. Jill Hammer, "The Red Heifer and the Cycle of Life and Death," http://telshemesh.org/earth/the_red_heifer_and_the_cycle_of_life_and_death.html; Starhawk, "Witchcraft as Goddess Religion," in *Spellbound: Women and Witchcraft in America* (Wilmington, Del.: Scholarly Resources, 1998), pp. 201–20. For alternate perspectives on feminist spirituality, see additional essays in the same volume.

59. Woolf, *A Room of One's Own*, pp. 85, 88. Woolf had, of course, done that in *Mrs. Dalloway*.

60. Alice Walker, "In Search of Our Mother's Gardens," *Ms.*, May 1974, reprinted in Walker, *In Search of Our Mother's Gardens: Womanist Prose* (San Diego, New York, London: Harcourt Brace, 1983), pp. 239–43.

61. Sandy and Elinah Grant, *Decorated Homes in Botswana* (Mochudi, Botswana: Phuthadikobo Museum, 1995), pp. 9–15, 47, 55–57, 105, 80–84.

62. Gary N. Van Wyk, *African Painted Houses: Basotho Dwellings of Southern Africa* (New York: Harry N. Abrams, 1998), pp. 33–34.

63. Suzanne Abel-Vidor, Dot Brovarney, and Susan Billy, *Remember Your Relations: The Elsie Allen Baskets, Family & Friends* (Berkeley, Calif.: Heyday Books, 1996), pp. 10, 20–21, 33, 37, 103.

64. Ibid., pp. 26, 63–65, 103–04, 107.

65. Shelly Zegart, "Since Kentucky: Surveying State Quilts," The Quilt Index, Projects of Alliance for American Quilts and Michigan State University Museum: http://www.quiltindex.org/since_kentucky.php; Gregg Stull, "The AIDS Memorial Quilt: Performing Memory, Piecing Action," *American Art* 15 (2001): 84–89; Christopher Capozzola, "A Very American Epidemic: Memory Politics and Identity Politics in the AIDS Memorial Quilt, 1985–1993," *Radical History Review* 82 (2002): 91–109; and the AIDS Project website: http://www.aidsquilt.org/history.htm.

66. Alvia Wardlaw, "Introduction: The Quilts of Gee's Bend," in John Beardsley, William Arnett, Paul Arnett, and Jane Livingston, *The Quilts of Gee's Bend* (Atlanta: Tinwood Books in Association with the Museum of Fine Arts, Houston, 2002), pp. 8–9. For the photograph that inspired Arnett, see Roland L. Freeman, *A Communion of Spirits: African American Quilters, Preservers, and Their Stories* (Nashville, Tenn.: Rutledge Hill Press, 1996), p. 338, and the discussion on pages 332–37. Freeman also explores the history of the famous "Bible Quilt" that Alice Walker mentioned in her essay.

67. *Gee's Bend: The Women and Their Quilts* (Atlanta: Tinwood Books in Association with the Museum of Fine Arts, Houston, 2002).

68. Nancy Callahan, *The Freedom Quilting Bee* (Tuscaloosa and London: University of Alabama Press, 1987), pp. 175–81. Callahan's account relies on the

recollections of Myles's niece by marriage, Lucy Mingo, who is pictured on p. 183 with a Pine Burr quilt made from 23,850 pieces. In contrast, *Gee's Bend: The Women and Their Quilts* documents Mingo's work through a workclothes quilt, p. 68, a random "Housetop," p. 281, a "Log Cabin" variation, p. 283, and (in a small inset in the essay on the Freedom Quilting Bee), a "Chestnut Bud." Her oral history, pp. 280–81, says nothing about her work with Myles.

69. Nancy Scheper-Hughes, "Anatomy of a Quilt: the Gee's Bend Freedom Quilting Bee," *Southern Cultures* (Fall 2004): 88–98.

70. Wardlaw, "Introduction," in *Gee's Bend,* p. 11.

71. Mayer, "It Had to Be Done."

72. Michael Michael, "The Iconography of Kingship in the Walter of Milemete Treatise," *Journal of the Warburg and Courtauld Institutes* 57 (1994): 35–47.

73. Pizan, *Book of the City of Ladies,* pp. 118–19 and following.

74. Sylvia Federico, "The Imaginary Society: Women in 1381," *The Journal of British Studies* 40 (2001): 159–83.

75. Laurel Thatcher Ulrich, *Good Wives* (New York: Knopf, 1982), pp. 193–94.

76. The classic statement of this argument is in Natalie Davis, *Society and Culture in Early Modern France: Eight Essays* (Stanford: Stanford University Press, 1975), pp. 124ff.

77. Anne Walthall, "Devoted Wives / Unruly Women: Invisible Presence in the History of Japanese Social Protest," *Signs* 20 (1994): 106–36.

78. Lynne Viola, "Bab'i Bunty and Peasant Women's Protest During Collectivization," *Russian Review* 45 (1986): 23–38.

79. For a concise summary that integrates women's activities into an overall discussion of the Revolution, see Janet Polasky, "The Legacy of the French Revolution," in William B. Cohen, ed., *The Transformation of Modern France* (Boston and New York: Houghton Mifflin, 1997), pp. 5–27. For more detail, see Darline Levy and Harriet Applewhite, *Women in Revolutionary Paris* (Urbana: University of Illinois Press, 1979); Lynn Hunt, *The Family Romance of the French Revolution* (Berkeley: University of California Press, 1992); Olwen Hufton, *Women and the Limits of Citizenship in the French Revolution* (Toronto: University of Toronto Press, 1992); Suzanne Desan, *Reclaiming the Sacred* (Ithaca, N.Y.: Cornell University Press, 1990); and Marilyn Yalom, *Blood Sisters: The French Revolution in Women's Memory* (New York: Basic Books, 1993). For a survey of feminist scholarship on the topic, see Karen Offen, "The New Sexual Politics of French Revolutionary Historiography," *French Historical Studies* 16 (1990): 909–22.

80. Desan, *Reclaiming the Sacred,* pp. 199, 202.

81. Clarina Nichols, in Lois Stiles Edgerly, ed., *Give Her This Day: A Daybook of Women's Words* (Gardiner, Me.: Tilbury House, 1990), p. 28.

82. Edgerly, ed., *Give Her This Day,* pp. 129–30.

83. Temma Kaplan, "Naked Mothers and Maternal Sexuality: Some Reactions to the Aba Women's War," in Alexis Jetter, Annelise Orleck, and Dianna Taylor,

eds., *The Politics of Motherhood* (Hanover and London: University Press of New England, 1997), pp. 209–22.

84. D'Arcy Doran, "Women Protesters Claim Victory in Nigeria," *Toronto Star*, July 22, 2002, p. A7; "Protesters Seize Nigerian Oil Company Facility Again," *Panafrican News Agency Daily Newswire*, July 30, 2002.

85. Dianna Taylor, "Making a Spectacle: The Mothers of the Plaza de Mayo," in *Politics of Motherhood*, 182–96. For fuller accounts, see Marguerite Guzman Bouvard, *Revolutionizing Motherhood: The Mothers of the Plaza de Mayo* (Wilmington, Del.: SR Books, 1994); Jo Fisher, *Mothers of the Disappeared* (Boston: South End Books, and London: Zed Books, 1989); Matilde Mellibovsky, *Circle of Love Over Death: Testimonies of the Mothers of the Plaza de Mayo* (Willimantic, Conn.: Curbstone Press, 1997).

86. Wangari Maathai, *Unbowed: A Memoir* (New York: Alfred A. Knopf, 2006), pp. 3–5, 36–37, 46–52, 98–114. Also see "Wangari Maathai: The Nobel Peace Prize 2004," Nobelprize.org, http://nobelprize.org/nobel_prizes/peace/laureates/2004/maathai-bio.html; http://nobelprize.org/nobel_prizes/peace/laureates/2004/maathai-lecture.html.

87. "The River Has Been Crossed: Wangari Maathai and the Mothers of the Green Belt Movement," Alexis Jetter interview with Wangari Maathai, in Alexis Jetter, Annelise Orleck, and Diana Taylor, eds., *The Politics of Motherhood: Activist Vices from Left to Right* (Hanover and London: University Press of New England, 1997), pp. 70–76.

88. Ibid., pp. 74–75, 70.

89. "The Green Belt Movement," http://www.greenbeltmovement.org/.

90. *Eighty Years and More*, pp. 342–43.

91. Sharon J. Wohlmuth, Carol Saline, and Dawn Sheggeby, *A Day in the Life of the American Woman: How We See Ourselves* (New York and Boston: Bulfinch Press, 2005), pp. 102–5, 142–45, 132–33, 152–57, 123, 34–35, 36, 66–67, 27.

92. Ibid., pp. 8, 9.

93. Ibid., pp. 110–11, 134–37.

94. Ibid., pp. 32–33.

95. Ibid., p. 8.

96. Ibid., pp. 56–57.

97. Red Hat Society official website, http://www.redhatsociety.com/info/WhatDoWeDo.html; Red Hat merchandise can be seen at http://www.earthsunmoon.com/products/item.php/865/1 and other places.

Chapter Six: Waves

1. Martha Lear, "The Second Feminist Wave," *New York Times* (Sunday) *Magazine*, March 10, 1968, electronic edition, ProQuest document ID:90032407, p. 1.

2. Ibid., pp. 1–2.

3. Ruth Rosen, *The World Split Open: How the Modern Women's Movement Changed America* (New York: Viking, 2000), pp. 6–7; Daniel Horowitz, *Betty Friedan and the Making of* The Feminine Mystique (Amherst: University of Massachusetts Press, 1998), pp. 2–5.

4. "Lois Wilson," in Ann Braude, ed., *Transforming the Faiths of Our Fathers: Women Who Changed American Religion* (New York: Palgrave, 2004), pp. 13–14; Susan Brownmiller, *In Our Time: Memoir of a Revolution* (New York: Delta, 1999), p. 3.

5. Leila J. Rupp and Verta Taylor, *Survival in the Doldrums: The American Women's Rights Movement, 1945 to the 1960s* (New York: Oxford University Press, 1987), pp. 176–77; "Martha Edna Wright Griffiths," in Suzanne O'Dea Schenken, ed., *From Suffrage to the Senate: An Encyclopedia of American Women in Politics* (Santa Barbara, Calif.: ABC-CLIO, 1999), I: 304–6; Rosen, *World Split Open,* pp. 63–74.

6. Rosen, *World Split Open,* pp. 74–76; Sara M. Evans, *Tidal Wave: How Women Changed America at Century's End* (New York: Free Press, 2003), pp. 24–26.

7. National Organization for Women, "Statement of Purpose," October 29, 1966, reproduced in Feminist Chronicles, Feminist Majority Foundation, website http://www.feminist.org/research/chronicles/chronicl.html.

8. Rupp and Taylor, pp. 134, 180–81; "Pauli Murray," website, "The North Carolina Writers Network," http://www.ncwriters.org/pmurray.htm; Evans, *Tidal Wave,* pp. 24–25; Rosen, *World Split Open,* p. 80.

9. Rosen, *World Split Open,* pp. 56–57, 110–14; Mary King, *Freedom Song: A Personal Story of the 1960s Civil Rights Movement* (New York: William Morrow, 1987), pp. 76–78.

10. King, *Freedom Song,* pp. 443–44, 450; Appendix 2, pp. 567–68.

11. Ibid., pp. 451–52.

12. "A Kind of Memo from Casey Hayden and Mary King to a Number of Other Women in the Peace and Freedom Movements," November 18, 1965, Appendix 3, King, *Freedom Song,* pp. 571–74. For an online copy of the memo, see Casey Hayden and Mary King, "Sex and Caste: A Kind of Memo," in Classic Feminist Writing, CWLU Archive, http://www.cwluherstory.com/CWLUArchive/memo.html.

13. King, *Freedom Song,* pp. 465–68.

14. Interview with Marilyn Webb, New York, Oct. 23, 1994, quoted in Brownmiller, *In Our Time,* pp. 14–15.

15. Rosen, *World Split Open,* pp. 108–10.

16. King, *Freedom Song,* 467–68, 473–74; Brownmiller, *In Our Time,* pp. 14–15; Rosen, *World Split Open,* pp. 121–24, 114.

17. Evans, *Tidal Wave,* p. 31; Rosen, *World Split Open,* p. 129; Rosalyn Fraad Baxandall, "Catching the Fire," and Barbara Winslow, "Primary and Secondary Contradictions in Seattle: 1967–1969," in *The Feminist Memoir Project:*

Voices from Women's Liberation (New York: Three Rivers Press, 1998), pp. 212, 230–33; "Carol P. Christ," in Braude, ed., *Transforming the Faiths of Our Fathers*, p. 99.

18. Charlotte Curtis, "Miss America Pageant Is Picketed by 100 Women," *New York Times*, September 8, 1968, p. 81; Evans, *Tidal Wave*, p. 40; Brownmiller, *In Our Time*, pp. 35–41; Carol Hanisch, "Two Letters from the Women's Liberation Movement," in *The Feminist Memoir Project*, pp. 199, 200.

19. Brownmiller, *In Our Time*, pp. 35–37; Hanisch, "Two Letters," p. 199.

20. Rosen, *World Split Open*, p. 140.

21. Robin Morgan, ed., *Sisterhood Is Powerful: An Anthology of Writings from the Women's Liberation Movement* (New York: Vintage, 1970); *Feminist Memoir Project*, p. 501.

22. On WITCH, see Brownmiller, *In Our Time*, p. 49.

23. Evans, *Tidal Wave*, pp. 31–39; Stephanie Gilmore, "The Dynamics of Second-Wave Feminist Activisim in Memphis, 1971–1982: Rethinking the Liberal/Radical Divide," *NWSA Journal* 15 (2003): 94–117. Brownmiller, *In Our Time*, shows the shifting boundaries among New York groups.

24. Evans, *Tidal Wave*, pp. 42–43.

25. Benita Roth, *Separate Roads to Feminism: Black, Chicana, and White Feminist Movements in America's Second Wave* (Cambridge, England: Cambridge University Press, 2004), pp. 107–10; Evans, *Tidal Wave*, pp. 77–78.

26. Roth, *Separate Roads*, pp. 165, 139–41, 152–53.

27. Brownmiller, *In Our Time*, pp. 180–85; Rosalyn Baxandall and Linda Gordon, eds., *Dear Sisters: Dispatches from the Women's Liberation Movement* (New York: Basic Books, 2000), pp. 120–21.

28. Isasi-Diaz, in Braude, ed., *Transforming Faiths of Our Fathers*, p. 87.

29. Evans, *Tidal Wave*, pp. 57–58.

30. Ibid., p. 88.

31. Roth, *Separate Roads*, p. 158.

32. Schlafley and "Henpecked Congress."

33. Rosen, *World Split Open*, pp. 243, 246.

34. Ibid., pp. 247, 242–43.

35. Evans, *Tidal Wave*, pp. 6, 109; Brownmiller, *In Our Time*, pp. 234–43.

36. Brownmiller, *In Our Time*, pp. 72, 82, 96–98; Radicalesbians, "The Woman-Identified Woman," in Baxandall and Gordon, eds., *Dear Sisters*, p. 107.

37. Rosalyn Fraad Baxandall, "Catching the Fire," in *Feminist Memoir Project*, p. 210.

38. Evans, *Tidal Wave*, p. 10.

39. "A Letter to the Editor of *Ms.*" in Alice Walker, *In Search of Our Mothers' Gardens* (San Diego, New York, London: Harcourt Brace Jovanovich, 1983), pp. 273–75. Also see Evans, *Tidal Wave*, pp. 77–78.

40. Roth, *Separate Roads*, p. 139.

41. King, *Freedom Song*, p. 0.

42. Jo Freeman, "On the Origins of the Women's Liberation Movement from a Strictly Personal Perspective," in *Feminist Memoir Project*, pp. 170–71.

43. Estelle B. Freedman. *No Turning Back: The History of Feminism and the Future of Women* (New York: Ballantine Books, 2002), p. x.

44. Evans, *Tidal Wave*, p. 14.

45. Scott tells her story in "The Southern Lady Revisited," an autobiographical afterword to the twenty-fifth anniversary edition of *The Southern Lady: From Pedestal to Politics, 1830–1930* (Charlottesville and London: University Press of Virginia, 1995), pp. 239–97.

46. Ibid., p. 241.

47. Ibid., pp. 242–44.

48. Gerda Lerner, "Women Among the Professors of History: The Story of a Process of Transformation," in Eileen Boris and Nupur Chaudhuri, eds., *Voices of Women Historians: The Personal, the Political, the Professional* (Bloomington and Indianapolis: Indiana University Press, 1999), p. 1. Gerda Lerner has also written about her life in *The Majority Finds Its Past: Placing Women in History* (New York: Oxford, 1979); *Why History Matters: Life and Thought* (New York: Oxford, 1997); and *Fireweed: A Political Autobiography* (Philadelphia: Temple University Press, 2002).

49. Joan Kelly, *Women, History & Theory: The Essays of Joan Kelly* (Chicago and London: University of Chicago Press, 1984), pp. xi–xiii, 19.

50. Nupur Chaudhuri and Mary Elizabeth Perry, "Achievements and Battles: Twenty-five Years of CCWHP," *Journal of Women's History* 6 (1994): 97–105; AHA website http://www.historians.org/info/AHA_History/index.htm; Gerda Lerner, "Women Among the Professors of History: The Story of a Process of Transformation," in Hewitt and Chaudhuri, eds., pp. 1–2; Eileen Boris, "In Circles Comes Change," in Hewitt and Chaudhuri, eds., p. 195.

51. "The Berkshire Conference of Women Historians," http://www.berks conference.org/history.htm.

52. Chaudhuri and Perry, eds., "Achievements and Battles," pp. 97–105. AHA website http://www.historians.org/info/AHA_History/index.htm; and OAH presidents' website http://www.oah.org/about/pastofcrs.html.

53. Hilda Smith, "Regionalism, Feminism, and Class: The Development of a Feminist Historian," in Hewitt and Chaudhuri, eds., p. 31.

54. Renate Bridenthal, "Making and Writing History Together," in Hewitt and Chaudhuri, eds., p. 80.

55. Ibid., pp. 77–84, 81.

56. Alden Whitman, "The Woman in History Becomes Explosive Issue in the Present," *New York Times*, November 2, 1974, p. 34.

57. Charity Willard, Foreword to Barbara K. Altmann and Deborah L. McGrady, eds., *Christine de Pizan: A Casebook* (New York and London: Routledge, 2003), pp. xi–xiii.

58. Natalie Davis, Foreword to Christine de Pizan, *The Book of the City of Ladies,* trans. Earl Jeffrey Richards (New York: Persea Books, rev. ed., 1998), p. xv.

59. Blanche Wiesen Cook, " 'Women Alone Stir My Imagination': Lesbianism and the Cultural Tradition," *Signs* 4 (1979): 730.

60. Brenda R. Silver, *Virginia Woolf, Icon* (Chicago and London: University of Chicago Press, 1999), pp. 40–45.

61. Beverly Guy-Sheftall, "Sisters in Struggle: A Belated Response," in *Feminist Memoir Project,* p. 487.

62. Interview with Susan Kohler, April 2, 2007. Although the agenda has varied over the years, *Exponent II* is still being published today. In 2007 it went from hard print to the web: http://www.exponentii.org/. For a discussion of conflict among Latter-Day Saint women over uses of the past during the battle over the ERA, see Martha Sonntag Bradley, *Utah Women, Religious Authority, and Equal Rights* (Salt Lake City: Signature Books, 2005), Chapter 1, pp. 1–28.

63. Renate Bridenthal, "Making and Writing History Together," p. 81; Renate Bridenthal and Claudia Koons, eds., *Becoming Visible: Women in European History* (Boston: Houghton Mifflin, 1977).

64. Estelle B. Freedman, *No Turning Back: The History of Feminism and the Future of Women* (New York: Ballantine Books, 2002), pp. x–xi.

65. Linda Kerber, "On the Importance of Taking Notes," in Hewitt and Chaudhuri, p. 50.

66. Hinding's guide was published in New York by R. R. Bowker in 1979.

67. Evans, *Tidal Wave,* p. 1.

68. In 1946, an earthquake near the Aleutian Islands produced fifty-five-foot-high waves in Hawaii five hours later. In Chile in 1960, a combination earthquake-and-wave killed two thousand people. Today, official warning systems use the Japanese term *tsunami* to describe these giant waves. The tsunami that hit Papua, New Guinea, in 1998 killed as many as three thousand persons. There is a great deal of information about tsunamis available online, including a basic website linked to the National Oceanographic and Atmospheric Administration, United States Department of Commerce: http://www.pmel.noaa.gov/tsunami/.

69. Evans, *Tidal Wave,* p. 1.

70. For a concise summary of changes, see Baxandall and Gordon, *Dear Sisters,* pp. 16–18.

71. Evans, *Tidal Wave,* p. 5.

Afterword: Making History

1. www.oneangrygirl.net, and e-mails to Laurel Thatcher Ulrich, September 3, October 6, 21, 22, 23, 2006.

2. "Christine de Pizan: The Making of the Queen's Manuscript" (Harley MS 4431), Arts and Humanities Research Council, University of Edinburgh, http://www.pizan.lib.ed.ac.uk/.

3. The Elizabeth Cady Stanton and Susan B. Anthony Papers Project, http://ecssba.rutgers.edu/index.html.

4. The Brown University Women Writers Project, http://www.wwp.brown.edu/.

5. Harriet Tubman Resource Centre, York University, Department of History, http://www.yorku.ca/nhp/intro.htm.

6. "The Quilt Index," http://www.quiltindex.org/about.php.

7. Harriet Jacobs Papers Project, http://www.harrietjacobspapers.org/.

8. "Introduction to the Oxford DNB," Digital Edition, October 2006, http://www.oup.com/oxforddnb/info/prelims/intro/intro5/#outcomes.

9. "Women Working, 1800–1930," http://ocp.hul.harvard.edu/ww/.

10. For example, a search in October 2006 produced, among 314 titles, such works as Nancy Scheper-Hughes, *Death Without Weeping: The Violence of Everyday Life in Brazil* (Berkeley and Oxford: University of California Press, 1992); Heba Azis El-Kohly, *Defiance and Compliance: Negotiating Gender in Low-Income Cairo* (New York and Oxford: Berghahn Books, 2002); and Rachel Ginnis Fuchs, *Gender and Poverty in Nineteenth-Century Europe* (Cambridge, England: Cambridge University Press, 2005), as well as a modern edition of the nineteenth-century classic by Alice Caldwell Hegan Rice, *Mrs. Wiggs of the Cabbage Patch* (Lexington: University Press of Kentucky, 2004).

11. In October 2006, I found in Oxford University's integrated catalog such works as Jacquie Sarsby, *Missuses & Mouldrunners: An Oral History of Women Pottery-Workers at Work and at Home* (Milton Keynes: Open University Press, 1988); Shirley Angell, *Pinnacle Club: A History of Women Climbing* (Glasgow: Pinnacle Club, 1988); Donna L. Halper, *Invisible Stars: A Social History of Women in American Broadcasting* (Armonk, N.Y., and London: M. E. Sharpe, 2001); Margarita Diaz-Andreu and Marie Louise Stig Sorensen, eds., *Excavating Women: A History of Women in European Archaeology* (London: Routledge, 1998); Birgitta Jordansson and Tinne Varrimen, eds., *Charitable Women: Philanthropic Welfare 1780–1930: A Nordic and Interdisciplinary Anthology* (Odense: Odense University Press, 1998); Heike Bauer, *Women and Cross-dressing 1800–1939* (London: Routledge, 2006).

12. Search conducted on Harvard University Libraries Catalog "Hollis" in the autumn of 2004.

13. Thanks to Adrian Finucane for tracking down T-shirts among the papers of twentieth-century activists and organizations. Like eighteenth-century printed handkerchiefs, these objects are both texts and textiles.

14. Gerda Lerner, *The Creation of Feminist Consciousness* (New York and Oxford: Oxford University Press, 1993), pp. 280–81.

15. Ann Gordon to Laurel Ulrich, e-mail October 31, 2006; Laura Ciampa, ed., "Inspired by Our Feminist Foremothers," *American Feminist* (Spring 2004): 5–10; "Feminists for Life," http://www.feministsforlife.org/covetable_stuff/index.htm. Although the quote attributed to Stanton on the coffee mug appears

in many places, including Wikipedia, the source given (a letter in a supposed 1873 diary of Julia Ward Howe) appears to be spurious. According to Mary Crane Derr, co-editor of *Pro-Life Feminism: Yesterday and Today,* an expanded edition (Sentinel, 2006), it was first used in the pro-life movement in the early 1990s by a researcher who said that she had lost the scrap of paper on which she wrote the reference. Derr's book includes other quotes from Stanton that *can* be documented (Mary Derr to Laurel Ulrich, e-mail, November 6, 2006).

16. *Christine de Pisan at Her Computer,* 1999, Mary Yaeger Gallery, http:// www.maryyaeger.com/pages/pisan.html.

INDEX

(Page references in *italic* refer to illustrations.)

A Note About the Author

LAUREL THATCHER ULRICH received her B.A. from the University of Utah, her M.A. from Simmons College, and her Ph.D. from the University of New Hampshire. She was previously professor of history at the University of New Hampshire and is currently Phillips Professor of Early American History and 300th Anniversary University Professor at Harvard University. Her book *A Midwife's Tale* won the Pulitzer Prize in history, the Bancroft Prize, and the American Historical Society's John H. Dunning and Joan Kelly Memorial Prizes. Ulrich's discovery of Martha Ballard and her work on Ballard's diary have been chronicled in a documentary film written and produced by Laurie Kahn-Leavitt, with major funding from the National Endowment for the Humanities and the *American Experience* television series. Ulrich is also the author of numerous articles and reviews, and the recipient of a MacArthur Foundation Fellowship and many other honors and awards.

A Note on the Type

This book was set in Fournier, a typeface named for Pierre Simon Fournier fils (1712–1768), a celebrated French type designer. Coming from a family of typefounders, Fournier was an extraordinarily prolific designer of typefaces and of typographic ornaments. He was also the author of the important *Manuel typographique* (1764–1766), in which he attempted to work out a system standardizing type measurement in points, a system that is still in use internationally. Fournier's type is considered transitional in that it drew its inspiration from the old style, yet was ingeniously innovational, providing for an elegant, legible appearance. In 1925 his type was revived by the Monotype Corporation of London.

Composed by North Market Street Graphics, Lancaster, Pennsylvania

Printed and bound by RR Donnelley, Harrisonburg, Virginia

Designed by Anthea Lingeman